Calculation and Morality

OXFORD STUDIES IN THE HISTORY OF ECONOMICS

Series Editor: Steven G. Medema, PhD, University Distinguished Professor of Economics, University of Colorado Denver

This series publishes leading-edge scholarship by historians of economics and social science, drawing upon approaches from intellectual history, the history of ideas, and the history of the natural and social sciences. It embraces the history of economic thinking from ancient times to the present, the evolution of the discipline itself, the relationship of economics to other fields of inquiry, and the diffusion of economic ideas within the discipline and to the policy realm and broader publics. This enlarged scope affords the possibility of looking anew at the intellectual, social, and professional forces that have surrounded and conditioned economics' continued development.

Calculation and Morality

The Costs of Slavery and the Value of Emancipation in the French Antilles

Caroline Oudin-Bastide
and
Philippe Steiner

OXFORD
UNIVERSITY PRESS

OXFORD
UNIVERSITY PRESS

Oxford University Press is a department of the University of Oxford. It furthers the University's objective of excellence in research, scholarship, and education by publishing worldwide. Oxford is a registered trade mark of Oxford University Press in the UK and certain other countries.

Published in the United States of America by Oxford University Press
198 Madison Avenue, New York, NY 10016, United States of America.

Library of Congress Cataloging-in-Publication Data
Names: Oudin-Bastide, Caroline, author. | Steiner, Philippe, author.
Title: Calculation and morality : the costs of slavery and the value of emancipation in the French Antilles / Caroline Oudin-Bastide and Philippe Steiner. Other titles: Calcul et morale. English
Description: New York, NY : Oxford University Press, [2019] | Includes bibliographical references and index.
Identifiers: LCCN 2018024944 (print) | LCCN 2018027737 (ebook) | ISBN 9780190856861 (UPDF) | ISBN 9780190856878 (EPUB) | ISBN 9780190856854 (hardcover : alk. paper)
Subjects: LCSH: Slavery—Economic aspects—France—Colonies. | Slavery—Moral and ethical aspects—France—Colonies | Slavery—France—Colonies—History. | Slavery—France—Public opinion—History. | Du Pont de Nemours, Pierre Samuel, 1739-1817—Influence.
Classification: LCC HT1180 (ebook) | LCC HT1180.O9313 2019 (print) | DDC 306.3/620944—dc23
LC record available at https://lccn.loc.gov/2018024944

CONTENTS

Calculation and Morality

Introduction

In 1771 Pierre Samuel du Pont published two articles in the *Éphémérides du citoyen* that introduced the issue of calculation into the debate over the abolition of slavery, a debate that had otherwise been dominated by moral considerations ever since the appearance of Montesquieu's *L'Esprit des lois* in 1748. Right up until 1848, when slavery was eventually abolished in France, the writings of both slavers and abolitionists presumed that calculation and morality were quite intimately connected.

Paul Hazard classically described the early eighteenth century in terms of a "crisis of the European mind"[1] in which many received ideas related to morality were put in question, especially those relating to religious belief and the hold it had over men and women. To analyze the way in which the meanings of words develop we need to be familiar with the representations that they carry. This approach, following from the work of Lucien Febvre,[2] can teach us a great deal about a controversy that unfolded during a period of intellectual innovation. It was no coincidence that three major dictionaries were published at this time—the *Dictionnaire de Furetière* in 1690, the *Dictionnaire de l'Académie française* in 1694, and the *Dictionnaire de Trévoux* in 1704. While the definitions of the words in these dictionaries hardly varied in subsequent editions up to the 1760s, the commentary added to them allows us to grasp and follow the movement of ideas.

MORALITY, LIBERTY, SLAVERY

These dictionaries tell us that morality is related to *moeurs* (*mores*); according to the *Dictionnaire de Trévoux*, it is "the art of living well; a science that teaches us how to lead our lives, how to guide our actions. Morality provides us with limits to our passions, it cultivates our virtues, and roots out our vices." The writer of this article retains the three theological virtues—faith, hope, and charity—and only two cardinal virtues (sobriety and justice). In conformity with the representations prevailing in the very Catholic kingdom of France, he emphasizes that only Christian morality is pure, everything else being no more than "pagan integrity." Belonging to the government of the self, morality is primarily something that is deeply internal, involving those motivations to action most privy to the individual: "Evangelical morality does not limit itself to outward regulation and external conduct so that one may acquire a good reputation among men; it holds sway over the heart and carries its flame right into this secret and hidden source of our actions. . . . The prime employment of morality is to provide precepts to regulate passions, and to disencumber reason of errors of sense and imagination." The ability to choose between Good and Evil with which God has endowed men and women is conditional upon rules for conducting life in a manner fitting to a struggle against passion, prejudice, and the errors of our senses. Moral liberty is thus indexed to religion: "In theology it is the natural state of man within which he freely exercises all movements of his will. It is a power, a faculty of being able to voluntarily distinguish the good or the bad in one thing or another." Liberty is not "the power of living out our fantasies" but the capacity to disengage oneself from passion. True liberty can therefore be distinguished from its semblance: "Liberty, Right, the legitimate power to do and think what one wishes, without constraint and without dependence. True liberty consists in serving no passion." Passion encumbers the individual in relation to the motives of others; it enchains the individual, and holds that individual in its power. Liberty is not, however, confined to the inner life, for it is also inscribed in the domain of civil and political life: "Liberty is also opposed to captivity, prison. Those taken by corsairs lose their liberty. The very best legacy that Romans bequeathed to their slaves was that of liberty." But also: "Liberty means peoples, it signifies independence, or less dependence; or dependence of a certain kind." The *Dictionnaire de l'Académie française* is here more precise: "When talking of a state, of a country, liberty takes the form of government in which the people has sovereign authority."

In the two meanings of liberty slavery is defined by default: first, a slave is someone who, by accident of birth or of war, finds himself or herself in the power of another; and second, an individual is subject not to another person but to his or her own passions.

The first meaning links slavery to dependence, being thrown into captivity by one's enemies, especially by the pirates of the Barbary Coast. By extension, it also designates "the excessive dependence . . . that arises when one is in the power of a prince whose might is too absolute." Here the sense is political, the sense that underwrites the premodern definition of political liberty that preceded the advent of liberalism.[3] Figuratively, slavery involves morality: "For morality, slavery implies figuratively the way that we allow our passions to sway us. Lovers complain that they are enchained, that they languish in slavery. Those who have ambition in Court are truly enslaved." One can also "Groan from an enslavement to sin." The writer of the entry "slave" notes the same duality, but in illustrating the moral meaning of the term introduces a notion of interest that is missing from the entry on "Slavery": "We are slaves of everything that we fear and desire. Interest renders one proud and vain, a worshipper is a vile slave of all who possess fortune."[4]

Slavery is therefore something which is at once moral and political: the submission of the vanquished can be assimilated to the way in which an apparently free man submits when he fails to conform to moral precepts. In its moral sense it applies to every human being who is prey to passions that can rob him or her of a liberty that is the gift of God. In the religious variant of this, slavery appears to be the common fate of humanity, but also the very thing against which the precepts of morality must struggle. Political meaning is more restricted, categorizing the beaten and defeated. The active traffic in black slaves in America illustrates this, modeled upon the captives of Algerian corsairs and the slaves of antiquity; their fall into servitude arouses no scorn. The definitions found in these dictionaries are otherwise in complete agreement with those ideas developed in the first half of the eighteenth century that we can call the "science of political commerce."[5] Jean-François Melon's *Essai politique sur le commerce* discusses the role of colonies and slavery from the perspective of the Prince, in terms of "Reason of State," a classical stance for this form of economic discourse. He takes a pragmatic approach: in a situation of commercial rivalry the interest of the Prince and of the nation prevail: "The fact that the use of slaves is authorised in our colonies teaches us that slavery is contrary neither to religion nor [to] morality. Hence we are free to examine whether it might be more useful to extend the use of slaves elsewhere."[6] While he condemns the absence of a proper legal framework in the case of oriental slavery, he sees great merit in the *Code Noir*, the regulations enacted by Jean-Baptiste Colbert for protecting slaves in French colonies from the possible exactions and abuses of harsh masters. Two decades later, when the science of political commerce flourished in the group formed around Jacques Vincent de Gournay, Inspector General of Commerce, slavery was not something to which there was any great moral objection: where competition existed between slave nations it was profit that was of greatest significance. In 1754 Gournay translated Josiah Child's *Discourse on Trade* (1693), and in writing a commentary upon it he found nothing that needed reformulating when it came to the maintenance of slavery. His disciple, François Véron de Forbonnais, took the same position in his entry on "Colonies" for Denis Diderot's *Encyclopédie*, republishing it in his influential work *Éléments du commerce*. In the pages that he devoted to slavery he emphasized the beneficial impact upon colonial agriculture of the low price of black slaves, and on the prospects of maintaining it at this level.[7]

There was, however, a notable shift in ideas about slavery during this period. At the point where the transatlantic slave trade was at its zenith, European philosophy thought of morality in terms of *autonomy*: no longer was morality treated as a duty of obedience to God and his terrestrial representatives, but rather as the capacity, shared by all humans, to conform to those principles or laws that man's reason found to be good.[8] Kantian philosophy seemed to be the culmination of this new conception of morality. Liberty was defined as a natural right, inalienable and universal.[9] This would be affirmed in the Declaration of the Rights of Man in 1789 as the leading legal principle, the condition from which all law was derived. It assumed a political dimension in the course of the century. In this context it is not surprising that slavery should in the eighteenth century be questioned in terms of morality. While words did not change their meaning, the underlying ideas did begin to change. This can be shown at work in some of the articles published in the *Encyclopédie*.

As with the dictionaries of the early part of the century, the author of the entry on "*Morale*" defined this as a science of wise conduct constantly beset by the needs of life, false interests, opinions, prejudice, and, above all, the passions. Without alluding to religion, the entry concludes by affirming the superiority of morality over faith. Moral liberty is always defined as the power of an intelligent being to do what it wants in conformity with its own determination; although the entry on "*Liberté, naturelle*" characterizes this as "the most precious of goods": "[this state] cannot be exchanged for another, it cannot be sold, it cannot be lost; for of course all men are born free; which is to say that they are not subject to the power of another, and that nobody has a right of property in them." While Christianity was to be commended for having abolished servitude as an outcome of defeat in war, the author asks why it is that Christian powers have treated servitude as compatible with the perfection to which Christian religion calls men: "They need their colonies, their plantations, their mines. *Auri sacra fames!*" A comparison of various texts making reference to slavery demonstrates that the development of ideas regarding this institution was not uniform.

If the entry "*Nègre (commerce)*" involved a negative judgment concerning negroid traits, the entry devoted to "*Nègre (esclaves nègres dans les colonies)*" confined itself, rather like Forbonnais's approach in his entry on "*Colonies*," to a description of the different activities occupying plantation slaves. By contrast, the articles of Louis de Jaucourt took their point of departure from Montesquieu and were resolutely anti-slavery. In the entry "*L'esclave*" he explained that the slave "is someone deprived of liberty and who is in the power of a master. According to natural law, all men are born free; the state of personal servitude is an invention of the rights of people." Forcibly stripped of his liberty, the slave's life itself is constantly under threat. As he wrote in his entry "*Esclavage*," "the moment that a man seeks to subordinate me to himself against my will I can assume that if I fall into his hands he will treat me according to his own caprice, having no scruple about killing me if the whim so takes him. In other words, liberty is the rampart of my self-preservation, and the foundation of all other things that belong to me." Slavery is an institution that is both useless and destructive of morality: "Together with this illustrious author [Montesquieu] we can state once again that slavery is useful neither to master nor to slave since they can do nothing through virtue—for the master, because with his slaves he is led into all sorts of vices and bad habits that are contrary to the law of society; insensibly, he becomes accustomed to the loss of all moral virtues; he becomes proud, hasty, choleric, hard, voluptuous, barbaric. All of which conspires to strip man of the dignity natural to him. All cry that one cannot strip him of the natural dignity that is his liberty, that the rule of justice is not founded upon power, but upon that which conforms to nature; slavery is not only a condition humiliating for the person subordinated, but for humanity itself which is thereby degraded." While the enslavement of the mind by the passions is touched on by other entries in the *Encyclopédie*, Jaucourt does not deal with this. Neglecting the uniquely moral sense of the term "slavery," he lays emphasis on the political sense: it is not the common humanity of sinners that captures his attention but the common humanity of liberty. In the article "*Traite des Nègres*" Jaucourt identifies this trade as "theft," "brigandage," a "crime" committed to satisfy the avarice and vanity of colonists. This assimilation of slavery to crime will remain a leitmotiv of abolitionist discourse right up to 1848.

ABOLITIONIST MORAL DISCOURSE

While Montesquieu's *Esprit des lois* created a way of making arguments against slavery, abolitionist discourse did not really begin to consolidate and develop until the early 1770s.[10] At the beginning of this decade Louis-Sébastien Mercier made himself the defender of a right of resistance to the oppression of slavery. He announced in his book *L'An 2440* the coming of an "avenger from the new world" able to lead his brothers to liberty, a theme taken up by Diderot in his *Histoire des deux Indes*, a book that itself went through three editions between 1770 and 1780.[11] These predictions of insurrection, repeated in the nineteenth century,[12] sought to demonstrate to colonists that their obstinacy in preserving the system of slavery would lead to the loss of the colonies. At the same time that Du Pont made his calculations the abbé Baudeau and the abbé Roubaud proposed a new international division of labor related to the emancipation of slaves, opening up a new way of thinking about the relationship of Europe with its American and African colonies that gained increasing influence among abolitionists. In 1781 Jean Antoine Caritat, marquis de Condorcet published his *Réflexions sur l'esclavage des Nègres*, opening with a moral condemnation of slavery, following that with a response to the prejudice that colonies could only be cultivated through the use of slave labor, and ending by outlining a project for the gradual dismantlement of slavery. The book was republished in 1788, shortly after the foundation of the Société des amis des noirs, of which Condorcet was a founding member.

The abolitionist movement had now assumed an organizational form. The objectives of the society, which remained active up to the autumn of 1791, were threefold: the immediate abolition of the slave trade; the gradual emancipation of slaves; and the creation of a new commercial international order based upon the introduction of the sugar industry to Africa, worked by free labor, together with the introduction of new crops to the islands. Faced with the slave revolt in Haiti, the Convention abolished slavery on February 4, 1794. In 1797 some members of the Société des amis des noirs formed a broader association that included, among others, Jean-Baptiste Say. However, the Société des amis des noirs et des colonies, whose purpose was to promote a colonial order based upon equality and free labor, proved short-lived. Napoleon Bonaparte restored slavery in 1802 and in January 1804 Haiti declared independence, events that for metropolitan opinion confirmed the failure of the abolitionist movement.

After a difficult period during the Empire, the movement saw a cautious revival during the Restoration, and consistent growth during the July Monarchy.[13] Organized within the Société de la morale chrétienne (1821–1834) and then as the Société française pour l'abolition de l'esclavage (1834–1850), the majority of whose members were politicians, abolitionists campaigned within local and national assemblies for the government to abolish the slave trade and permit the gradual emancipation of slaves. Despite the rise to power of prominent members of the movement (including King Louis-Philippe), this approach had only mixed results. Having taken effective measures to close down clandestine trading in slaves, and having given equality of rights to freed black slaves, the July Monarchy made no further positive initiative regarding the issue of slave emancipation. Instead, after the abolition of slavery in British colonies,[14] it limited itself to passing several laws aimed at improving the condition of slaves and preparing them for liberty. Envisaging only a gradual process of abolition, the actual proposals advanced by parliamentary commissions[15] remained a dead letter. Abolition would finally be decreed on April 27, 1848, only as a result of another revolution. Nonetheless, during the last decade of the July Monarchy the debate on slavery did find a place in political institutions.

The acquisition of wealth through "cruel and criminal paths"; "horrible atrocities"; "piracy"; "Europe's shame": this was the terminology used by those agitating against slavery during the revolutionary period. Nineteenth-century abolitionists adopted an approach that allowed the most radical among them to forcefully declare the unreformable nature of servitude. In 1840 Victor Schœlcher noted the apt expression of an English writer: "You cannot regulate slavery in a humane way because you can't regulate assassination." This became a political slogan, and in 1846 was used as the title-page epigraph in a pamphlet published by Commandant France, and then in the following year in the two volumes of Schœlcher's final abolitionist work. It also had a place in the petition that the same Schœlcher addressed in August 1847 to the Chambre des pairs (Upper House) and to the Chambre des deputes (Chamber of Deputies) through the good offices of the Société pour l'abolition de l'esclavage.[16]

CALCULATION, INTEREST, AND ECONOMIC GOVERNMENT

During the last third of the eighteenth century another strong argument was added to the moral and political condemnation of slavery: that of calculation. It would remain in place right up to the point of slave emancipation. How could this association of calculation and morality come about? How can we explain the sudden appearance of calculative rhetoric in the early 1770s, when no trace of it can be found either in the dictionaries of the time or in the *Encyclopédie*?

The scientific revolution of the seventeenth century lent a new impulse to the idea that God wrote the world in geometrical language, to repeat the expression used by Galileo in his *Discorsi e dimostrazioni matematiche intorno a due nuove scienze*. This is a formulation that echoes the phrasing in the Apocrypha, that God "has regulated all things in measure, and number, and weight,"[17] a phrasing upon which Catholic theologians have sometimes commented. The New Science emerged in a world not yet divided clearly into disciplines, and its quantitative approach was quickly taken up to take account of social and political life. One prominent example of this in the latter seventeenth century was William Petty, a very active member of the Royal Society who set himself the task of measuring the balance of forces between Britain and its adversaries by calculating their respective economic and demographic powers. Slipping into the language of the new scientific regime created by natural philosophy, political calculation was seen as a way of overcoming arguments both verbal and verbose:

> The Method I take to do this, is not yet very usual; for instead of using only comparative and superlative Words, and intellectual Arguments, I have taken the course (as a Specimen of the Political Arithmetick I have long aimed at) to express myself in Terms of *Number*, *Weight*, or *Measure*; to use only Arguments of Sense, and to consider only such Causes, as have visible Foundations in Nature, leaving those that depend upon the mutable Minds, Opinions, Appetites, and Passions of particular Men, to the consideration of others; Really professing my self as unable to speak satisfactorily upon those Grounds (if they may be call'd Grounds), as to foretel the cast of a Dye; to play well at Tennis, Billiards, or Bowles, (without long practice,) by virtue of the most elaborate Conceptions that ever have been written *De Projectilibus & Missilibus*, or of the Angles of Incidence and Reflection.[18]

In the eighteenth century the word "calculation" had a dual signification: the *Dictionnaire de l'Académie française* defined it both as a hypothesis (*supputation*) and as an "account" (*compte*).[19] The first meaning suggests that calculation does not necessarily rely upon numbers and measurable quantities. The term rather implies a form of reasoning in which different kinds of facts are considered in order to determine a course of action, the best way to deal with a project or an idea; poor calculation thus leads one "to deceive oneself, to be mistaken in whatever matter." Alongside this general meaning, which was always valid, the sense of "account" emerged, presuming a sequence of operations on the basis of measurable quantities that were capable of being defined exactly, operations that enabled a numerical result to be arrived at: "Account. *Exact calculation. To calculate some sum.*" Calculation was incarnated in the person of the astronomer, "a great and good calculator," something which is no surprise in Newton's contemporary work *Principia Mathematica*. The entries in the *Encyclopédie* are elaborated more technically since Jean-Baptiste le Rond d'Alembert was a skilled geometer, but the entries for "*Calcul*" and "*Calculer*" also invoke the figure of the astronomer, although also introducing practitioners in the "arts" such as mechanics and clockmakers. However, calculation was not only a matter of planetary orbits, the order of the cosmos, and the measurement of time; it came down to earth to deal with political order, commerce in goods and, more generally, human action. In so doing it passed from a divine order, regulating the course of the planets, to the political order that regulated human behavior; and here calculation encountered morality. The rubric "political arithmetic" is one of the very many subentries in the *Encyclopédie* under "*Arithmétique*," detailing the different forms taken by the science of numbers, including differential calculus. Political arithmetic is "that which has as its aim investigations of use to the art of governing peoples, such as the number of persons living in a country; the quality of the food that they must consume; the work that they can do; the length of time they live, the fertility of land, the frequency of catastrophes, etc." William Petty is treated as the person introducing this new domain. Diderot, the author of this entry, wrote that a clever minister could gain from this great benefit for government; but many imagined that they were possessed of a natural genius that made such a careful and detailed approach redundant, also thinking that the nature of the affairs with which they dealt hardly ever allowed or required geometric precision. Diderot concluded: "However, if the nature of affairs requires it and permits it I have no doubt at all that one will not conclude that the political world, as well as the physical world, in many respects can be regulated by weight, number and measure."[20]

There is a long history to this way of cloaking economic thinking with the language of science and calculation, with the intention of silencing opinions and the rhetorical artifice behind which interests are concealed. It can be found flowing from the pen of François Quesnay, who in the mid-1750s abandoned the medical science at which he excelled to elaborate a theory of "economic government." This was intended as a way of rebuilding the kingdom of France during the Seven Years' War (1756-63), when it was confronted with the naval and financial power of Britain. Like Petty, Quesnay used many calculations in his articles for the *Encyclopédie*.[21] With Quesnay and the group that formed around him—the "Philosophes économistes," the "Économistes," or later the Physiocrats—calculation became the language enabling access to truth, defense of its rights and preeminence in the public domain.

In the "Introduction" to *Philosophie rurale*, a joint work by Quesnay and Victor Riqueti de Mirabeau but which was published under the name of the latter, the motivation of this option was outlined:

> Economic politics is henceforth subject to calculation; for we cannot call too many witnesses for the proof of truth, too many enthusiasts for instruction in the science of demonstration. Calculation is to economic science what bones are to the human body. . . . Economic science is extended and developed by inspection and reasoning; but without calculation it would always be an uncertain science, confused and everywhere prey to error and prejudice. The more that calculations are unshakable in their foundation, sequence and duration, the more that those who think themselves interested in preventing the explosion of enlightenment rush to openly maintain that calculations are false. . . . Calculation can only be attacked with other calculations."[22]

Calculations thrived in two socially distinct spaces: while some were used to support the administration, others founded political and moral arguments. An administrator had to render account, detail his resources and the use made of them to his hierarchy; but these calculations, like those of merchants or engineers, did not circulate beyond a small number of persons engaged in practical matters.[23] The memoranda on conditions in slave colonies addressed to the Minister of the Navy and Colonies by Pierre-Paul Le Mercier de la Rivière illustrates this calculative practice within the administration. Le Mercier, a prominent Physiocrat, was Intendant for Martinique (île du vent) from 1759 to 1762 and then again from 1763 to 1764, and in his memoranda he constantly made use of calculations in order to determine the condition of the territory and population for which he was responsible, but also to establish the best way in which he might structure taxation.[24] Calculation seemed to be a mode of government, both in its object and in its form: it justified decisions that had been taken as far as central authority was concerned, but it also justified these decisions to those upon whom these decisions would bear—citizens required to pay taxes—and, ultimately, demonstrated the rationality of royal authority. For this, data were needed capable of testifying to administrators and to the minister of the crown the positive view that the Intendant had of the islands, also confirming his ability to raise the tax required while at the same time preserving the productive potential of the territory.

Alongside this form of administrative calculation, a tool of government aimed at taking and justifying decisions, there emerged economic calculation as an instrument of public debate. In the latter case, it served first of all to compel an adversary who sought to enter the terrain of political economy to respond to calculations with alternative calculations. It thus became a way of making someone do something: calculations showed what individuals themselves had to do once their interests had been made explicit by calculation. Numbers became new and powerful rhetorical and pragmatic instruments. In the articles that Quesnay published in the *Encyclopédie*, at a time that the costs of the Seven Years' War were weighing on the monarchy, Quesnay made calculations that defended agriculture and demonstrated the resources that the free export of grain would not fail to create for the nation.

Administrative and economic calculation did, however, rapidly converge upon the point at which there was significant interaction between administration and science.[25] The governmental practice of calculation did not exclude recourse to the rules and principles of political economy that permitted calculations to be structured while providing arguments with which they could make sense.[26] In this respect the memoranda that Le Mercier drafted are exemplary.[27] Administrative calculation is here structured according to the principles of political economy. And, in spite of his denunciation of the Physiocratic mania for calculation, Anne-Robert-Jacques Turgot himself followed the practice of Quesnay when he was seeking to persuade the Controller General of the relevance of the policy of free trade.[28]

However, the promotion of calculation by the Économistes is not reducible to a merely arithmetical dimension, in the sense that it was a matter of finding a result that derived from a series of known quantitative facts. The novelty and the power of this calculative impulse came from its association with a political doctrine that the interests of the various social classes (farmers, landed proprietors, merchants) could be represented in numbers. Self-interest was understood to be the political lever capable of creating the cohesion necessary for the power of the nation. It was a matter of calculating self-interest in such a way that an "economic government" might be established whose decisions could be of benefit to all. This objective guided thinking about the liberalization of the grain trade, a significant political reform which was of central importance for both public and government in the second half of the eighteenth century. The approach was given theoretical formulation by Le Mercier de La Rivière, who based politics entirely upon self-interest, instead of placing it, as with Montesquieu, under the aegis of honor, or of virtue as Rousseau wished. The first two pages of the "Discours préliminaire" of his most important text are explicit on this point:

> I write in the interests of kings, since I deal with the means by which their wealth, their power, and their authority might be raised to the greatest degree possible. . . . I write . . . in the interests of landowners, since I deal with the means by which all land might be brought to deliver to them the greatest possible income. . . . I write . . . in the interests of this class [wage-earners], since I deal with the means by which the mass of workers' wages can be increased in all ways to the greatest extent possible. . . . I write . . . in the interests of the destitute, since I deal with the ways in which one might secure harvests of the greatest possible abundance. . . . I write . . . in the interest of merchants, since I deal with the ways in which the greatest possible reproduction might be secured, and the greatest possible consumption of all the wealth that can enter the kingdom. . . . I therefore write in the interest of the entire body of society.[29]

This connection between calculation and interest has decisive importance for understanding how calculation and morality are joined together in the debate over the abolition of slavery.

"Interest" is of course a generic term that applies to any form of attachment that an individual might have with worldly affairs. The *Dictionnaire de l'Académie française* defines it as a "passion" whose sense is "what matters, what is appropriate in any matter whatsoever, whether to the honor, or to the utility, or to the satisfaction of someone." Beyond its legal usage ("to remove all interest," meaning to provide compensation), and its commercial sense ("the profit that is made upon money that has been lent"), interest acquires a sense related to a form of social relationship:

> It is also said, to take an interest in a matter, in a person, meaning to have affection for them, to take care of them, to take their part in seeking success. . . . One also says, to take an interest in the pleasure or the affliction of someone, in the loss that they have suffered, the disgrace that has come upon them, meaning to be touched by it, to be sensitive to it.

Besides these meanings, the dictionary notes a specific sense that is today the dominant one: "Interest is also sometimes taken as meaning that which concerns the sole utility." The term can also be used to describe, positively or negatively, individual behavior: "He is a man above all interest, he allows nothing to depend upon interest"; "He will betray his best friend for an interest of five sols." It can, however, assume a general sense: "Most people conduct themselves, govern themselves only by interest, only through interest"; "it is interest that governs everything." For its part, the *Dictionnaire de Trévoux* echoed the lengthy debate between moralists, represented primarily by François de La Rochefoucauld and Charles de

Saint-Évremond; and theologians including François de Salignac de La Mothe-Fénélon and Jacques Bénigne Bossuet (who were adversaries in the dispute over pure love). Following on from Saint-Évremond, the writer of the dictionary entry noted that "It is from interest alone that we act, even in those things in which we seem the least interested."

Albert Hirschman analyzed the development of the notion of interest in the eighteenth-century moral and political domain.[30] He demonstrated how Occidental thought quite gradually came around to the view that interest was the legitimate motivation of human action. United in believing that passions endangered the liberty of the individual and of his relationship to God, moralists took different positions upon the way in which morality could govern human beings. Some of them considered that reason should be called upon to moderate the passions; a solution that suppressed the problem rather than dealt with it, the property of passion being exactly to dominate reason. Others sought to contrast "good" and "bad" passions, the first acting as a counterweight to the second—a fragile solution given the delicacy of the mechanism to be set to work. The solution to the problem was eventually found in the promotion of the notion of interest, a third term, never clearly defined, inserted between passion and reason. As Hirschman wrote, "Interest was seen to partake in effect of the better nature of each, as the passion of self-love upgraded and contained by reason, and as reason given direction and force by that passion."[31] The course of conduct dictated by interest showed itself to be as predictable and constant as that of a virtuous man. Everyone could calculate their own interest—Prince, farmer, landowner, but also the slaveowner.

The significance of Quesnay's "science of economic government" was precisely related to the junction that it created between material interest and calculation. The latter appeared to be the means of defining the true interests of different classes, allowing the Prince and wise ministers to preside over their harmonization. Touchstone of the good government of the nation, interest is equally the guarantee of an individual's morality: having become conscious of his true interest, man leads his life in a wise manner, in conformity with the natural order. The calculation of these interests became a morality, a form of life conduct that could be recommended: calm, restrained, predictable, and profitable to all. By demonstrating what the interests of both the governing and the governed were, calculation provided political effects: it gave all actors an incentive to act according to that which political economy prescribed as the most useful. It created an *ethos*, right conduct; it was therefore a source of morality. Contemporary French utilitarians, notably Claude-Adrien Helvétius,[32] used it as such before Jeremy Bentham, the father of modern utilitarianism, had taken up the issue.

CALCULATION, MORALITY, AND THE ABOLITION OF SLAVERY IN FRANCE

The purpose of this book is to bring to light an important, if neglected, aspect of the secular controversy over the emancipation of blacks opened up in 1748 by Montesquieu's comments in *L'Esprit des lois* and closed in 1848 by an abolition decree promulgated by the Provisional Government of the Republic. The calculation of the costs of free labor as opposed to those of slave labor became a feature of political debate that had, up until then, worked purely in terms of moral issues, sometimes reinforced by an appeal to emotion. This does not involve us in conducting a cliometric study of the kind made by Robert Fogel and Stanley Engerman in their book *Time on the Cross*, where the authors showed that slave labor was, because of its great productivity, profitable to those plantation owners whose return, they calculated, on investment in Mississippi increased by 16 percent, a rate of return higher than that of industry not only in the South, but also in the North.[33] While we emphasize the gaps and assumptions in contributions using calculation made by many different actors taking part in the debate over slave emancipation in French colonies, we do not seek to resolve the question of the relative profitability of free and of servile labor. The aim of our study is to show how calculations that were introduced into debate alongside moral arguments became critical social objects, having their own consistency and tangible effects.

The term "calculation" is meant here in the sense employed in the sociology of sciences and of economics.[34] First of all, it deals with the operations through which entities that are thought relevant are grouped into the same class, together with the reasons for their having been retained. Second, the categorized elements are enumerated in respect of their scale, making it possible to manipulate them mathematically in a manner appropriate to clarification of the phenomenon studied. Categorization and quantification are of equal importance. We will employ this duality in studying the calculations set to work to analyze the relative costs of slave and free labor in the works published by various protagonists in the debate over the abolition of slavery: economists, abolitionists, colonists, administrators—all using them to defend their own points of view in an impassioned debate. The intervention of calculation in the controversy on the comparative costs of free and servile labor was made possible by their dual dimension, by the diverse sources that they were able to take into account, but also by the technical simplicity involved at this time—essentially, all that they involved were the four rules of arithmetic. Easily used by economists and administrators, but also by militant abolitionists and the representatives of colonists, the introduction of calculation excluded no one from debate. Those intervening were understood by and responded to their adversaries by referring, explicitly or not, to their writings: the calculations of one side were countered with calculations from the other. Our study is restricted to France, and involves the works of economists, politicians, administrators, and publicists active during the period writing pamphlets expressing the urgency of political debate, but also contributing to important periodicals; and it also takes into account the reports of parliamentary commissions, royal or republican, that appeared from the later 1830s onward. This allows us to establish, over a period of a little more than sixty years, *a series of calculations that are connected together by public discussion*. We do not claim that this series is exhaustive—there are probably more calculations to be discovered in archival documents that we have not been able to find, or did not know how to—but it allows us to tie together quite solidly facts that have usually been treated as unrelated to each other.

The calculations that we have studied were produced in two distinct phases. During the Ancien Régime the administration gathered together a great deal of material that already possessed a great deal of homogeneity—population changes (births, deaths, marriages), the course of food prices (especially cereal prices)—but were not intended to be made public. During this phase the calculator could limit himself to defining the principles applicable to the examination of a problem, principles suited to lead to quantification, but where this was not of absolute necessity. However, if he had obtained data through contacts in the administration or his links with those prepared to share their archive with him (accounts of the management of economic initiatives, information collected from travelers) he might be able to extend his work of categorization and arrive at some kind of numerical representation. Quantitative information that was used was rarely linked to a verifiable source; it circulated among an enlightened public that assumed it was valid. At the end of the eighteenth century this is the material on which the calculations of Du Pont, Condorcet, the members of the first Société des amis des noirs, and also those produced by colonists were all based.

The imperfect quality of the numbers used in the calculations made raised problems of which those who made calculations were well aware. The period can be treated as pre-statistical: Jean-Claude Perrot's investigation of the statistics used in the first dictionary of political economy that was published in France[35] shows that only a third of them were official, and that more than half of them came from the stories of travelers or were collected by economists, or by the author himself.[36] To deal with this problem some writers, like Arthur Young in his *Political Arithmetic*,[37] distinguished calculations involving the manipulation of numerical data from calculation as a mode of reasoning. In the latter case it was not the exactness and precision of the numbers employed that was important, but instead the intellectual reasonings that were based upon them in the expectation that, where necessary, one would be able to employ well-founded numerical data. In his preface to his own *Political Arithmetick* William Petty provided an audacious justification for this approach that dealt with any objection that might be raised to the numbers he used:

> Now the Observations or Positions expressed by Number, Weight and Measure, upon which I bottom the ensuing Discourses, are either true, or not apparently false, and which if they are not already true, certain, and evident, yet may be made so by Sovereign Power, Nom id certum est quod certaum reddi postest, and if they are false, not so false as to destroy the Argument they are brought for; but at worst are sufficient as Suppositions to show the way to that Knowledge I aim at.[38]

This rather unheroic epistemological admission does make a useful distinction between an ideal calculation based upon verifiable numbers and one elaborated using conjectural figures—the intermediate case being to take account of incorrect data that was however susceptible to become exact if the government were to employ those able to make them so, something that was beyond the power of a single individual. *In every case* the principles of reasoning conducted upon "objective foundations," which henceforth would be numerical, are an essential component of calculation. In the final remark of his famous *Tableau Économique* Quesnay made the same plea:

> Under these conditions [twenty-three hypotheses relating to the functioning of the French economy] the agriculture that one presumes in the *Tableau* to produce exactly in the same way as in Britain would be a fiction; but that does not make the principles any less certain, nor any less the true principles of the science of economic government, which is not here to be confused with the trivial science of specious financial operations, whose only object is the nation's savings and the movement of money through commerce; in which credit, the lure of interest, etc. produces no more than sterile circulation, as in a game.[39]

Du Pont adopted a similar point of view when he joined Quesnay's circle at the beginning of the 1760s. His book on the promotion of the commercialization of grain[40] is a good example of the sophisticated calculations associated with what he called the "new science" of political economy.[41] These calculations made no claim to being a rigorous account of precise empirical cases but were a guide for government in respect of food security, showing economic elites where their real interest lay. He used the same procedure in his study of roads,[42] aimed at landowners, where he imposed on his reader long series of numbers, noting that he would spare his reader the detail of fastidious calculations, which he would only publish if anyone sought to contradict him.[43] He did not, however, demonstrate such reticence in the analysis he made of the costs of servile labor in *Éphemérides du citoyen*, the physiocratic periodical of which he had become editor. The calculations that he there put forward were presented as complementary to literary works, intended to capture the interest of the reader who would then be prepared to take the time to consider the arid speculations of the calculator, adding the weight of numbers to that of words.

After the Restoration, data collected by the administration increasingly gained a wider public circulation; a process that Alain Desrosières has called "the politics of large numbers" characterizing a world in which the government of human collectivities was effected through the increasingly massive use of quantitative data which, classified and measured by and for calculation, became an indispensable tool of government. To begin with, calculators like Jean-Baptiste Say and Jean Charles Léonard Simonde de Sismondi adhered to the approach taken by their predecessors in the eighteenth century; only Charles Ganilh took the trouble to relate the arguments he advanced to precise numerical data drawn either from previous writers or from data collated by the administration. From 1830 onward official statistics were made available; calculators relied upon them in all economic matters, especially those arising from the abolition of slavery. During the final decade of servitude numbers were used not only as rhetorical arguments but also as instruments of government. In dealing with the question of sugar production, in 1838 the Minister of the Navy and of the Colonies commissioned Paul Lavollée, an Inspector of Finance, to study conditions of cultivation and production in Martinique and Guadeloupe. In 1839 a report written by Alexis de Tocqueville for the parliamentary commission investigating Victor Destutt de Tracy's project for the progressive abolition of slavery used the figures and calculations of Lavollée, together with a great mass of statistics relating to British islands where emancipation had already taken place. The commission established by royal decree on May 12, 1840, and charged with examining "questions relating to slavery and to the political constitution of colonies" (the de Broglie Commission) based much of its work upon quantitative information. The publication of Lavollée's report in 1841 followed a request made by this commission, and was made by order of the Minister of the Navy and Colonies. The three volumes presenting the findings of the commission were a veritable hymn to statistics. The framework for the reform of administration and of colonial political representation was first established with the aid of many tables, followed first by a review of British colonial statistics and then by a series of calculations aimed at establishing the costs of gradual abolition (compensation for slaves, the support of children and old people) that employed a study of the dynamic development of the slave population, taking into account the rates of emancipation and of death (using Duvillard's mortality tables). The commission appointed by the provisional government in 1848 "to prepare the *immediate abolition* of slavery"—and not, like those that had preceded it, to establish a project for emancipation—also sought to prove its interest in the economic repercussions of the decision that had been taken. It twice interviewed Paul Lavollée who made presentations of various statistical tables, which were then partially included in the appendices to the report that appeared under the name of Victor Schœlcher, the commission's president.

Given that calculation was a common factor in two periods differing both in the scale of production of quantitative data and in their mode of diffusion, this provides for the historian and sociologist a unique perspective upon debates arising from social and economic problems.

Calculations produce a "knowledge effect" insofar as they bear upon complex questions. What goes to make up the price of servile labor? How can this be placed in relation to free manual labor when the employment of free workers is extremely limited and restricted to specialized activities in slave colonies? What magnitudes should be taken into account in estimating the productivity of the slave and of the free worker? How can the profitability of work be estimated if it is allowed that it does not only depend upon its price but also on labor productivity?

Calculations also have political effects. Introduced into public debate, calculative rhetoric presents itself as a *guide to action*. The calculations of labor cost has for a long time been treated as a minor part of social activity. Businessmen seeking to gauge the extent of their wealth do nonetheless pay attention to it, and hardly bother about the nature of the living conditions of those to whom it is applied. The ideas that developed in the course of the eighteenth century and which became known as political economy, the moral and political sciences, or even economic philosophy did on the other hand place calculation firmly within the tradition of moral philosophy. This can be seen both in the writings of Quesnay's disciples—the Physiocrats—and in those of Adam Smith who was, we should remember, a professor of moral philosophy; and it is also something that we can see in the writings of French liberal economists during the nineteenth century. Calculations came to be mobilized to establish the "just price" of manufactured products.[44] Those which were made in relation to the analysis of the slave system were not, however, aimed at establishing an economic magnitude (price) that would be morally acceptable (just). For those opposed to the slave system, the aim was to demonstrate that the interest of the slave, of the colonist, and/or of the nation lay in abolishing the injustice involved in the putting a price on a human being; and for those who hoped to be able to preserve servitude, to demonstrate that this price was, ultimately, the condition of a situation that suited everyone morally and politically, including slaves themselves.

The economic argument was never detached from the moral context in which it had been developed, that of opposition to a system that became increasingly denounced as inhuman. In the eighteenth as in the nineteenth century, protagonists in the debate sought to demonstrate *the articulation of calculation and morality*. Both were put on the same level.

Rather than seeking to distance economic calculation from morality, our study emphasizes the way in which economists, militant abolitionists, and also colonists bound them closely together. Calculations of labor costs were continually linked with a questioning of the morality of economic activity based upon the deportation of individuals torn from their roots and their social relationships, to be sold in the colonies and then forced through violence to work. By demonstrating that masters and/or the entire nation would find it in their interest to employ free manual labor abolitionist calculators claimed to reveal the irrationality of colonial or metropolitan defenders of servitude. Their aim was to enlighten different collectivities regarding their real interest, and to show that this coincided with justice. Colonists, for their part, accused those opposed to slavery of allowing themselves to be blinded by their philanthropic principles, and argued that the slave system was perfectly rational and the only means, at least in the short run, of upholding the interests of everyone. In addition, the calculations of abolitionists depended on a *deontological ethics* that was more Kantian than utilitarian. The emancipation of slaves was judged not only in terms of its consequences; abolitionists never ceased arguing that it had become an obligation independent of the interests (colonial or metropolitan) that it might harm. Colonists, by contrast, pointed constantly to the harm that would be done to everyone by abolition—planters, merchants, consumers and metropolitan manufacturers, the slaves themselves—and so took a *pragmatic ethical* position.

One social category was, however, excluded from this controversy: the slaves themselves. Placed at the center of debate, and objects of calculation, they were never in a position to offer their own calculation. Were they unable to calculate?

From the eighteenth-century interest, rationality and calculation became constitutive elements of the economic and moral modernity of the subject who was charged with calculating the best course of action in the various markets in which that subject participated. All those involved in this controversy invoked this logic but came to diametrically opposed conclusions. While colonists emphasised the "laziness" of the Black, abolitionists explained this by servitude. In their eyes, "laziness" was the outcome of a rational calculation: as a foe of the master the slave had an interest in serving him badly; concerned with protecting himself, he worked just enough to save himself from the harshest punishments. This argument was a decisive one. The capacity of the slave to calculate, while at the same time subject to terrible conditions, was evidence of the slave's humanity. This calculation could then be treated dynamically: freed, the slaves would understand, from the example set by the white worker, that the gain made from working could lead him out of poverty into a life of ease; he would use his own potential for labor for his own best interests. He would in this way achieve complete economic rationality and also the morality associated with it. The calculation of interest highlighted a "freeing" of the slaves that would be of advantage to planters, to the nation, to the entire globe, to the greater material and moral good of humanity as a whole.

Analysis of the controversy over the abolition of slavery cannot therefore treat calculation and morality separately.

From 1771 to 1848 *calculations were used to answer calculations*. They became embedded in public debate and became tied up with moral argument in order to make more obvious the force of the antislavery cause, or to defend the retention of servitude. Calculation and morality were the two indivisible faces of political debate over abolition.

NOTES

1. Paul Hazard, *La Crise de la conscience européenne*, Boivin, Paris 1935, translated in 1952 as *The European Mind, the Critical Years, 1680–1715*.
2. Lucien Febvre, *Pour une histoire à part entière*, SEVPEN, Paris 1962.

3. Re-interpreting Roman historians, philosophers define the liberty of a state in terms of its autonomy, that is, its capacity to determine the laws according to which its subjects are governed—see Quentin Skinner, *Liberty before Liberalism*, Cambridge University Press, Cambridge 1998.
4. In unison with this, the *Dictionnaire de l'Académie française* gives as the second figurative meaning: "It is also said that a man is slave to favour, to his interests and his passions, meaning that he does everything in the service of favour, for his interests, or for his passions."
5. Philippe Steiner, "Commerce, commerce politique," in Loïc Charles, Frédéric Lefebvre, Christine Théré (eds.) *Le Cercle de Vincent de Gournay, Savoirs économiques et pratiques administratives en France au milieu du XVIIIe siècle*, INED, Paris 2011.
6. Jean-François Melon, *Essai politique sur le commerce*, Paris 1734, p. 48.
7. "The trade in negroes must therefore be considered, favoured and maintained as the necessary basis of colonial cultivation. The certain means to make it flourish are our fleets and the greatest possible competition between merchants; but this is not always enough. It is still more important to enable merchants to trade in slaves as cheaply as other nations." François Véron de Forbonnais, *Éléments du commerce*, vol. 2, Leiden 1754, pp. 33–34.
8. Jerome B. Schneewind, *The Invention of Autonomy. A History of Modern Moral Philosophy*, Cambridge University Press, Cambridge 1998, Ch. XXII.
9. Oliver Grenouilleau, *Qu'est-ce que l'esclavage? Une histoire globale*, Gallimard, Paris 2014, pp. 48–57.
10. Montesquieu's analysis largely formed the basis for Jaucourt's *Encyclopédie* entry on "*Esclavage*." We might note that if Montesquieu did present a rough critique of the slave trade and of servitude in Book XV of *Esprit des lois*, he framed this in terms of a theory of climates; while he considered slavery "contrary to nature," he did, however, treat it as "based upon natural reason" in those countries with a warm climate where men only worked if they were forced to.
11. For an account of the development of anti-slavery arguments in the eighteenth century see Marcel Dorigny, "La Société des Amis des Noirs: antiesclavagisme et lobby colonial à la fin du siècle des Lumières (1788–1792)," in Marcel Dorigny, Bernard Gainot (eds.) *La Société des Amis des Noirs*, Éditions de l'UNESCO/EDICEF, Paris 1998, pp. 16–19.
12. The idea that colonists were living on top of a volcano was developed by the abbé Grégoire in particular—*De la noblesse de la peau: du préjugé des Blancs contre la couleur des Africains et de celle de leurs descendants noirs et sang mêlé* [1826], Jérôme Millon, Grenoble 1996, p. 88; and also by the abbé Dugoujon in his *Lettres sur l'esclavage dans les colonies françaises*, Pagnerre, Paris 1845, p. 93.
13. For a very detailed analysis of this, see Lawrence C. Jennings, *French Anti-Slavery: The Movement for the Abolition of Slavery in France, 1802–1848*, Cambridge University Press, Cambridge 2001.
14. Britain enacted the Slavery Abolition Act in 1833, which provided for the continuation of urban slavery to 1838, and rural slavery to 1840. The final abolition for all slaves in fact took place on August 1, 1838.
15. Commissions were headed by Charles de Rémusat in 1838, by Alexis de Tocqueville in 1839, and by the final de Broglie royal commission on questions relating to slavery from 1840 to 1843.
16. Nelly Schmidt, *Abolitionnistes de l'esclavage et réformateurs des colonies, 1820–1851*, Paris, Karthala 2000, p. 879.
17. Wisdom of Solomon xi, 21.

18. Charles Henry Hull (ed.), *Economic Writings of Sir William Petty*, vol. I, Cambridge University Press, Cambridge 1899, p. 244.
19. "**Calcul**, s.m. *Supputation, compte*. Exact calculation. To calculate a sum. From my calculation I find that etc. Error of calculation. To be misled by one's calculation. Used proverbially and figuratively. To be misled by one's calculation means to deceive oneself, to be mistaken in whatever matter. Calculator, someone who calculates. This astronomer is a great and good calculator." Le *Dictionnaire de Trévoux*, published in 1704, dealt with the definition in the same terms—we leave aside here the French medical meaning of calcul (stone).
20. This rubric is mostly duplicated under "Politique arithmétique" that can be found under the entry for "Politique." The text is in places identical—criticism of Petty and a quick presentation of the work of some of his successors (Charles Davenant, Gregory King). But he does make some more precise comments: "Political arithmetic, that is the application of arithmetical calculation to political subjects or employments; such as public revenue, number of inhabitants, the extent and value of land, taxes, arts, commerce, manufactures; everything relating to power, force, wealth etc. of a nation or a republic."
21. The articles "Fermiers (Économie politique)" and "Grains" in Vols. VI and VII of the *Encyclopédie* in 1755 and 1756. He also wrote additional articles for the *Encyclopédie*: "Hommes," "Impôt," and "Intérêt de l'argent," but these were not published by Quesnay, since he was linked to the court of Louis XV and no longer wished to contribute to Diderot and d'Alembert's project when its royal authorization was withdrawn. These texts are all available in the two volumes of *Œuvres économique complètes et autres textes de François Quesnay*, INED, Paris 2005.
22. Victor Riqueti de Mirabeau, *Philosophie rurale ou Économie générale et politique de l'agriculture*, Amsterdam 1763, pp. xix–xx.
23. There is some literature relating to the diffusion of accounting methods among merchants and traders; for engineers' calculations, especially in relation to costs, see Hélène Vérin, *La Gloire des ingénieurs. L'intelligence technique du XVIe au XVIIIe siècle*, Albin Michel, Paris 1993; and also Anne Cochon on the corvée, *La corvée des grands chemins au XVIIIe siècle. Economie d'une institution*, Rennes, Presses universitaires de Rennes 2016.
24. Pierre-Paul Le Mercier de la Rivière, *Mémoire sur la Martinique*, 1762; *Procès verbal de l'assemblée convoquée en exécution de l'arrêt concernant une imposition de 500 000 livres*, 1763; *Observations sur l'imposition ordonnée par le roi*, 1763, in *Mémoires et textes inédits sur le gouvernement des Antilles*, vol. 2, Éditions du CNRS, Paris 1978.
25. As happened during the 1770s between the administration and the Academy of Sciences through the mediation of Condorcet—see Éric Brian, *La Mesure de l'État. Administrateurs et géomètres au XVIIIe siècles* t. 2, Éditions du CNRS, Paris 1978.
26. Le Mercier de la Rivière, *Mémoire sur la Martinique*, p. 141; *Procès verbal de l'assemblée*, pp. 157–158.
27. Le Mercier de la Rivière, *Observations sur l'imposition ordonnée par le roi*, pp. 192–196.
28. Anne-Robert-Jacques Turgot, *Lettre au Contrôleur Général sur le commerce des grains* (1770), in *Œuvres de Turgot et documents le concernant* t. 3, Alcan, Paris 1919.
29. Pierre-Paul Le Mercier de la Rivière, *L'ordre naturel et essentiel des sociétés politiques* [1767], Fayard, Paris 2001, pp. 9–10.
30. Albert Hirschman, *The Passions and the Interests. Political Arguments for Capitalism before Its Triumph,* Princeton University Press, Princeton, NJ, 1977. See also Johan Heilbron, "French Moralists and the Anthropology of the Modern

Era: On the Genesis of the Notion of 'Interest' and 'Commercial Society'," in J. Heilbron, L. Magnusson, and B. Wittrock (eds.) *The Rise of the Social Sciences and the Formation of Modernity. Conceptual Change in Context, 1750–1850*, Kluwer, Dordrecht 1998; Gilbert Faccarello and Philippe Steiner, "French Philosophie économique: Sensationism, Interest and the Science of the Legislator, 1695–1830," *European Journal of the History of Economic Thought*, vol. 15 (2008), pp. 1–23.

31. Hirschman, *Passions and Interests*, p. 43.
32. Claude-Adrien Helvétius, *De l'esprit* [1758], Fayard, Paris 1988 and *De l'homme* [1773], Fayard, Paris 1989.
33. Robert W. Fogel, Stanley L. Engerman, *Time on the Cross. The Economics of American Negro Slavery*, Little, Brown & Co, Boston 1974.
34. Alain Desrosières, *La politique des grands nombres. Histoire de la raison statistique*, La Découverte, Paris 1993, and *Gouverner par les nombres*, Presses de l'école des Mines, Paris 2008; Wendy Espeland, Mitchell Stevens, "Commensuration as a Social Process," *Annual Review of Sociology* (1998); Michel Callon, Fabian Muniesa, "Les marchés économiques comme dispositifs collectifs de calcul," *Réseaux* (2003); François Vatin (ed.) *Evaluer et valoriser. Une sociologie économique de la mesure*, Presses de l'Université du Mirail, Toulouse 2009.
35. This relates to the four volumes of *L'Encyclopédie méthodique. Economie politique et diplomatique*, edited by Jean Nicolas Desmenier and published between 1784 and 1788.
36. Jean-Claude Perrot, *Une histoire intellectuelle de l'économie politique, XVIIe–XVIIIe siècle*, Éditions de l'EHESS, Paris 1992, p. 131.
37. "The observations that I made in my journies through the kingdom, fixed my opinions concerning the population—the inclosure and division of landed property—the prices of the earth's products, etc. I found the language of plain facts so clear, that I could not but listen and be convinced, and I laid the facts before the world on which I founded my opinions: In opposition to these facts, those writers have offered reason upon reason, argument upon argument, and have given elaborate disquisitions on those subjects which demanded facts alone." Arthur Young, *Political Arithmetic, Containing Observations on the Present State of Great Britain; and the Principles of Her Policy in the Encouragement of Agriculture*, London 1774, p. ix. Arthur Young (1741–1820) was a distinguished British agriculturalist and agronomist.
38. William Petty, *Political Arithmetick*, in *Economic Writings of Sir William Petty*, vol. I, Cambridge University Press, Cambridge 1899, pp. 244–245.
39. François Quesnay, *Tableau économique*, 3rd version, 1759, in *Œuvres économiques complètes*, vol. 1, pp. 437–438—the second version also made this point about the difference between numerical data and principles; see *Œuvres économiques complètes*, vol. 1, p. 411.
40. Pierre Samuel Du Pont, *De l'importation et de l'exportation du blé*, 1764. In this book Du Pont calculated the impact of a rise in the price of wheat for the different categories involved in its production. The complexity of his calculation is owed to the way that he examines the successive and diminishing impact of an increase in price. For an assessment of his calculations and his standing as a calculator see François Etner, *Histoire du calcul économique en France*, Économica, Paris 1987, chap. 2.
41. Pierre Samuel Du Pont, *De l'origine et des progrès d'une science nouvelle* [1768], CUECM, Catania 1992.

42. Pierre Samuel Du Pont, "De l'administration des chemins," *Éphémérides du citoyen*, t. V (1767).
43. "I have not wished to overload this little work with the details of fastidious calculations; but if it finds those who contradict it, I would have the honor of responding, and publishing the elements of my calculations and justifications." Ibid., p. 197.
44. François Vatin, *Morale industrielle et calcul économique dans le premier* XIX*e siècle. L'économie industrielle de Claude-Louis Bergery (1787–1863)*, L'Harmattan, Paris 2007.

CHAPTER 1
Du Pont, or

The Economic Error of Slavery, as Demonstrated by Calculation

Du Pont was not the only Physiocrat to take an interest in the question of slavery; he was preceded in 1766 by the abbé Baudeau in the *Éphémérides du citoyen*, and in 1771 by the abbé Roubaud in the *Journal du commerce, de l'agriculture et des finances*.[1]

That Physiocrats took a close interest in the question of servitude is linked to the importance they gave to property rights; this presumed above all the right of property in oneself, something that the social and political order of slavery entirely violated. To demonstrate the irrationality of this system Du Pont made use of a strategy that had already proved itself in the hands of Physiocrats in seeking to establish, sometimes with very sophisticated arguments, that landowners acted contrary to their own interest when they refused to pay tax.[2] Du Pont had made use of the same approach in his study of the construction and maintenance of highways, arguing with calculations that the employment of forced labor—the *corvée*—was more costly for landowners than the payment of a tax that could be used to finance works using wage labor.[3] The same argument was used in his article informing readers that Pennsylvania Quakers had abolished slavery;[4] and then again, in a more elaborated manner, in the texts that he published against slavery during 1771: that despite all appearance, the use of wage labor was economically preferable to the use of servile manual labor. Here again it was a matter of demonstrating to the slave owners where their real interest lay, an interest which could be shown to be in conformity with morality.

The text that Du Pont published in 1771 in Volume VI of the *Éphémérides du citoyen* differed from his earlier writings in that it transferred a mode of argument commonly used among Physiocrats into a domain where moral argumentation generally predominated. This did not mean that moral argument was superseded; Du Pont's piece was preceded by a lengthy narrative by the Marquis de Saint-Lambert entitled *Ziméo*,[5] in which the author sought to show that blacks, like whites, displayed intelligence, sensitivity, a sense of honor, and above all courage, that it was circumstance and not nature that had given the whites superiority over the blacks. *Ziméo* concludes with an appeal to respect the principles of natural law: "Civilized people, Enlightened people, take care—you only have morality, good government and *mœurs* where the principles of natural law are familiar to all men; and where you and your legislators would constantly apply them to your conduct and your laws." Printed immediately after *Ziméo*, Du Pont's text opens with an advertisement to the reader warning that in the following essay the reader would not be charmed by entertaining and flowing eloquence; the work of the "sublime poet" [Saint-Lambert] was followed by the work of "calculators who are not cold, but who are rigorous." Scientific work appears as the counterpoint to literary work; it contrasts with it while not competing with it, each contributing in its own way to the general efficaciousness of anti-slavery discourse. Before presenting the calculation that would be the heart of his argument, Du Pont first affirmed the superiority of the moral principle: while admitting that slave labor was more profitable than free labor, slavery would nonetheless have to be abolished, and the fact that more would have to be paid for sugar accepted, or otherwise go without. The enslavement of a man in order to obtain his work cheaper was no more acceptable than murdering a traveler on the road in order to steal his money. The reader was, however, immediately reassured: it would not be necessary to give up colonial goods, since the science of political economy rigorously demonstrated that injustice is always very expensive, whereas with benevolence everything could be acquired cheaply. The study of man and nature "turns to the public good the very passions [ambition, greed] which, in ignorance, degrade the earth, and disturb society."[6] "What is the medium," he added, "which acts with equal force on people and nobles, on the weak man and on the man of character, on well-born souls and on the wicked? It is the gift of God, it is interest."[7] The science of political economy must therefore enlighten this interest, always placing it in accordance with justice, and most often with charity. Du Pont set out to demonstrate the truth of these assertions through an examination of black slavery, maintaining in addition that the study of any other problem of political economy would lead to the same conclusion. *Calculation comes into play!*

Du Pont's aim was to prove that the cost of slave labor was more than that of free labor. The fact that a slave was not paid a wage did not mean that his labor was free. Du Pont enumerated the following elements of the cost of slave labor: the purchase price of the slave; the costs arising from maintenance, but also from the need for an overseer whose lash is the only stimulus to work; and the costs arising from the latent state of war between masters and their slaves.

The purchase price of a slave (put at 1,200 *livres*)[8] could be offset against ten years that Du Pont estimated was the average length of a slave's working life, so that the first element in a slave's *direct cost* was 120 *livres* per year. To that could be added the costs that the death of the slave occasioned, which could be set at 120 *livres* more. This doubling of the capital cost was often forgotten by later calculators, and at first sight it does seem surprising. Du Pont was a faithful disciple of Quesnay, who had calculated in this way when comparing the cost of farming with horses and oxen;[9] and he not only took account of the capital locked up by the purchase of the slave and so no longer available for investment in other economic activity (the "opportunity cost" in modern economic terminology), he also took account of the fact that the capital would have to be replaced at the end of ten years, following the death of the slave. He therefore provided both for the depreciation to zero of the capital invested in the slave over ten years and for the capital cost of purchasing a replacement slave at the end of this period. To the final annual capital cost of 240 *livres* there could be added the maintenance costs of the slave (food and clothing), estimated at 100 *livres* per annum. The *annual direct cost* of a slave was therefore 340 *livres*.

An artificial source of stimulation was required because slave labor was neither prompted nor sustained by the self-interest of the worker. Hence account had to be taken of the cost of an overseer, "half overseer, half bully," who would lash those in his charge to their work. His purchase price, at 1,800 *livres*, was higher than that of the other members of the team, but since he was better fed and dressed than the others (the cost of his annual maintenance being as high as 120 *livres*) he lived longer (fifteen years, instead of ten). Divided up among the ten slaves in his charge, the cost of the overseer, or the indirect annual cost, was 42 *livres*.

But Du Pont did not stop there; he also wanted to take into account the costs of interior defense of the colony made necessary by the dangers that maroons slaves presented to plantations. Here he ran into a problem: if up to this point Du Pont had been able to put numbers on things by reference to commercial transactions that had actually been made (the purchase of slaves, the cost of food), he now had to find a way of estimating the cost of protecting plantations, given the absence of a market for the provision of security to slave plantations. Here Du Pont was as inventive as modern economists who, when faced with this kind of problem, estimated the cost of a nuisance in terms of how much the individuals were willing to pay for the nuisance to be nullified. A number could be put on this virtual cost, or contingent estimate, by a sample from those persons affected by the problem. Obviously Du Pont could not carry out a survey like this himself; instead he proposed a sum equal to one-tenth of the annual cost of slave labor, which was 38 *livres*. This is, he thought, was a suitable sum as a rule of thumb, although he did not exclude the possibility that he might revise it: "If they [the planters] turn down this offer, then our estimate is too high; if they do want to do so, then it is not only right, but possibly too low."[10]

Du Pont also noted the existence of other costs, such as the damage to tools resulting from a lack of care and the losses arising from negligent harvesting, but he chose not to include these in his calculations, holding them back so that he might "stop the mouths of those who would contest the results."[11] He had assembled the elements that he needed to make his point, and he ignored those that are secondary, as a physician would do. The elements of the calculation that Du Pont finally retained are presented in Table 1.1.

The labor costs of a slave as calculated (420 *livres* per annum, or 28 *sols* a day) were much higher than the payments made to many Europeans (between 20 and 25 million of them having, according to Du Pont, barely 30 *livres* a year to live on); and so he demonstrated that slave labor was relatively more costly than free labor.

The calculative eloquence of Du Pont in favor of free labor was in no respect diminished by the way in which he added together direct and indirect labor costs. There was another factor that reinforced the demonstration that free labor was more efficient than slave labor: the productivity gap between the two. Idle "because idleness is his sole pleasure, and the only way

Table 1.1 DU PONT'S CALCULATION

Interest on fixed capital	120 *livres*
Cost of replacement of capital	120 *livres*
Maintenance	100 *livres*
Cost of overseer	42 *livres*
Cost of security	38 *livres*
Total cost	420 *livres*

in which he can regain from his master some of the person that the master has stolen wholesale," inept because he had no interest in improving his intelligence, and poorly motivated because he lived in a permanent state of war with his master, the slave was a worker whose productivity was low. Free workers owned what they gained, the ambition to increase their income and to be preferred over their competitors made them active and intelligent, they worked for less and produced *twice* the amount that slaves did—and at the same time became less fatigued, thanks to the constant improvement of their working methods.

This ratio of 1:2 between the productivity of the slave and that of the worker—a ratio that was simply stated without any figure being advanced in support—very much augmented the relative efficiency of free labor. Since its cost was not higher than that of slave labor, according to the calculation presented, the wages of free workers compared with the product of their work would be about *half as cheap*. Planters would therefore have a very great interest in employing them, even if they had to pay them much more than black slaves, something that would seem impossible given the level of wages in Europe. The bottom line was that the interest of the planters coincided with that of workers.

It would furthermore be easy to transport men from Europe and set them to work in plantations if they could be interested in being paid the 420 *livres* annually that slaves cost. Du Pont here parried "the constantly-repeated objection" that whites could not work in the sultry climate of the Antilles by noting that these colonies had been founded by whites—pirates, buccaneers, tobacco planters—adventurers for the most part "lost from previous debauchery" who had recovered their health in the islands where they had labored. He did not shrink from adding that the European showed himself a much more robust worker that the African, the Asiatic Indian, or the Native American, even in their own climates. While claiming that black slaves were lazy because of their status, Du Pont did not, however, count on them as the source of free labor in the plantations. Only European migrant labor would be effective.[12] The need for this substitution was not, however, explained—the dubious argument concerning the physical superiority of the whites over other peoples was not an essential point in the argument. Du Pont seems to have presumed that this superiority was obvious. The free laborers who, given their readiness to work and their intelligence, would do twice the work of the black slaves would essentially be Europeans.

The aim that Du Pont had set for himself was achieved: he demonstrated the superiority of free labor and the self-interested behavior over slave labor driven by violence. Calculation showed that the damage done by slavery to morality was not only unprofitable but was, on the contrary, "terrible for those who are its victims, and damaging and ruinous for those who impose it."[13] This result, however, not only discredits the practice of slavery by colonial planters; it generally places in question the relationship of Europeans to other peoples, whereby the former "seem to have only taken from their spirit, their arts, and their industry the odious privilege of setting everything in flames and causing the misfortune of their fellows from one end of the earth to the other."[14] The constant demand for new slaves gave rise to wars among the various peoples of the African coast, wars that were waged to produce captives, half of whom would then die on slave ships during the Atlantic crossing. The colonization of America had resulted in the extermination of its native inhabitants who would have asked for no more than the chance to sell their products. To escape from this "half civilization" that had brought harm to everyone without being of any benefit to themselves, Europeans needed to not only abolish slavery, they needed to promote a new international division of labor. Sugar plantations had to be established on the African coast, something that presumed a peaceful approach, capital, and commercial knowledge; while the agriculture of the colonies should be renewed, since the exhaustion of the soil by sugar cane demanded that production be altered. This was a grand project that aroused the enthusiasm of the projector. Suddenly Du Pont's accent became prophetic: the first sovereign who enabled Africans to sell syrup rather than slaves will show the way to other nations; he would be the "benefactor of Europe and of Africa" "favoured by God and by man"; "his virtues and his enlightenment [would] bring rewards in Heaven, the gifts of nature to his estate and to those of his neighbours."[15] In conclusion, Du Pont enjoined colonists to understand that "political arithmetic" proved the need for abolition, and led governments to see that "ignorance fostered injustice, and that injustice protected ignorance"; that all citizens who were "enlightened and sensitive" would work in favor of "such a desirable revolution."[16] Calculation and justice most decidedly spoke with one voice: self-interest had to become enlightened to fully realize its beneficial work.

Du Pont wrote more on the subject. In the eighth volume of the *Éphémérides* he wrote a long review of a novel called *Lettres africaines, ou Histoire de Phedima et d'Abensar* whose author, Jean-François Butini, advocated the abolition of slavery and argued that it would be of advantage to the slavemaster.[17] Du Pont wrote that Butini added his voice to the struggle against slavery waged by a small number of authors: Montesquieu who, in his *L'Esprit des lois*, "ridiculed the pretence at reasoning" of slavers; de Jaucourt, who had shown with "strong arguments" in his *Encyclopédie* articles that the state could emancipate slaves; the abbé Baudeau, who had demonstrated the illegitimacy of slavery through invoking the "principles of natural law"; Saint-Lambert, who had in his poem highlighted the humanity of black; and finally the abbé Roubaud who, in the *Journal du commerce, de l'agriculture et des finances*, had explained that it would be preferable for Africans to trade in the sugar they had learned to produce instead of selling slaves.[18] He did omit to note Mirabeau's contribution to the anti-slavery movement in his *L'Ami des hommes*, a book that was widely read.[19] Having commented on the merits of each, Du Pont stated what his own contribution was: "We have proven that the work of black slaves is more expensive than that of free men; that It is at least 28 *sols* per day; that there is therefore no interest, even apparently, in violating all divine and human laws in order to obtain through the unhappiness of one's fellows workers at such a high price."[20] In the midst of long extracts from Butini's book he goes back to the argument in which he had estimated the cost of servile labor at 420 *livres*. Without drawing attention to it, he did, however, modify his earlier exposition: he no longer based the viability of colonial export-based agriculture on the large-scale migration of poor European workers but on the use of former slaves in situ. Moreover, he extended his initial calculation by considering the future course of wages and its impact on settler income. Better-nurtured and better-dressed than the slave, the free black would see his wage increase and become closer to a European wage: "Assuming that his personal consumption rises to *150 livres* as is happening in France for the average worker; *one hundred livres* added to this amount for the expenses that he may have to lay out and to begin his savings, this only comes to *250 livres* a year, or about 17 French *sols* per day of work for women, or for a black fieldworker or one of average talent; because, in total, each has *17 sols* per head, while each now costs in fact 28 *sols* each to spend. This would at least be the pay for a wife, that the father of the family has more than half in addition, and children less."[21] Their talents and enthusiasm for work being stimulated by competition, black would soon merit much larger wages; these could be equal to the cost of slave labor (28 *sols* per day per head) but no more than that, "because the competition of great numbers of poor Europeans would be in opposition to it."[22] In the second as in the first case, the master would find it to his advantage to employ free manual labor: if the wage were fixed at 17 *sols* per day "there would be a *hundred and seventy livres* per year profit on each worker for the master, while the welfare of the worker would nonetheless be increased in the proportion of 5 to 2 [17 *sols* compared to the 6.6 *sols* maintenance cost of a slave]";[23] If the wage were to reach 28 *sols* per day (the cost of the slave), the master would benefit from the fact that his workers would do twice the work, while their income would be quadrupled.

The problem of the economic profitability of slave labor was raised once more in the last volume of the *Éphémérides du citoyen* published in 1771, which contains an anonymous text intended to complement and strengthen the calculation presented by Du Pont, and also in *Ziméo*. This article examined the nature of the slave trade,[24] and the author wrote that: "This trade, Monsieur is not merely a scandal; you have proved how expensive it is for the owners of plantations whose exploitation is effected by slaves. It is also easy to prove that traders buying and reselling these slaves derive only a modest amount from doing so, and that these are not the kind of profits they would have that dazzle those who are not familiar with this matter."[25] The author produced a lengthy calculation on the armament of a slave ship, the costs of the crew, the food for the slaves, and the gain made from their sale in the islands, showing that the gains from the slave trade were much less than was said—it brought a profit of 9.5% on 200,000 *livres* of capital advanced, and he argued that the gain was essentially made on the profits of the sugar trade. He also mentioned elements of the cost of slave labor that Du Pont did not take into account: losses due to sickness and suicide among slaves, and the poll tax on slaves (9 *livres*). Du Pont added a note at the end of this text welcoming the assistance provided by this "traveller," expressing his hope that slavery would soon be abolished: "We hope, before dying, to see slavery eradicated from those countries subject to European rule. But we are at least certain to have demonstrated with the greatest amount of evidence that its abolition will be as useful as it is just, and much easier than it is thought."

In these two founding texts Du Pont tied morality and calculation with a triple connection: through *valuation*, *evaluation*, and *valorization*.

Du Pont mobilized *valuation* when he emphasized the moral importance of slavery. In 1771 there were few enough members of the republic of letters in France prepared to grant the issue sufficient importance to write two articles upon it. By taking the trouble to do so, Du Pont showed that, among the various things with which he was concerned, slavery involved a moral imperative. Hence he made clear the axiological value that he gave to abolition as a political economist. Moving to the decisive phase of *evaluation*, he introduced into the debate an approach that was quite original by comparison with the small number of writers who had previously defended the antislavery cause. Evaluation was aimed at reinforcing the axiological value of the abolition of slavery by showing what the "new science" could introduce by way of calculation: an empirically based comparison of the costs of slave and free labor indicated that colonists ignored their real economic interest. With calculation, political economy added the weight of numbers to morality, demonstrating the most profitable form of cultivation. Based upon the logic of self-interest, the principle of all economic behavior and so of the slaveowners themselves, calculation defined a common standard for both moral and economic actions. This way of approaching the question would mark debate during the later eighteenth century. However, evaluation should not be reified: it was important neither to isolate it from the valuation that preceded it nor to detach it from the phase that followed that of *valorization*. In this final phase Du Pont made use of economic calculation as a rhetorical instrument: through his calculation he introduced an argument that he thought essential to moral and political debate that turned on the question of slave emancipation. The fact that he circulated his draft before publishing it in 1771 shows that he sought to gain the support of those committed to this cause. The rhetorical valorization of calculation was intended to project the moral problem into public debate and, by extension, place it on the agenda for government action.

The sequence valuation-evaluation-valorization that Du Pont initiated can be found in the writings of abolitionists who, whether explicitly or not, took up the path it lays out. Lacking the social pressure that would have made the emancipation of slaves a cause with its own inherent dynamic, the relatively small number of those who became involved in the struggle against slavery in French colonies made axiological valuation their prime approach. Nevertheless, evaluation became a structuring element in the debate that, until the definitive decree abolishing slavery in 1848, opposed the followers of emancipation on the one hand to the colonists on the other. This was, intellectually, a generally creative initiative: lacking adequate commercial magnitudes, Du Pont turned to the economic principle that estimates the cost of a nuisance according to the price someone is prepared to pay to remove it. In the last days of slavery new ways of calculating the net value of the slave *qua* capital were developed, and workers' budgets were used to determine the level of well-being necessary for emancipated slaves. Responding to the many objections regarding calculatory procedure and the enumeration of elements, calculators established a close connection between evaluation and valorization. This type of rhetoric found a particular echo during the years of the Revolution preceding the initial abolition of slavery; and then, following a fallow period in the abolitionist movement, during the last two decades of slavery.

* * *

Following on from Du Pont, we will examine how the essential elements of his argument were discussed, transformed, and contested. We will observe how abolitionists, colonists, and economists exploited or abandoned the calculative thread of their thinking on the relative costs of free and slave labor, thinking that was quite plainly determined in large part by their own moral and political presuppositions. We will show the effort made by some abolitionists to measure the productivity gap between slave and free labor, a key element in the greater efficiency of the latter with respect to the former. We will study the process that led the relation between productivity and self-interest—the latter being closely connected to the constraint represented by needs—becoming central to the debate over the possibility of free colonial labor. We will show that propositions concerning the origin and status of free manual labor were, following emancipation, articulated around the question of self-interest, stimulating productivity. We shall see that the global and civic dimension of Du Pont's propositions remained an important element in debates over slavery in the industrial order that developed from the Restoration onward.

Du Pont's exposition is suffused with the conviction that economic calculation and justice go together—this is presented as an analytical result, while at the same time embodying the assumption that political economy and morality are ultimately one and the same thing. Our study of those writings from the debate over slavery that tended to neglect the path that Du Pont opened up—whether to extend the debate or to close it—will, finally, help us understand how these authors saw the relationship between justice and utility.

NOTES

1. On Physiocratic writing devoted to the issue of slavery see Michèle Duchet, *Anthropologie et histoire au siècle des Lumières*, Albin Michel, Paris 1995, chap. 3; and Pernille Roge, "The Question of Slavery in Physiocratic Political Economy," in Manuela Albertone (ed.) *L'economia come linguaggio politica nell'Europa del Settecento*, Feltrinelli, Milan 2009. The eighteenth-century economic literature on slavery is presented by "Slavery and French economists, 1750–1830," in *The Abolitions of Slavery. From L. F. Sonthonax to V. Schœlcher, 1793, 1794, 1848*, UNESCO Publishing and Berghahn Books, Oxford 2003.
2. Philippe Steiner, *La «science nouvelle» de l'économie politique*, Presses universitaires de France, Paris 1998, chap. 3.
3. The abolition of the *corvée*, a form of forced labor applied to free men, also gave rise to a debate among calculators; on this occasion Du Pont clashed with the engineers of the Ponts et Chaussés, adversaries who were better armed technically than colonists.
4. Pierre Samuel Du Pont, "Affranchissement des nègres en Pennsylvanie," *Ephémérides du citoyen*, vol. 9 (1769).
5. This novel has recently been republished with an introduction by Youmna Charara in *Fictions coloniales du XVIIIe siècle. Ziméo, Lettres africaines, Adonis, ou le bon nègre, anecdote coloniale*, L'Harmattan, Paris 2005, chap. 1.
6. Pierre Samuel Du Pont, "Observations importantes sur l'esclavage des nègres," *Les Éphémérides du citoyen*, vol. VI (1771), p. 220.
7. Ibid., p. 222.

8. So that we can make our calculations comparable we have opted to give all figures in *livre tournois* (this was the French currency divisible into 20 *sols*, and the sol into 12 *deniers*). To do this we have converted data that are presented in terms of colonial *livres*. Lacking sufficient coinage to manage their own transactions, colonies quickly made use of foreign tender at a legal and compulsory rate of exchange. At the same time, they adopted a monetary unit (the colonial *livre*) as a common unit of account. This was given a fictitious value higher than that of the *livres tournois* used in France. In 1760 the legal rate of exchange was 150 *livres coloniales* to 100 *livres tournois*. In 1803 it rose to 166 2/3 for 100 in Guadeloupe, and in 1805 in Martinique; then, in 1817, it rose to 185 for 100 in Guadeloupe and 180 in Martinique. These legal provisions were not always observed in private transactions. A royal ordinance of August 30, 1826, ended these variations by applying the monetary rules of metropolitan France to its colonies. Some foreign currencies did, however, continue to circulate and were duly recognized.
9. Quesnay [1756] "Fermiers. Economie politique," in F. Quesnay (ed.), *Œuvres économiques complètes*, INED, Paris 2005, p. 133.
10. Du Pont, "Observations importantes sur l'esclavage des nègres," *Les Éphémérides du citoyen*, vol. VI (1771) p. 232.
11. Ibid., p. 233.
12. Ibid., pp. 235–238.
13. Ibid., p. 240.
14. Ibid.
15. Ibid., p. 244.
16. Ibid., p. 246.
17. The text is reprinted in Charara, *Fictions coloniales du XVIIIe siècle*, ch. II.
18. Du Pont, "Lettres africaines," *Les Éphémérides du citoyen*, vol. VIII (1771), pp. 76–79.
19. Victor Riqueti, marquis de Mirabeau, *L'ami des hommes, ou traité de la population*, 3rd edition, vol. 2, Chrétien Hérold, Hamburg 1758, pp. 389–394.
20. Pont, "Lettres africaines,"p. 78.
21. Ibid., p. 101.
22. Ibid., p. 103.
23. Ibid., p. 101.
24. The transatlantic slave trade involved about 1 million captive slaves between 1519 and 1675, 6.6 million between 1676 and 1800, and 3.4 million between 1801 and 1867. About 1 million were transported to the French islands where the trade in black slaves ended at the beginning of the 1830s. See Olivier Pétré-Grenouilleau, *Les traites négrières. Essai d'histoire globale*, Gallimard, Paris 2004, pp. 164–165.
25. "Lettres d'un voyageur à l'Auteur des *Éphémérides* au sujet des observations sur l'esclavage des nègres insérées dans le sixième tome de l'année 1771," *Les Éphémérides du citoyen*, vol. 12, (1771), p. 53.

CHAPTER 2
The Proliferating Use of Calculation among Eighteenth-Century Abolitionists

Those champions of the moral and political sciences who supported the abolitionist cause adopted the calculative rhetoric that Du Pont had introduced. However, elaborating the calculation of the comparative costs of free and slave labor was not something that could be done unproblematically. It was possible to calculate the basic elements of the costs of manual slave labor and put numbers on them, but it was not so simple to estimate the costs of free labor for a post-abolitionist colonial society. The certainty with which Du Pont had identified justice with utility diminished in the course of subsequent argument.

TURGOT VERSUS DU PONT

The debate got off to a bad start. Du Pont was no doubt rather disagreeably surprised to find his model calculation rejected by one of his closest friends, Anne Robert Jacques Turgot, Baron d'Aulne and at the time *intendant* in Limousin.

Turgot had followed with interest the development of political economy by Quesnay and his small band of disciples; while not allowing himself to be completely swayed by their thinking, his approach to political and economic theory was very much influenced by them. Had he read the calculation that Du Pont had drafted in 1769 and "frequently discussed with all his friends"?[1] There is nothing in the correspondence that would allow us to assume he had, but it is highly likely that Du Pont had raised the issue with him. Whatever the case may be, one year *before* the appearance of the article Turgot had, in his correspondence with Du Pont, criticized the principle and factual foundation exposed in it.

Turgot's letters raised two contentious points. In the first place, he objected to the modifications made to a text that he had sent to Du Pont for the pages of the *Éphémérides du citoyen* which Du Pont had so much trouble filling. This related to a manuscript that Turgot had written in 1766 entitled "*Réflexions sur la production et la distribution des richesses*" (*Reflections on the Formation and Distribution of Wealth*), one of the major texts of eighteenth-century political economy. When Turgot received his copy of *Éphémérides du citoyen* he noticed that his friend had altered two passages. The first and most important alteration, in his view, does not directly concern us here: it involves the theory of property and of capital from which he derived a justification for the existence of rent, the remuneration received by landowners. The second passage related to slavery. In this section, which was one stage of a conjectural history of economic development, Turgot explained the appearance of slavery by the difficulty that landowners had encountered in finding workers to cultivate the land available. Violence was used to force manual laborers to work for others for an income that was "the least admissible for subsistence."[2] This was a mode of cultivation that had been adopted in antiquity, and which was associated with constant wars waged to generate the manual slave labor required for cultivation, the excessively hard labor imposed by greedy masters leading to the premature death of very many slaves. Turgot did not conceal his opposition to modern slavery:

> This form of brigandage and this trade still prevails in all its horror on the coasts of Guinea, where Europeans encourage it by travelling there to buy blacks to work on the land in the American colonies.[3]

He explained that this institution had declined in Europe thanks in part to the progress made in the form of cultivation (the employment of draught cattle) and of civilization (the exchange of prisoners of war), both of which had contributed to a reduction in domestic slavery; and also by the way in which slavery had been transformed into vassalage and glebe slavery.[4] However, Turgot objected to the changes made to his text:

> You have now very much altered the section on slavery. What you have said on its origins is not too dissimilar to my ideas, apart from which I would not say that one can only fight out of weakness, but above all I would not substitute a piece of eloquent prose for a marginal summary.[5]

Du Pont probably tried to justify, in a reply that has not survived, the ideas that he had published in place of what his friend written. Whatever the case may be, Turgot came back to the subject in another letter to make clear that he believed, contrary to Du Pont, that *slavery is profitable for entrepreneurs*:

> Regarding the article on slaves, I told you what I thought of your addition. I would have preferred it if you had kept it back for the extract from *Ziméo*. Franklin has also shown[6] that the work of blacks is more costly than it at first seems, because of the need for replacements, but I don't think any less that in our islands there is an advantage in holding slaves, not for the colony, but for the owner who wants goods of great venal value so that he can make a quick fortune through this trade. I believe that I have provided in my text those reasons making the work of slaves useful in a country where one wishes wealth and commerce to promote population. You know that in the islands a good worker is paid 6 *livres* a day, which makes 1500 *livres* per year.[7]

The modifications that Du Pont made to Turgot's text do not in fact state the argument that slave labor is more costly than free labor; Du Pont limits himself to the idea that slaves "produce very little," and that this system of cultivation "is costly and of little profit." Instead, it was as an outcome of this exchange that Du Pont elaborated his particular line of argument and, in turn, Turgot his own. This is confirmed by the letter closing the exchange between the two men on the matter:

> I have received the start of my manuscript; if I had a little more time I would also, for my part, write a large book to prove to you that there is no need to correct me: 1. that there is no need to conclude from what I have said that slavery would be good for any society, even in its infancy. As for the people who have slaves, that is something else. I wish you were right in arguing that slavery is of no benefit to anyone because it is an abominable and barbaric injustice, but I'm afraid that you are wrong, and that this injustice is not infrequently useful to those who commit it. The human race is not so fortunate that injustice finds immediate punishment. There are enormous numbers of injustices, and some injustices have certainly procured those who commit them great satisfaction. Sometimes remorse may be a compensation for those satisfactions that are the fruit of injustice, but when injustice is not recognized by opinion, it does not excite remorse. . . . I no longer believe that, among those peoples where slavery is established, their masters have any scruples about owning slaves. It is undeniable that injustice is often useful to he who commits it, and that the injustice of slavery is just like any other.[8]

One year before Du Pont published his calculation in *Éphémérides du citoyen* he found himself opposed on two key points: that free labor in the Antilles *was more expensive than slave labor, and that an unjust institution could remain profitable for those who practiced injustice*. This twin affirmation by his friend Turgot did not shake his convictions; he went ahead and published his calculations and thoughts regarding the equivalence of political economy and morality, of justice and utility.

What was Turgot's reaction to the appearance of the 1771 article? As might have been expected, he was not impressed by his friend's calculations, and continued the discussion that had been started by the alterations made to the text of his *Réflexions*:

> I read your piece on the negroes and I find that you have not dealt with the matter at all. I am cross about that, because there will be criticism, and unfortunately they will be right. . . . Messieurs Les Économistes, never allow yourselves to talk of facts where you might at any moment be proved wrong, when you could instead rely upon demonstrative arguments.[9]

Turgot did not repeat the argument he had made against his friend in February 1770, that the wage of a worker in the Antilles was 1500 *livres*, three and a half times what Du Pont estimated as the cost of maintaining a slave. Instead, he suggested that it was a mistake to try to base an argument on real numbers; these were hard for Du Pont to evaluate, and he ran the risk of seeing his argument undermined and ridiculed by those able to show that the magnitudes he used were erroneous. He argued that Du Pont would be better off developing "demonstrative arguments," in other words, a theoretical argument based on principles. Du Pont could respond, in the style of Petty or Quesnay, that the data he had used were not false in relation to the argument for which they had been collected, and if they were, then they did at least help in developing assumptions that would allow understanding of the problem to advance.

In the following letter Turgot renewed his opposition to the calculations made by his friend, noting in particular and not without a touch of malice that he preferred the chapter that another Physiocrat, the abbé Roubaud, had devoted to slavery in a book that had also just been published.[10] Nothing more can be learned from the correspondence; Turgot quite clearly did not wish to pursue the discussion through an exchange of letters with his friend that was so "full of rumblings and inflexibility," given also that he was moving close to Paris. It can be seen that he found numerical calculation unconvincing, seeing it as full of dangers intrinsic to the information upon which it was based; and also because he considered that a better approach would be through analysis based upon principles. It is true that Turgot rarely used calculations in his writings, preferring instead to develop the "demonstrative reasoning" at which he was a master and which he recommended to Du Pont for his own writing.

Nonetheless, it seems that there was a degree of partiality in the way that Turgot dealt with his friend. Where did the figure of 6 *livres* a day for a "good worker" in the islands come from? Was it as well founded as he appeared to think? If it was allowed that wages in the islands had reached this level, was that not a reason to look for explanation of why the labor force was so expensive? Is the argument that Turgot made sufficient to demolish Du Pont's own case? That is not at all certain. Du Pont would have been able to answer by arguing that work on the plantations did not need "good workers," but instead unskilled agricultural workers, and that the price cited by Turgot is unreliable since it is itself a reflection of slave-based production that needed to be abolished. There were very few free "good workers," black or white, in the colonies; the restricted labor market allowed them to demand a high level of remuneration. Alongside these free workers there was a small number of urban "rental slaves"[11] whom Le Mercier de la Rivière had criticized when he was *intendant* of Martinique in 1763 as a factor in the increasing labor costs of the island. Their wages supported their maintenance as well as that of their master, together with the payment of interest on the capital invested in their purchase. The price of this fee-paying slave labor force is therefore much higher than that of free laborers who would only have been able to support their own needs.[12] From this Le Mercier de la Rivière concluded that it would be possible to reduce wages maintained at an artificially high level by introducing white workers into the colony, while at the same time taxing urban slave labor very heavily. Such measures would have a dual positive impact: the imposition of a significant tax would eradicate any interest in owning these kinds of slaves, who would return to agricultural cultivation where there was a lack of labor; while the large numbers of white workers arriving from France and for whom skilled employment would be reserved would consider themselves "obliged to work for a price that was fair for them and for everybody else."[13]

We do not know if Du Pont sought to respond directly to Turgot's argument regarding the high price of manual labor in the Antilles. He was not in any case indifferent to the question it raised: evidence of this concern can be found in his review of *Lettres africaines* (*African Letters*) where he suggests that after emancipation the wages of free workers in the colonies would be held down by the potential competition of the European poor.

CONDORCET AND THE ABOLITIONIST CURRENT

Turgot's stance regarding the profitability of slave labor for the slaveowner was for the time being expressed only in his private correspondence with Du Pont. It was, however, introduced into the public domain a dozen years later by someone to whom he was close—the Marquis de Condorcet, who published a book under the pseudonym "Pastor Joachim Schwartz"[14] that had a great impact not only on those who supported the abolition of the slave trade and of slavery, but also on the defenders of colonial slavery. The book was republished in 1788, shortly after the creation of the Société des amis des noirs; Condorcet added several notes to it, among which was a comment on Du Pont's calculation that he had not mentioned at all in the first edition. This was an astonishing lacuna, given that the two were acquainted through their connection to the group of collaborators formed around Turgot when he became Controller General. A difference of opinion, or perhaps rivalry, accounts for this delayed recognition for Du Pont's calculation.

While Condorcet did, in the sixth chapter of his book, reproduce the argument that the free worker, having labored to secure his subsistence, was prompted to work more in a quest for leisure to the extent that he might be allowed it,[15] he did not present a comparison of the costs of free and slave labor. What he introduced to the debate involved *the distinction between the net and the gross product* resulting from the passage from slave labor to free labor:

> In fact, with cultivation by slaves the net product will be greater, because the cost of cultivation will be the lowest possible. You will only give your slaves the least amount of food necessary, you will choose the most common and least expensive, they will only have a hut for a home, at worst you will have to give them coarse clothing. A day labourer very desperate for work still needs a higher wage. Moreover, a day labourer wants to earn more money to raise some capital, sometimes he wants time for his own entertainment; if he exerts himself, your money will be needed to compensate him for not sinking into idleness. With slaves you use a stick, which is cheaper. In cultivation based on free labour it is the mutual competition of owners and workers that fixes the price. In slave cultivation, the price depends absolutely on the owner's greed. But also in slave cultivation the gross product is lower; for in cultivation based on free labour the gross product will be much greater. So it is not an interest in increasing cultivation that prompts the defence of negro slavery, but an interest in the increase of income for colonists. So this is not a patriotic interest that is more or less well-founded, but simply the avarice and the barbarism of the slaveowners. The

destruction of slavery would ruin neither colonies nor trade; it would make the hills more flourishing, and it would increase the trade.[16]

Following Turgot, Condorcet defends the idea that slave labor is profitable to slaveowners, but neither to the colonies nor to metropolitan France. While the cost of free labor depends on the power relationships of the labor market and on conventions relating to the level of an adequate wage capable of providing the necessary stimulation to the zeal of workers for gain, the cost of slave labor depends only on the cupidity of the owner. Cultivation performed by slaves provides a relatively small output (the gross product of the colonies was therefore small), but it was enough to meet the interests of slaveowners who, in using slave labor, gained a net product higher than that they would have had by employing free laborers. In reverse, more expensive, but more productive, free labor would allow an augmentation of production capable of satisfying the collective interest that Condorcet thought appropriate to feed the size of population suited to this enlarged output. Without explicitly saying so at this stage of his argument, he suggests that the cost of free labor is greater than that of slave labor, which leads to a distinction between gross and net product:[17] by increasing production costs through the rise in the price of labor, abolition will result in the reduction of the net product for the owner. This is a line of argument that is difficult to support, in that Condorcet asserts that free labor, being more expensive than slave labor, will also be more productive than the latter: the decoupling of the gross from the net product depends on the assumption, not explicitly stated by Condorcet, that the increase in productivity generated by the establishment of free labor is not enough to cover the increase in the expenditure it will bring about. If the proposition is reversed, this means that the relative weakness in productivity of slave labor is largely offset by the very low costs it incurs. *Condorcet's reasoning leads implicitly to the idea that slave labor is of greater economic efficiency.*

In a later chapter Condorcet introduced the elements of a calculation contrasting free with slave labor which was made without any definite numbers; this avoided the use of numbers that could be contested by opponents, as Turgot had suggested. For the master, the slave cost him first of all the purchase price, to which should be added the cost of feeding the slave or that of the land granted to the slave for his support, and that of older slaves. There was no purchase price for the free laborer, but the wage paid to him had to be sufficient not only for him to feed himself, but also to support his wife and children, to provide for older parents, or to save for his own old age. Ultimately, the costs are quite similar: Condorcet wrote that "These two things can balance out. . . . Cultivation with free negroes is not necessarily any more expensive than with slaves."[18] He claims, in a somewhat contradictory manner, that this is in conformity with the argument about the distinction between net and gross product, which is based upon the higher cost of free labor:

> [Cultivation by black slaves] is not [more expensive] as we have said, that because of the division of the gross product made in the condition of liberty by virtue of a free agreement, and in slavery by the whim of a master's avarice; and that in a condition of liberty it is the mutual competition of workers and owners that sets the price of wages, and not a calculation made by greed, to the state of distress to which a man can be reduced, without diminishing in greater proportion the quantity of labour that can be gained from him by the stroke of a whip.[19]

In the second edition of the book Condorcet added a note to Chapter VI in which he commented on the calculation that Du Pont had made:

> In the fifth volume of the *Éphémérides du citoyen* can be found a calculation that is very well done, showing that a negro costs 420 *livres*; which would lead to the same result [that the costs of slave labour is higher than that of free labour]. But it should be noted that the calculation presumes that all dead negroes are replaced by newly-purchased negroes, when experience seems to show that a plantation supported only by these means would only be of low productivity. The calculation would in this way demonstrate more the lack of utility in the slave trade in negroes than the lack of utility of slavery.[20]

Is this conclusion valid? The idea that slaves are reproduced on the plantation means that the 120 *livres* that Du Pont set aside for purchasing a replacement for a deceased slave can be eliminated, but it also requires that the costs related to the improvement of the material situation of adults so that they can raise children be added. If this latter cost comes to the same amount as the former, then Du Pont's calculation is not undermined. Furthermore, in the same note Condorcet raised once more the important point involving the comparative productivity of the two kinds of labor:

> The question therefore comes down to knowing if the work of a slave is sufficiently inferior to that of a free man to at least compensate for the difference between the price set by competition and that which the economy establishes by reducing slaves to a simple necessity; or in other words, if a free man, to whom one would attribute what it would cost the master per working slave, would do more or less work. *It is quite probable that he would do less.*[21]

In this very important passage Condorcet set to one side the case where free labor was more productive because of the incentive of gain, an idea that itself led to the decoupling of net from gross product (the former falling following a rise in productivity that was weaker than the rise in the price of manual labor); instead he examined the case where the wage cost of a free man was equal to the cost of setting a slave to work. His response is striking: *the free worker who is spurred on neither by self-interest nor by the whip would produce less than the slave.*[22] Hence in the second edition of his book Condorcet does not alter his position, even if he does add some remarks that lead to an ambiguous conclusion: "Without finally deciding which of the two forms of cultivation is of advantage to the proprietor, the difference between the two seems to us too small to offset the pecuniary advantages that are consequent upon liberty."[23]

Condorcet came back to the question a third time after Malouet had in 1788 replied to the *Réflexions sur l'esclavage des nègres*.[24] He explained in a personal letter that he could not undertake "to respond to these arguments [of Malouet] to prove that 2 plus 2 did not make 5."[25] Condorcet considered that the arguments advanced by his opponent ran into incontrovertible truths. Firstly, there was no doubt that "a crime remained a crime, no matter how great the number of those who shared in its profits. . . . It was therefore necessary to prove to M.M . . . that decent people do not negotiate over moral principles."[26] It was quite obvious that freed slaves would work if they had an interest in so doing:

> It is impossible, according to Mr. M . . . , to cultivate, to base the cultivation the land in the islands on the work of free negroes. So we must prove to Mr. M . . . that money does to white men what blows do to slaves. Do you mete out a few lashes? You will need to add little to the wage to obtain the same amount of work from the emancipated slave; do you mete out a lot? The increase will be even greater. A quantity of sugar costs the manufacturer a hundred francs and negroes a hundred strokes of the whip; eliminate the whip and the same amount of work will cost one hundred and fifty, two hundred *livres*. So it is a matter of choosing between lashes of the whip for a negro and a loss of ten or twenty *sous* for a white manufacturer. That's the entire question."[27]

Condorcet is equivocal: free labor seems here to be no more productive than slave labor, but more costly; it causes a reduction in the net product gained by the white manufacturer.

Condorcet was a philosopher revolted by the slavery that Europeans had introduced to the New World, and to some extent he was following in the footsteps of Du Pont: both demanded that the inalienable right of the individual to himself be respected; both considered that the masters had no claim to indemnification when slavery was abolished. But there was one critical point on which the writers disagreed: while Du Pont insisted that the interests of owners and the nation, measured in terms of the net product, coincided, Condorcet argued that slaveowners had no interest in emancipation because their net product would fall, but that the "patriotic interest" would be satisfied by a rise in the volume of the gross product. This distinction had profound consequences—the increase of the gross product sustaining the increase of the size of the population—and so was of great interest to the nation: *wages are no longer treated as a cost, but as revenues*, permitting the formation of a virtuous circle. Condorcet's demonstration of this was poorly understood by those who later referred to his work to reinforce their arguments in favor of free labor.

The distinction between gross product and net product can also be found in a speech by André-Daniel Laffon de Ladebat, a member of the Société des amis des noirs at the Bordeaux Académie royale des sciences et belles-lettres on the eve of the Revolution,[28] although De Ladebat did not ascribe the importance to it that it had in Condorcet's analysis. He also shared the idea that "slave labour is never as productive as that of the free man,"[29] although he assigned variable numbers to this, drawing upon English figures in the work of Arthur Young. He retained a ratio of 1 to 2, and then proposed a ratio of 1 to 3.6 based on the comparison of the product per head of slaves in some Caribbean colonies and that realized on average by a French farmer. He in turn made a comparative calculation of the costs of slave and free labor:

> It is said that slave labour is less expensive than that of the day labourer, and it is much less the absolute product of cultivation that is important for the master than the gain that he makes from it. If the interest on the value of a slave is calculated, the price of necessary replacements, and the cost of food and hospital, it will be seen that this cheapness is only an illusion and that each working negro costs his master annually over 500 *livres*.[30]

He developed his calculation in a note at the end of this excerpt:

> It is therefore necessary to prove once more that the slave's work is more expensive than that of the waged cultivator. The negro whose work I estimated as 1,200 *livres* is worth at least 3,000 *livres*. The interest on this sum is 8 per cent in the colonies, the risk of replacement is 5 per cent, together making 13 per cent or 390 *livres*; If only 110 *livres* are added for maintenance and food, it will

> be found that every slave, a good worker, will cost at least 500 *livres*, while the price of a day labourer in France is only 300 to 350 *livres* for his annual labour.[31]

The elements selected, therefore, are as presented in Table 2.1.

All that is missing here from the calculation of Dupont are the costs associated with the supervision of work and for the protection of masters, given the dangers facing settlers living in the midst of the slaves. The bottom line is very similar: slavery is more expensive than free labor.

In a book written for the abolition of the slave trade and of slavery Benjamin-Sigismond Frossard,[32] a member of the Société des amis des noirs, repeats the argument concerning the decoupling of the net and gross product developed by Condorcet, employing a calculation of the same type as that performed by Du Pont.

Frossard explains the advantage of using free workers by their eagerness to work and their interest in the plantation's success; while slaves do not derive any gain from an increase in output, and so are generally quite uninterested in the fate of the plantation. The free worker is actively working to "provide for his own subsistence and that of his family," but also "to deserve the benevolence of the owner who lets him live."[33] The competition to which it is subject is a strong stimulus:

> The free man . . . sure to be dismissed if his services fail to satisfy, and always having the hope of advancing himself, is encouraged to work by the most powerful motives, and he does not need the rigour of an overseer to do his task. Does one not notice a great difference between a labourer paid by the day and a labourer paid by piece? The latter does not need supervision, nor any goad to work.

Using this classic argument Frossard maintains, like Du Pont, that there is a ratio of 1 to 2 between the product of slave and free labor, an assertion based on the observations of James Ramsay, a settler in Jamaica.[34] To support his analysis he proceeded, in a much less sophisticated way than Du Pont, to a make a calculation proving that the employment of wage workers, whether black or white, would be profitable to settlers.

Table 2.1 LADEBAT'S CALCULATION

Interest on fixed capital	240 *livres*
Cost of replacement of capital	150 *livres*
Maintenance	110 *livres*

Frossard first takes into account the interest on the capital fixed in the purchase of the slave (1,440 *livres* at a rate of 15 percent), which is 216 *livres* annually. He also values the maintenance of the slave at the relatively low amount of 72 *livres*. The annual cost of the slave is therefore 288 *livres* (see Table 2.2).

He relates this cost to that of a free worker whose daily wage is fixed at 30 *sous*, which is an annual salary of 390 *livres* for 260 days of work.[35] The result of his calculation is therefore contrary to that of Du Pont. He foresees the danger of being criticized for setting the price of labor at too low a level compared to that observed in the colonies, arguing that the price of day laborers will decrease as they become more numerous. The extra cost of free labor will rise to 102 *livres* per annum, but will be largely offset by the fact that it will double the amount produced by slave labor; *the master will therefore benefit from abolition*. Frossard does not understand that Condorcet's argument regarding the decoupling of gross and net product, which he cites in the course of his work to reinforce his point, opposes the interests of the masters and that of the nation, whereas he himself concludes that by liberating their slaves by degrees masters can "satisfy their heart without harming their interests."[36]

Continuing his argument in this vein, he advances the idea that some of the workers' consumption would return to the master through purchases amounting to about 200 *livres* that workers would make from the master.[37] The argument he makes is odd: the plantation being organized for the production of sugar, and so an export monoculture, it is not evident how this interchange between employees and settlers could arise, apart from assuming a peonage system where the worker would only be paid in vouchers to be spent in a shop owned by the planter. But other factors do support his conclusion: the shift to free labor would release planters from the need to set aside large capital sums for the purchase of slaves, sums which dissolved with the death of the slave; and the labor force would no longer be subject to the mortality and absconsion typical of the slave system. He finally noted that the dangers slavery presented to the wealth and life of the masters had to be taken into account. That the abolition of the slave trade would lead planters to renew their labor force through

Table 2.2 FROSSARD'S CALCULATION

Interest on fixed capital	216 *livres*
Maintenance	72 *livres*

natural reproduction could make slave cultivation more profitable, but it would not diminish the insecurity in which they lived or the reproach of bad conscience. *Ultimately, calculations showed that abolition would benefit everyone: slaves obviously, then masters, and finally the nation, since the decline in the cost of sugar production in the colonies would result in a lower price paid by consumers in the metropolis.*

Eighteenth-century British writers did not generally follow the strategy of calculation adopted by French abolitionists. James Anderson was an exception. Manchester campaigners against slavery, being persuaded of the immoral and impolitic nature of slavery, appealed to this "gentleman so distinguished in the science of Political Œconomy."[38] Responding to their request, Anderson followed a line of reasoning similar to that of Du Pont:

> Say that a good negro slave costs at his first purchase fifty pounds. This sum, at the rate of eight per cent, the legal rate of interest in the West Indies, would yield four pounds a year. The life of a slave cannot, I presume, be reckoned, on an average, after the time he is purchased, to amount to the full extent of ten years. Say ten years compleat. Fifty pounds, the capital being sunk, in that time, say five pounds a year, which with interest is nine pounds. For maintenance during this time, say six pounds a year—and for the charges of overseer, surgeon and other contingencies, two pounds more. At this rate, the annual expense of a slave would be seventeen pounds. Say farther, that after deductions for sickness, bad weather and other accidents, it should be found that in the course of a year, the slave performed two hundred and ninety full days of labour and no more; at this rate it would cost his owner, upon the whole, at the rate of a trifle more than fourteen pence a day; which multiplied by three, produces three shillings and six pence, the daily earnings of a free man for producing an equal quantity of work. But as I conceive three shillings and six pence to be more than the daily earnings of a free man in Britain, who have not been bred to any particular craft, I would thence infer, that labour performed by the slave costs considerably higher, than if the same labour were performed by free men.[39]

Like Du Pont, Anderson calculates the annual cost of slave labor by adding the interest on the capital locked up in the slave (£4), the cost of replacing the capital (£5), of maintenance (£6), and of supervision (£2)—without, however, including here the security costs that Du Pont allowed for. This all adds up to £17, or 14d. per day. Taking into account that work paid by piece and which prompts a personal interest in the work done is three times more productive than that work paid by day, he multiplies the daily cost of slave labor by three to establish the cost of the same work done by a free worker paid by piece. The sum he arrives at, 3s. 6d., is much higher than the average daily wage of an unskilled British worker. By introducing a dynamic element into the calculation Anderson can confirm that the cost of free labor is lower, and that the interest of the planter would therefore be to employ free, and not slave, labor.

HOW TO CALCULATE?

The calculation made by Du Pont did not really persuade anti-slavery writers, for whom he was supposed to represent a source of argument.

Turgot thought that his rhetorical strategy was flawed: by using figures whose reliability was not certain Du Pont had opened a Pandora's box; it would, he suggested, be better to base arguments upon principles. He also raised doubts about the identity of justice and utility, noting that moral precepts and economic practices did not always coincide: slavery was profitable for the masters. Morality did not conform to the perspective of the calculator.

Condorcet got around the issue with numerical magnitudes by using approximations that still allowed him to decouple gross and net product, but without being explicit about the exact conditions. Frossard and Ladebat, like Du Pont, resorted to numbers; and like him their calculations aimed at showing a convergence between self-interest and morality, utility and justice, a convergence that provided reinforcement for their advocacy of the abolition of slavery. All the same, when examined more closely the calculations created to resolve one set of problems created others in their stead.

These writers employed different elements in their calculations, and put them together differently too. All of them took into account the capital cost of buying a slave, and the price of the food that had to be given to him. Only Du Pont and Ladebat took account of the capital cost induced by the need to replace dead slaves; while Frossard did include a rate of interest on capital invested (15 percent) much higher than the sum of the two rates identified by Ladebat (13 percent). Only Du Pont and Condorcet took into account the costs of supervision. Frossard made his calculation more complex (see Table 2.3) by emphasizing how the master gained from the birth of children to slaves—a "positive element" neglected by other calculators—but he did not seek to quantify this gain, that was neutralized by the lack of security that the master suffered.

Besides the differences in the elements taken into account, there is also the differences in the magnitudes assigned to them: the price of purchasing

Table 2.3 ELEMENTS FOR SETTING THE PRICE OF SLAVE LABOR IN THE ABOLITIONISTS' CALCULATIONS

	Du Pont	Condorcet	Frossard	Ladebat
Cost:				
Capital	X	X	X	X
Replacement of capital	X			X
Maintenance	X	X	X	X
Coercion	X	X		
Security	X		X	
Benefit:				
Children born from slaves			X	

Table 2.4 DIVERGENT RESULTS IN THE ABOLITIONISTS' CALCULATIONS

	Du Pont	Condorcet	Frossard	Ladebat
Cost of free labor	**Cheaper** than slave labor; in the long run the two are **equal**	**More than, or as expensive as,** slave labor	**Cheaper** than slave labor	**More expensive** than slave labor
Productivity of free labor	Higher (×2)	Higher (not calculated, or ×1.6)	Higher (×2 or ×3.6)	Higher (×2)
Abolition of slavery	Masters and nation **gain**	Masters **lose** and the nation **gains**	Both masters and nation **gain**	Both masters and nation **gain**

a slave varies considerably (from 1200 *livres* to 3000 *livres*), as does the amount allocated to their maintenance (from 72 *livres* to 110 *livres*). There is also a significant variation in the rate of interest that determines the annual cost of capital (from 8 percent to 15 percent).

Given these differences it should not be surprising that the results arrived at diverge: for Du Pont the cost of slave labor reaches 420 *livres*, for Ladebat it is 500 *livres*, while for Frossard it is only 288 *livres*. Even worse: while Du Pont and Ladebat maintain that the cost of slave labor is higher than that of free labor, Condorcet comes to the conclusion that they are either equal or that slave labor is more costly than free labor, with which latter calculation Frossard agrees. The general conclusions to which these writers come can be summarized as shown in Table 2.4.

This disparity between conclusions is not only due to variations in the results obtained in respect of the price of slave labor—it is just as much related to the difficulty that the writers have in estimating the level of pay that free workers might expect in a competitive colonial labor market. No one could accurately judge what this would be so long as the colonial labor market had only a small number of free workers and rental slaves, as shown by Le Mercier de la Rivière in his report of 1762. Calculators would deal with this difficulty in a variety of ways.

Having first determined the cost of slave labor, Du Pont then deducted from it the cost of the daily wage that a white European immigrant worker might be given. Such workers had come from a Europe in which some twenty or twenty-five million individuals earned no more than 30 *livres* per annum, something like fourteen times less than the 420 *livres* that a slave cost his master. This gap was so great that it would operate as a powerfully attractive force inducing the European poor to seize the opportunity of working in the colonies. Ladebat's calculations followed the same line of thinking, while using different figures: he estimated the cost of slave labor at 500 *livres* per annum, and the wage of a European immigrant worker at 300 to 350 *livres*. On the other side of the channel Anderson adhered to the same approach.

Du Pont set no store by the idea that there would be massive immigration by white workers to the colonies; but he did revise his position in the calculation that he inserted into his presentation of Butini's novel: the wage paid to free blacks in the colonies would progressively converge with the cost of slave labor, the existence of an agricultural reserve army in France limiting any movement to excessive remuneration.

Condorcet proposed two different solutions that depended upon verbal reasoning rather than figures. In the first edition of his book he presumed that the competitive labor market relationship would lead to an increase in the cost of free labor. In the second edition, he presumed that free labor was as badly paid as slave labor, and came to the conclusion that slave labor was less productive that free labor. Supposing the cost of free labor to be 102 *livres* greater than that of slave labor, Frossard based his advocacy of free labor on the rise in productivity that he thought might satisfy the interest of the proprietor. His argument is not sophisticated by comparison with that of Condorcet, whose work he did, however, claim as his inspiration.

All the same, there were major differences among the calculations made by abolitionists. Du Pont, Ladebat, and Frossard considered that abolition would be profitable for all parties, including the colonists; Condorcet, on the other hand, taking a cue from Turgot, developed the idea that slavery was profitable for colonists who would consequently lose economically from abolition. He did, however, employ various qualifications to obscure a conclusion that would not have been popular among the abolitionists who were his friends.

And so anti-slavery writers were divided into two camps. One group's calculation coincided with morality because free labor, which was morally preferable, was more productive and less costly than slave labor. The other group considered slave labor to be less costly than free labor, so that there was an a priori divergence of economic interest and moral principle. The latter group got over this problem by assuming that free labor was more productive, a postulate that allowed them to avoid considering the very awkward possibility that slave labor was cheaper and more productive than free labor, which is what Fogel and Engerman argued in relation to plantations in the southern United States and in the West Indies. Fogel sought to deal with this moral paradox by disassociating morality from efficiency, a move that eighteenth-century French abolitionists were not prepared to make.[40]

* * *

Two decades after the publication of Du Pont's calculation the close connection between calculation and morality that he claimed to have found showed itself to be fragile. Calculators kept on running up against the difficulty of mastering an exercise whose procedures were not properly settled, and also of finding reliable figures than would make it possible to evaluate them.

Nonetheless, despite its weaknesses calculation had entered the debate and taken its place. Colonists who sought to respond to abolitionists' writings that had very much increased with the advent of the French Revolution followed the argument of Quesnay, who had argued that calculations could only be attacked using other calculations. They entered the calculatory joust with the intention of demonstrating the need to maintain slavery.

NOTES

1. Pierre Samuel Du Pont, "Observations importantes sur l'esclavage des Nègres," *Les Éphémérides du citoyen*, vol. VI (1771), p. 179.
2. Anne Robert Jacques Turgot, 1766, *Réflexions sur la formation et la distribution des richesses*, in *Œuvres de Turgot*, t. II, Alcan, Paris 1914, p. 547.
3. Ibid.
4. Ibid., pp. 547–548.
5. Ibid., p. 374. To see the original text of Turgot and the version modified by his unfaithful editor, see pp. 547–548. Section XXI (Second Approach: Slave Cultivation) of Turgot's text was rewritten by Du Pont and divided into three sections: XXI—Another approach which is very wrong, that was unfortunately very widespread during the centuries of barbarism and which, to the shame of humanity, still

exists in many countries that are neither enlightened nor well-civilised; XXII—The portion of the product of their work that nature secures to cultivators, even slaves; XXIII—How much of the cultivation done by slaves is barely profitable and expensive both for masters and to humanity. Only the title of this last section introduces the idea that servile labour is less profitable than free labour.

6. Turgot is referring to Benjamin Franklin's "Observations Concerning the Increase of Mankind, Peopling of Countries, etc.," which was published in 1751: "12. Tis an ill-grounded opinion that by the labour of slaves, *America* may possibly vie in cheapness of manufactures with *Britain*. The labour of slaves can never be so cheap here as the labour of working men is in *Britain*. Any one may compute it. Interest of money is in the Colonies from six to ten per Cent. Slaves one with another cost thirty £. Sterling per head. Reckon then the interest of the first purchase of a slave, the Insurance or risque on his life, his cloathing and diet, expenses in his sickness and loss of time, loss by his neglect of business. (Neglect is natural to the man who is not to be benefited by his own care or diligence), Expence of a Driver to keep him at work, and his pilfering from time to time, almost every slave being *by Nature* a thief, and compare the whole amount with the wages of a manufacturer of iron or wool in *England*, you will see that labour is much cheaper there than it ever can be by negroes here." Franklin does not go on to make any numerical calculation in the way that Du Pont did, but the list of elements that he takes into account to support his assertion is very close to that of the Physiocrat.
7. Turgot, Letter to Dupont, February 6, 1770, in *Œuvres de Turgot*, vol. III, p. 375.
8. Turgot, Letter to Du Pont, February 20, 1770, ibid., p. 378.
9. Turgot, Letter to Du Pont, October 15, 1771, ibid., p. 497.
10. Abbé Roubaud, *Histoire générale de l'Asie, de l'Afrique et de l'Amérique, contenant des discours sur l'histoire ancienne des peuples de ces contrées, leur histoire moderne et la description des lieux, avec des remarques sur leur histoire naturelle, et des observations sur les religions, les gouvernements, les sciences, les arts, le commerce, les mœurs, les caractères, etc., des nations*, Des Ventes de la Doué, Paris 1770–1775. This book inspired Diderot when he radicalized the critique of slavery that he added to the third addition of the abbé Raynal's *L'histoire des deux Indes* of 1780—Ann Thompson, "Diderot, Roubaud et l'esclavage," *Recherches sur Diderot et sur l'Encyclopédie*, No. 35 (2003), pp. 69–94. We will come back later to this reference to Roubaud's book.
11. "Rented slaves" were usually skilled slaves who had come to an agreement with their masters authorizing them, in exchange for the payment of a fixed fee, to live and work in a situation of semi-liberty (they enjoyed freedom of employment and of residence but also of movement thanks to a permit issued by their master). They were quite numerous in towns where some free inhabitants lived entirely off the "rents" paid by several slaves.
12. "The price of the black labour force including both the cost of feeding them and maintaining their masters, who were more significant consumers than simple white workers, and in addition covers the interest on the prime purchase price of the negro, where this interest has to be placed in relation to a capital subject to damage, daily depreciation, and total extinction, such labour must necessarily be much more expensive than work performed by the whites." Le Mercier de la Rivière, *Mémoire sur la Martinique*, p. 161.
13. Ibid., p. 162.
14. Schwartz [Condorcet], *Réflexions sur l'esclavage des nègres*, Neuchatel 1781. The pseudonym was quickly enough seen through, since a pamphlet of the Société

des amis des noirs gave Condorcet as the author nine years later: Anon., *Liste des ouvrages sur la traite et l'esclavage*, Paris 1790, p. 2.

15. Schwartz [Condorcet], ibid., p. 21.
16. Ibid., pp. 25–26.
17. This type of argument is the basis of a shift in classical economics relating to the impact of the introduction of machinery on the working classes. In the early nineteenth century economists thought that the price reductions brought about by the use of the machinery served the collective interest, represented by consumers. Workers, also being consumers, benefited from this reduction and therefore had nothing to complain about. David Ricardo repeated the argument in the first two editions of his famous work on the *Principles of Political Economy and Taxation*. In the third edition of 1821 he changed his view and emphasized the difference between the gross and net product: he now argued that the employer could introduce a machine that reduced the gross product (and the number of workers employed) while increasing the net product (the rate of profit), the ultimate criterion of the rational capitalist. The development of machinery leads to a reduction in the number of jobs that is not compensated by the lower price for the consumer: the opposition of workers to machinery is thus justifiable.
18. Schwartz [Condorcet], *Réflexions sur l'esclavage des nègres*, p. 64.
19. Ibid., p. 65.
20. Schwartz [Condorcet], *Réflexions sur l'esclavage des nègres*, 2nd edition [1788], Harmattan, Paris 2003, p. 19.
21. Ibid., p. 20, our emphasis.
22. We can find this argument again advanced by Pierre Dockès, who employs this passage as the basis for the theory of efficiency wages, where a rise in wages brings about a rise in productivity, and not the reverse. See Pierre Dockès, "Condorcet et l'esclavage des nègres ou esquisse d'une économie politique de l'esclavage à la veille de la Révolution française," in Jean-Michel Servet (ed.) *Idées économiques sous la Révolution, 1789–1794*, Presses universitaires de Lyon, Lyon 1989, p. 115.
23. Schwartz [Condorcet], *Réflexions sur l'esclavage des nègres*, 2nd edition [1788], p. 20.
24. This book is analyzed in detail in chapter 3.
25. Letter of Condorcet to a marquis [La Fayette?] concerning a work by M.M. . . .?, published by Léon Cahen, "La société des amis des noirs et Condorcet," *La Révolution française* 50 (1906), p. 498. We thank Nicolas Rieucau for drawing our attention to this correspondence that draws the links between calculators that we are examining in this book much closer.
26. Letter of Condorcet in Cahen, ibid., p. 500.
27. Ibid., pp. 501–502.
28. André Daniel Laffon de Ladebat, *Discours sur la nécessité et les moyens de détruire l'esclavage dans les colonies*, Bordeaux 1788. In his postscript the author declared that he only came across the book by Schwartz after his own had gone to press. He praised "its clarity and the lucidity of its principles" (p. 42), but added that the means of emancipation presented by Condorcet seemed to him less suited to readying the slaves for liberty than those which he had himself put forward (the progressive abolition of slavery after a period of glebe servitude).
29. Ibid., p. 17.
30. Ibid., p. 20.
31. Ibid., p. 38. The writer varies in the numbers he gives, since ten pages later he gives the price of a slave as 2,000 *livres*.

32. Benjamin-Sigismond Frossard, *La cause des esclaves nègres et des habitans de la Guinée, portée au tribunal de la justice, de la religion, de la politique ou Histoire de la traite et de l'esclavage des nègres, preuves de leur illégitimité, moyens de les abolir sans nuire ni aux colonies, ni aux colons*, Lyon 1789. See for Frossard the book by Robert Blanc, *Un pasteur au temps des Lumières, Benjamin-Sigismond Frossard 1754–1830*, Honoré Champion, Paris 2000.
33. Frossard, *La cause des esclaves nègres*, vol. 2, p. 178.
34. James Ramsay, *Objections to the Abolition of the Slave Trade with Answers to which are prefixed Strictures on a late Publication, intitled, "Considerations on the Emancipation of Negroes, and the Abolition of the Slave Trade," by a West India Planter*, London 1788, p. 2; and *An Essay on the Treatment and Conversion of African Slaves in the British Sugar Colonies*, London 1784, pp. 120, 123. To arrive at this ratio Ramsay made comparative calculations of the area cultivated by a slave and that cultivated by a free labourer; this is the same type of calculation that had been conducted by Alexandre Moreau de Jonnès in his *Recherches statistiques sur l'esclavage colonial et les moyens de le supprimer*, Paris 1842.
35. Frossard, *La cause des esclaves nègres*, vol. 2, pp. 181–182.
36. Ibid., p. 181. This misunderstanding persists and one can find it in modern commentators: Joseph Jurt, "Condorcet: l'idée de progrès et l'opposition à l'esclavage," in Pierre Crépel et Christian Gilain, *Condorcet mathématicien, économiste, philosophe, homme politique*, Minerve, Paris 1989, p. 391.
37. Frossard, *La cause des esclaves nègres*, vol. 2, pp. 182–186.
38. James Anderson, *Observations on Slavery particularly with a view to its effects on the British colonies in the West Indies*, Manchester 1789, p. 2.
39. Ibid., pp. 9–10.
40. "The paradox is only apparent. It collapses under scrutiny, not because the new economic findings are false, but because the paradox rests on a widely held assumption that technological efficiency is inherently good. It is this beguiling assumption that is false, and when applied to slavery, insidious." Robert William Fogel, *Without Consent or Contract. The Rise and Fall of American Slavery*, W. W. Norton, New York 1989, p. 10; also pp. 409–410.

CHAPTER 3
Colonists Also Calculate

The writers whose work is presented in this chapter *explicitly* presented themselves as spokesmen of colonists in the Antilles. Their calculations were presented with a political aim: to defend the established social condition of slavery. Taking their data from sets of accounts established to manage their plantations, they claimed to be better equipped than their adversaries in reaching results that could be open to no doubt.

In their opposition to abolitionist discourse they were more concerned to rebut claims made about slavery than examine any possible internal contradiction in its claims. All the same, the way in which they went about making their calculations sheds light on the way in which justice and utility might, from their point of view, be related.

ÉMILIEN PETIT AND THE ERRORS AND OMISSIONS OF DU PONT'S CALCULATIONS

Toward the end of the 1770s the lawyer Émilien Petit published a compilation of legal texts on the "government of slaves" in which he took up the challenge posed by Du Pont.[1] He dealt at length with the long article of Du Pont in t. 6 of the *Éphémérides du citoyen* without, however, mentioning the elaboration of this argument included in the review of Butini's *Lettres africaines*.

To begin with, Petit summarized in five pages the content of the article, in so doing outlining the conclusions to which Du Pont's calculation led, but without giving any numerical details. In his introduction he maintained that the proposed reform would aggravate the evil it claimed to destroy; and the way he went about this involved an approach that Albert Hirschman labeled as typical of reactionary thought.[2] Petit supported his initial statement by claiming that the lot of slaves in the colonies was better than it would have been had they remained in Africa where they would, as captives, suffer "torments and certain torture." As such, this claim was not a new one: it is one that can be found in many colonial texts of the late eighteenth century, especially in those of David Duval de Sanadon.[3] It remained a key element of slaver argument right up to 1848. Petit had no scruples about defending "the current righteous prejudice of the difference between white and black bloods, and the superiority of white blood,"[4] and he devoted a great deal of his text to a point that Du Pont had neglected. In his first calculation seeking to demonstrate that a free labor force was cheaper, Du Pont had assumed that it would be enough for the poor populations of Europe to be told of the wages they might expect in the colonies for them to emigrate and replace freed slaves. But, argued Petit, this substitution would incur a cost that the "writer of this dissertation" had neglected.

> Suppose that emigration were possible on a scale involving as many whites as there were blacks in the colonies—which is to say, around 370,000 whites. How might they all be transported? At whose cost would they be brought to a port and maintained there, their passage paid and their food during the passage be paid for? That would be a considerable sum for the government; if the government were not prepared to advance it, there would be few proprietors, if any, able to reimburse the expenditure occasioned by the men he would employ. If owners were authorised to make deductions on the wages they paid, these wages would not be enough to support the men; and their death would leave masters without hope of recovering any money so invested.[5]

Immigration of this kind would bring with it several costs: the construction of accommodation for newcomers close to their places of work, and the consequent loss of land for cultivation; the cost of shelter, furniture, food, and tools would exceed the 28 *sols* that Du Pont had thought sufficient; the support of older white retired workers, or of sick workers; the maintenance of their families which they would not neglect bringing with them, or of households that they formed in the colony. Also the need to maintain order among "a number of whites far in excess of the masters able to exercise only a very weak authority over them" would lead to additional costs related to police and justice.[6] What would one do with freed slaves? How could they become small farmers if there were no land for them? How, if one took the tough decision to return them to Africa, could they be made to embark? How would this be organized—with what ships, to which regions, and at whose cost? How also might one deprive masters of property acquired at such great expense, and which formed the most important part of their wealth?

Having argued at great length about the obstacles that obstructed the implementation of the substitution of European workers for slaves, Petit noted ironically that masters had not had to wait for Du Pont's calculations to realize the cost of slave labor. He detailed the elements in the same manner as Du Pont: "The sums expended on the purchase [of slaves], the replacement costs, police, subsistence."[7] All that was missing was the cost of setting people to work under threat of violence. Petit added, not without some provocation, that the costs that Du Pont took into account were pitched too low. Furthermore, the result of his calculation was undermined by his failure to take into account the benefits[8] that masters derived from their employment of slave labor. Children born to slaves working on the plantation were undoubtedly a benefit; reducing the cost of replacing dead slaves, although not eliminating it. Moreover, a slave labor force was constantly available for work on the plantation, itself a necessary condition for a form of production that for certain periods called for a large and available workforce. Concurring also with the conceptions of a domestic economy, Petit finally pointed out that slaves acquired through the slave trade were not paid for with money but rather with the products of the plantation; by providing an outlet for products, purchase in kind appeared to be less costly than an exchange involving money. The conclusion was inescapable: masters were right to use slave labor whose annual profit was ten times more than the expenditures of food and clothing they involved.

The third point made by Petit involved the activity of white wage workers. He maintained that the motivation to work through self-interest assumed by Du Pont simply did not exist:

> The white worker who is only paid for his subsistence by the master has no more interest in the product of his labour than the slave that the master has to feed and maintain. Fear of preference will not spur the White to any more activity than it does to the slave; since for this to have any effect, the White would have to be, like the slave, at the service of his chosen master for some period of time; or alternatively, there would need to be a reserve of Whites sufficient to create competition for employment: but where to accommodate, how to feed, and how to divert these numbers of additional workers waiting upon employment?[9]

In short, in the absence of what Karl Marx would call a "reserve army of labour" the spur of competition would not work; the incentive to work for the wage laborer and the increase of productivity would not happen.

New elements entered into the controversy over calculation. It was not only a matter of taking account of the way in which colonists benefited from slavery, something that Du Pont had not included in his calculation; it was also necessary to evaluate the social costs of wage labor, something that Du Pont had not dealt with at all.

Petit's calculation wrong-footed that of Du Pont, who had not simply estimated the direct capital cost of the slave, and the indirect cost arising from the coercion required to keep him working, but had gone on to assess *the social costs of the employment of slave labor* arising from the fact that the master lived among his slaves and required protection from them. Petit rather deftly reversed the question, while taking account of the direct costs of the slave but also the benefits arising from his employment: he took account of *the social costs of employing free labor*. These costs involved the increased cost of accommodation and maintenance related to the higher level of needs of the European population; the need to create order through public security; the risk that wages would escalate because of the absence of a reserve army of agricultural workers, the creation of which would itself bring their own costs and dangers.

Petit's response to Du Pont's text shows that calculation immediately became an object of controversy. It questioned the elegant results that Du Pont considered a keystone in the abolitionist cause, which had previously rested entirely upon moralistic argument. Having not read Du Pont's second calculation, Petit is here responding to a proposition that Du Pont no longer held himself.

THE CALCULATIONS OF THE MASTERS

Thirteen years later, the speeches and pamphlets circulated by the Société des amis des noirs contained no comparable analysis of the costs of slave and free labor. Limiting their argument to the equality of the rights of free men of color with those of whites, and in particular to the abolition of the slave trade,[10] they made use of calculation to highlight the economy it represented for colonists. By encouraging the reproduction of their slaves in the islands, masters had to treat them better, but they would save on the capital cost of periodically replacing their dead slaves.[11] They otherwise denounced the short-term view taken by masters who, interested only in getting rich quickly, surrendered themselves to "the most horrible of calculations" by drawing up an account in which "those who provided *forced slave labor* and who often had to be replaced are set against the expenditure on their replacement, where work is less excessive and conducted with humanity."[12]

The colonial calculators did not even try to respond to this line of argument. At a time when progressive projects for slave emancipation were being presented to the public and to the Assembly[13] they took up the pen to demonstrate the economic impossibility of maintaining colonial cultivation while employing a labor force of free men.

Nicolas-François Jacquemard, in a book supposedly translated from the English, stated that the price of free workers was very much above that of slaves:

> . . .their labour only costs the owner the interest on this sum [that of their purchase - £50 on average] added to which there is the insurance premium, and the cost of maintenance; and this is a mere bagatelle in comparison with what it would cost to employ free men.[14]

The calculations of colonists were made from the perspective of the master to demonstrate the absurdity of abolition, and they were based on numbers that seemed to have originated in the account books of a plantation. Having listed the dangers of colonial life (hurricanes, earthquakes, wars), Dubuc de Marentille put the product of a plantation employing eighty slaves at 26,660 *livres* (deducting losses and replacements, but not the cost of feeding slaves). He estimated that the weakest and most incompetent free black would not work for less than 20 *sols*, or 360 *livres* per annum. The wage bill for the eighty day laborers who would replace the slaves would come to 28,800 *livres* for the plantation in question.[15]

His calculation is excessive in two respects. First, the estimate for the day laborer's annual wage at 360 *livres* is based upon a working year of 360 days; calculated on 300 days, the number of days actually worked according to Du Pont, leads to a sum total of only 300 *livres*, enabling the master to derive a small, but nonetheless positive, net product of 2,660 *livres*. Second, Dubuc de Marentille does not seem to have understood that calculation should relate to the *difference* between the labor cost of the slave and the wage of a free laborer. He does deduct the costs related to slave losses and their replacement from the net income, but he takes no account of their maintenance costs. How can this kind of approach be explained? It could simply be an error, of advantage when it was a matter of showing the unrealizability of employing free labor. But it is more likely that this omission related to the management practices prevailing in the Antilles: the subsistence of slaves being provided to a great extent through work that they did themselves, thanks to the granting of a patch of land,

and with both Saturday and Sunday as free days, the master had little need to spend any more money on the food and clothing of his slaves. He could therefore maintain the fiction that their cost of maintenance was zero.

The same type of calculation was put forward by François-Pascal Delattre de Montfleury in a memoir that he authored under his initials, M.DL.DMFY.[16] While these are more sophisticated that those of Dubuc de la Marentille, the text is likewise based on speculations regarding the wage of a free worker, and not on the difference between the cost of this to the master as compared with the labor cost of a slave.

Delattre de Montfleury estimated the agricultural production of a slave at 466 *livres*, and so a gross product of 46,600 *livres* for a plantation of 100 slaves; from which he had to subtract one quarter for costs, the value of the harvest then being 35,000 *livres*. The cost of capital invested was set at 20,000 *livres* (5 percent of a capital of 400,000 *livres*). The net product was therefore 15,000 *livres*. The annual attrition among slaves was 5 percent, seven negroes replacing five lost from death because of the high rate of mortality among new arrivals. Assuming a standard price of 1,733 *livres* per slave, the net product of the plantation was only 2,870 *livres*. The calculation led to the absurd rate of return of 0.7 percent on a capital of 400,000 *livres*. On this basis Delattre de Montfleury established two different calculations to demonstrate the impossibility of introducing wage labor to the Antilles, and hence the inanity of abolition (see Table 3.1).

In his first calculation he takes into account the wages paid to free blacks taken on by planters when the harvest calls for an increase in the workforce available, amounting to 2 *livres* a day. If all workers on the estate were paid at this rate that total annual wage bill would rise to 60,000 *livres*, a

Table 3.1 FRANÇOIS-PASCAL DELATTRE DE MONTFLEURY'S CALCULATIONS

	First Calculation	Second Calculation
Receipts		
Gross product	46,600 livres	46,600 livres
Compensation for emancipation	10,000	
Expenses		
Costs (25%)	11,600	11,600
Cost of capital	—	20,000
Wages	60,000	15,000
Net product	–15,000	0

sum higher than the net product (without depreciation) of 35,000 *livres*. The deficit created by working the plantation for one year would be 25,000 *livres*. Taking into account that the government would pay the owner a compensation at a rate of 5 percent for the loss of capital invested in slaves (200,000 *livres*), the colonist would experience a loss of 15,000 *livres*.

Might it, however, be possible to work the plantation while paying less than 2 *livres* to day workers? In a second calculation Delattre de Montfleury struggles to show that this is not possible.

If the estate's black slaves were transformed into day laborers, the 15,000 *livres* of the net product would allow payment of a daily wage of no more than 10 *sols* for the 300 working days of the year. This would be an inadequate income for the free worker, but too much for the master, who would not be able to derive anything for his personal consumption, nor be able continue in business with a rate of depreciation on capital (buildings and livestock) of 10 percent. The colonist would therefore experience a loss.

The two calculations come to the same result: slavery is the sine qua non of cultivation in the islands. Under any other conditions cultivation would hardly be profitable for most colonists:

> It can be established that in general the cultivation of colonial products provides a return of less than 4% to colonists, given the losses they experience. Cultivation is therefore entirely to the advantage of the nation. If some colonists make fortunes, this is due to the good quality of the land they possess; but many more colonists do not benefit from the same advantage.[17]

As for replacing blacks with Europeans, the climate is against the idea entirely. This substitution would have two disastrous outcomes: the abandonment of land in France, and the quick death of immigrants in the colonies.

Another writer adopted an approach very close to that of the abolitionists. Paul Edme de Saint-Cyran, an engineer, supposed a working day of twelve hours for the slave and valued it at 8 *sols*; and he compared this to a wage of 40 or 50 *sols* paid to soldiers authorized to engage in wage labor for nine or ten hours a day for planters when they were not required for military duties.[18] On this basis he advanced financial and economic arguments that made a progressive transition to wage labor impossible. It was mistaken to think that planters could raise capital sufficient to pay wages, because it was "impossible to find [in the colonies] the immense amount of cash that does not exist, nor could ever exist in lands permanently indebted to metropolitan France."[19] The excessive rise in costs brought about by wage labor would not allow the colonies to challenge competition from other foreign colonies that continued to employ slave labor. Besides that, it would prove impossible to maintain a stable workforce of wage laborers in the colonies; the rigors of the climate would kill the white immigrants, and the blacks, whose needs were very limited, would refuse to work on the plantations after their liberation.

THE MAINTENANCE OF PLANTATIONS AND THE GRANDEUR OF FRANCE

In his response to Du Pont, Petit remarked that the costs of the slave to his master "exceeded the evaluation made by the writer"[20] but added that he had not included in his calculations the economic benefits that would ultimately offset them. The calculating colonialists who responded to the writings of Condorcet and of members of the Société des amis des noirs never risked making a monetary estimate, nor did they give a precise list of the elements of the cost of slave labor that would enable them to arrive at a total cost.

Dubuc de Marentille provided no kind of estimate for the expenditure related to the replacement of slave labor, and he omitted that which was necessary to feed them. While he did take account of the death of slaves, Delattre de Montfleury never provided a precise amount for their subsistence, which he probably included in their accommodation costs. Saint-Cyran quite plainly only took into account the maintenance costs of the slave, and estimated the daily cost of slave labor at 8 *sols*. Rather than establish a basic price for slave labor, colonists preferred to demonstrate that the planter could not pay wages without ruining his business, a conclusion that demonstrated, a posteriori, the low cost of slave labor. While their point of reference was the income of the planter upon whom the upkeep or the disappearance of the plantation depended, they claimed to have in view a much more general object: behind the interest of the colonial owner there was that of France.

Delattre de Montfleury's calculations were intended to explain that cultivation done by wage laborers would not be profitable, and that colonists, with the exception of a small number fortunate enough to work especially fertile estates, profited very little from it. The modesty of the returns, which were estimated at 4 percent of the capital invested, meant that "the cultivation of colonial products is therefore entirely to the advantage of the nation."[21] The calculations of Dubuc de Marentille were made to prove that the introduction of wage laborers would bring about an excessive increase in costs that would be ruinous for planters, and would therefore destroy their plantations, and so they led to an obvious conclusion: "the balance of this account will certainly not induce anyone to continue a business of this kind, and the cultivation of coffee and sugar will necessarily be succeeded by that of manioc and potatoes."[22] Cessation of cultivation for export would reduce France's economic interest in colonies to nothing. This was an interest that Petit had sought to demonstrate was much greater than just the consumption of colonial products:

> No doubt one could do without sugar, indigo, coffee and cotton, since one went without them previously; but the prime purpose for the establishment of our colonies, and the trade in blacks so engendered, was not so that these goods might be consumed in France, whatever it might be that created a demand for their use. The maintenance and expansion of a navy, the sale of foodstuffs and metropolitan goods, the balance of trade between one nation and another, the useful occupations that result from this trade for a great number of persons of all kinds; a resort for so many families who have not found fortune in France; all this has laid an imperious law upon France to take all possible means to prevent the exclusive possession of these foodstuffs by rival nations, or enemies to France's power.[23]

In turn, Saint-Cyran emphasized the economic consequences of rising prices for colonial products that would follow from the establishment of wage-earners: "What price would colonial foodstuffs produced by new means have to bear, and how would such goods fare in the great markets of the competitive world against those of other nations who continued to manufacture by ordinary methods."[24] Faced with the constraint of competition, the reformers would have to admit that "the entry of a wage culture into our colonies would mean prompt and unfailing ruin."[25]

This shift in perspective was the response to the approach taken by Condorcet, who argued that net and gross product could develop in a contrary fashion, slavery serving the interests of the master but not those of the nation. In contrast, the calculations of the colonists showed that the ruin of slaveowners would bring about the ruin of France itself. The coincidence of the interest of the master with that of the nation remained a key feature of arguments in favor of slavery right up to its abolition.

THERE IS ONLY FORCED LABOR

The discourse of the colonial lobby had an entirely different perspective on the relation of slave and free labor to that taken by Du Pont and the abolitionists of the Société des amis des noirs. To respond to those who condemned them politically and morally for employing forced labor they simply adopted a radically different viewpoint: they maintained that both in Europe and in the colonies all labor was forced labor, even if the means of coercion might vary from one continent to another. Having put slavery and wage labor on the same footing, they went on to argue that the situation of free European laborers was worse than that of slaves.

Petit used the argument in his response to Du Pont:

> The slave is fed, treated when sick, and aided by the grant of a small allotment that is for his own use. It is the masters who provide these conditions, moderating the nature of the work and its duration. The master is not opposed to the diversions that slaves provide for each other during saint's days. The peasant and wage labourer can both be exposed to want. The most comfortable peasant is not as happy as the domestic slave who serves his master faithfully.[26]

This argument was taken up in an especially striking way by Pierre-Victor Malouet, a colonist in Saint Domingo who published a response to Condorcet's text.[27] Malouet stressed the high cost of slave labor and the attention that the master gave to his slaves, something that was indispensable for the proper functioning of the plantation. Malouet was in favor of retaining slave labor and the slave trade, and proposed that legislation be introduced to counter the abuses arising in an institution that was terrible in principle but whose destruction would undermine the entire social edifice.[28] The key argument of his *Mémoire* is that the slave and the poor French worker are maintained in an equivalent state of subjection: "Subordination and labour are the essential attributes of slavery, as well as for the majority of free men. The negro is like your small peasants."[29] Whatever their condition might be, all workers are subject to the same inexorable law: "*Work for me, and I will feed you: that is the universal pact between Rich and Poor*."[30] What difference is there, posits Malouet, between the tacit market that links the owner to the wage laborer and the market that links the owner to the slave beyond the fact that only the master has to spend 1,500 *livres*—the purchase price of a black—with the additional duty of feeding the slave that he sets to work? The interest of the planter also imposes upon him obligations that do not at all encumber the entrepreneur using wage labor: he must care for the slave when he is sick, maintain him in his old age, while indigent workers, dismissed by their employers, line the roads of France. Accusations of violence in the treatment of slaves are of little weight: in America the black who shows himself unwilling is chastised like a schoolboy who has not done his work; if he steals he is given a few cuts of the lash. In Europe, the wage laborer who cannot work, or who does not want to work, dies of hunger; the peasant who steals is hanged, while the poacher is sent to the galleys. The conclusion is unavoidable: "The negro, his subsistence secure, is happier than the wage labourer, who does not have the same certainty. That is what I have stated and proved."[31]

The idea that social oppression was a natural state was elaborated by several colonial writers. J.-Félix Carteau wrote that

> It remains proven it seems to me, that it is in the nature of the human species that great societies be composed of *people of leisure*, and of others *compelled to labour*; and so the first are called the *rich* and the second the *poor*; whether they are called *bourgeois* and *day workers*, or *masters* and *slaves*, is ultimately all the same: the only difference is in the names. The poor, slaves or wage labourers are truly only ever the same class of men: those destined by the social condition to serve others.[32]

In 1810 Richard de Tussac went further, claiming that the use of destructive force, present universally in nature, was in principle part of the harmony decreed by God. He used an animal metaphor: "The timid sheep becomes the prey of the ferocious tiger, the Creator removes its means to defend itself and gives the tiger an enormous mouth filled with sharp teeth to which there is no resistance." The dove is food for the sparrowhawk, the insect food for the bird, the fly for the spider: "all that has come into existence can only sustain itself through the destruction of living beings like itself. There we doubtless find evident contradiction: but is it not these supposed contradictions that engender the admirable order that maintains the universe?"[33]

At the dawn of the nineteenth century Jean Barré de Saint-Venant based his advocacy of slavery on Malouet's demonstration, which he cited at length. He extended the argument by adding it to a calculation modeled on the one made by Du Pont in which he sought to prove, rather paradoxically by comparison with previous writings of colonist calculators, that the cost of free labor was less than that of slave labor, the differential being 1:7 since the first cost only 65 *livres* and the second more than 400 annually. The "wage of the negro" is calculated as shown in Table 3.2.[34]

Modeling himself on Du Pont, Barré de Saint-Venant took account of maintenance costs—which he estimated at a far higher level than Du Pont had done—and of the cost of capital (15 percent of the price of a slave, the higher rate reflecting that this is an annuity). The total sum is much higher than the 420 *livres* which Du Pont had arrived at. However, Barré de Saint-Venant did not take into account the costs of setting the slave to work reflected in the cost of employing overseers, nor the costs of security;

Table 3.2 JEAN BARRÉ DE SAINT-VENANT'S CALCULATION

Rent of allotment	30 *livres*
Rent of accommodation	18
Cloth	8
Wool vest	4
Hat	3
Hospital and sickness	20
Tools and instruments	16
Meat or salt fish	18
Lemonade	22
Rum grog	4
Salt	4
2 days a month	22
Total	169 *livres*
Capital cost (2000 *livres* at 15%)	300 *livres*
Total	469 *livres*
Not counting firewood, and the marriage gift of the master in pigs, chickens, etc.	30 *livres*

the costs of coercion in the social condition of slavery are quietly brushed under the carpet.

While maintaining the need to retain slavery, Barré de Saint-Venant re-establishes Du Pont's results: the cost of slave labor is higher than that of free labor. However, the introduction of Malouet's argument into his demonstration allows him to reach conclusions diametrically opposed to those of the Physiocrat. All work being forced, slavery is a choice imposed on the colonies where, given the climate, coercion by the needs prevailing in Europe cannot occur. The condition of the black in America is better than it would be in Africa, and much better than that of the laborer or small farmer in Europe. Since a slave is very expensive, the rationality of the colonist could be relied upon to ensure the maintenance of his capital, which was essential to the operation of the plantation.

* * *

In his response to the "defenders of the blacks" David Duval de Sanadon likewise aligned himself with Malouet, suggesting that the condemnation of men on all continents to hard and almost continual labor was "the inevitable effect of society,"[35] placing on a common footing the complaints of slaves regarding their masters, the poor about the rich, the lower classes in respect of the powerful.[36] He countered the writings of abolitionists with the moderation shown by Jacques Necker, "one of the most skilled ministers," when he addressed the Estates General at their opening: "Perhaps the day will come when, joining with the deputies for the colonies in your deliberations, you will seek to moderate a system of slavery thought to be necessary."[37] Suppressing the passages in this discourse that would unsettle the colonial lobby,[38] Duval de Sanadon added that the colonists had already adopted "this just and human aspiration." The reference to Necker was not by chance: lacking all obligation, his pious wish suited the colonists, since it was careful not to make any imposition on them. This can also be found in Malouet who, after expressing his rejection of the physiocratic system whose "rigorous application. . . to taxation and the freedom of trade will long be a chimera," stated that he preferred the principles of Necker which could be more easily adapted to the administrative needs of the established social order. While some abolitionists, in particular Condorcet, were close to the Physiocrats, the colonists drew part of their argument from writers, such as Linguet and Necker, who were major adversaries. The political cleavage was doubled by the cleavage that existed between differing economic theories.

Physiocracy no longer dominated economic thought after the French Revolution. In what respect was thinking about the relative profitability of slave and wage labor modified?

NOTES

1. Émilien Petit, *Traité sur le gouvernement des esclaves*, Paris 1777.
2. Albert Hirschman, *The Rhetoric of Reaction. Perversity, Futility, Jeopardy*, Harvard University Press, Cambridge, MA, 1991.
3. David Duval de Sanadon, *Réclamations et observations des colons, sur l'idée d'abolition de la traite et de l'affranchissement des nègres*, 2nd edition, 1789, pp. 19–23.
4. Petit, *Traité sur le gouvernement des esclaves*, vol. 2, p. 30.
5. Ibid., vol. 2, pp. 30–31.
6. Ibid., vol. 2, p. 33. Petit also raises the issue of security to justify his book: "The need for slaves for the exploitation of land in our colonies, and the consequences for public safety of a police that is more or less rigorous in respect of this class of men, led me to study the laws constitutive of the government of slaves." Ibid., vol. 1, p. 1.
7. Ibid., vol. 2, p. 36.
8. Abolitionists generally neglected these benefits, apart from the first (natural reproduction), of which only Frossard took account.
9. Petit, *Traité sur le gouvernement des esclaves*, vol. 2, p. 37.
10. Société des amis des noirs, *Adresse à l'Assemblée nationale pour l'abolition de la traite des noirs*, Paris, Imprimerie Potier de Lille 1790; Étienne Clavière, *Adresse de la Société des amis des noirs à l'Assemblée Nationale, à toutes les villes de commerce, à toutes les manufactures, aux colonies, à toutes les sociétés des amis de la Constitution. Adresse dans laquelle on approfondit les relations politiques et commerciales entre la métropole et les colonies, etc.*, Paris, Imprimerie du patriote François 1791. Clavière

emphasizes this here and returns to the point three times in his *Adresse*, pp. 19, 76, 106.
11. Société des amis des noirs, *Adresse*, p. 12.
12. Clavière, *Adresse de la Société des amis des noirs à l'Assemblée Nationale*, pp. 79–80.
13. Marcel Dorigny, "Mirabeau et la Société des amis des noirs: quelles voies pour l'abolition de l'esclavage?" in *Les abolitions de l'esclavage*, Presses universitaires de Vincennes et UNESCO, Paris 1995.
14. Nicolas-François Jacquemard, *Réflexions d'un cultivateur américain sur le projet d'abolir l'esclavage et la traite des nègres*, Londres et Paris 1788, p. 9.
15. Dubuc de Marentille, *De l'esclavage des Negres dans les Colonies de l'Amérique*, Pointe-à-Pitre Guadeloupe 1790.
16. MDLDMFY, *Mémoire sur l'esclavage des nègres contenant réponse à divers écrits qui ont été publiés en leur faveur*, 1790. The book is tortuous in composition, running together various calculations that we here distinguish to make sense of the argument.
17. Ibid., p. 25.
18. M. de Saint-Cyran, *Réfutation du projet des Amis des noirs sur la suppression de la traite des nègres et sur l'abolition de l'esclavage dans les colonies*, Devaux 1790, p. 17. He gives figures in *livres tournois* without any further explanation. It can be assumed that he did not make any changes in the money of account he used in his calculations.
19. Ibid.
20. Petit, *Traité sur le gouvernement des esclaves*, vol. 2, p. 35.
21. MDLDMFY, *Mémoire*, p. 25.
22. de Marentille, *De l'esclavage des Nègres*, p. 25.
23. Petit, *Traité sur le gouvernement des esclaves*, p. 27.
24. Saint-Cyran, *Réfutation du projet*, p. 17.
25. Ibid., p. 18.
26. Petit, *Traité sur le gouvernement des esclaves*, vol. 2, p. 39.
27. Pierre-Victor Malouet, *Mémoire sur l'esclavage des nègres dans lequel on discute des motifs proposés pour leur affranchissement, ceux qui s'y opposent, et les moyens praticables pour améliorer leur sort*, Neuchatel 1788. In a preamble Malouet stated that his text had been drafted in 1775 and had not initially been intended for publication; the appearance of the work by "Pastor Schwartz" had prompted him to publication.
28. "It is no doubt terrible to calculate as if men had become commodities, and to find oneself drawn by the imperious law of necessity to such saddening results; but I reason according to the principles that I have presented in my memoir [need for slavery, of the slave trade, the general law of submission, easing the fate of slaves]" (ibid., p. 13). Posing as a man of the Enlightenment, Malouet favored, contrary to the opinion of the majority of planters in Saint Domingo, the greater intervention of legislative powers between colonists and their slaves, the only means that he thought possible of improving the lot of the latter.
29. Ibid., pp. 17, 28. He here repeats, without explicitly citing, the argument advanced by the lawyer and polemicist Simon-Nicolas Linguet in his *Théorie des lois civiles, ou principles fondamentaux de la société* [1767], Fayard, Paris 1984. Devoted entirely to the issue of slavery, the latter part of the text develops arguments that can be found in Malouet: "All that they [day labourers, wage labourers] here have gained [from the suppression of slavery] is to be at every instant tormented by the fear of dying of hunger. . . . They are exposed to all

of the worst treatment associated with slavery, and they do not even have the certainty of life as compensation. The slave is fed even if he does not work, like our horses who are fed hay on saints' days. . . . But the free wage labourer who is often paid badly when he works, what happens to him when he does not work? Who takes an interest in his fate? Who bears the cost when he expires from fatigue and poverty?" (*Mémoire sur l'esclavage*, p. 583). This argument was also defended by the abbé Mably, a stern moralist, who suggested the extension of slavery on the grounds that freedom in Europe was nothing but the freedom granted to the servants of the rich to break free from their chains in order to seek a new master. *Le droit public de l'Europe fondé sur les traités*, in *Collection complète des œuvres de l'abbé de Mably*, imprimerie de Ch. Desbrières, an III, vol. 6, pp. 480–482.

30. Malouet, *Mémoire*, p. 25.
31. Ibid., p. 36.
32. J.-Félix Carteau, *Soirées bermudiennes, ou Entretiens sur les événemens qui ont opéré la ruine de la partie française de l'isle de Saint-Domingue*, Paris 1802, p. 282.
33. François-Richard de Tussac, *Cri des colons contre un ouvrage de M. l'évêque et sénateur Grégoire, ayant pour titre "De la littérature des nègres,"* Paris 1810, pp. 84–85.
34. Jean Barré Saint-Venant, *Des colonies modernes sous la zone torride et particulièrement celle de Saint-Domingue*, Brochot, Paris 1802.
35. Duval de Sanadon, *Réclamations et observations des colons*, p. 23.
36. Ibid., p. 12.
37. Necker, *Ouverture des États généraux à Versailles le 5 mai 1789*, Imprimerie royale, Paris 1789, p. 82.
38. "Humanity is already defended in the name of interest and political calculation, and this excellent cause will not be delayed in appearing before the tribunal of all nations" (ibid.).

CHAPTER 4
Moving away from the Rhetoric of Calculation

How were the calculations comparing free and slave labor that Du Pont and Condorcet had made received in the first half of the nineteenth century? The loss of Saint Domingo, the abolition of slavery in 1794, and then its reinstatement in 1802 in the bloodbath of Guadeloupe changed things.[1] Running counter to contemporary politics, anti-slavery argument became an impossibility during the First French Empire (1804–1814). And during the Bourbon Restoration (1815–1830) abolition was associated with republicanism and regicide, so that the politics of a status quo ante prevailed.

The theoretical points of reference had also changed. The star of physiocracy waned and that of *Wealth of Nations* waxed; it was translated into French and became the subject of commentary.[2] Adam Smith was no great admirer of political arithmetic, and he spurned the calculatory rhetoric that Quesnay and many of his disciples had so admired. The British economists who took an interest in the slavery question were likewise uninterested in this form of demonstration. Numerical calculation no longer had the same attraction for French writers; they relied more on narrative, giving priority to the kind of "demonstrative arguments" that Turgot had recommended. On the other hand, in line with the *Compte rendu au Roi* and *De l'administration des finances de la France* initiated by Necker at the end of the Ancien Régime, the reconstruction of administration initiated by the French Revolution was associated with a significant effort in the collection of statistical data. Central administrators demanded that prefects organize their tables in terms of the new unit of local government, the Department. The resulting *Statistique des préfets* was, however, only made partially available, since the administration did not want to feed public debate on sensitive political issues.[3] This situation fostered a split between those economists who would use administrative statistics and those who refused to do so on methodological or political grounds. Hence Jean-Baptiste Say opposed the statistical approach of writers like Charles Ganilh or Charles Dupin—the latter later becoming a resolute defender of the slave system in France's colonies on the grounds that the political interests of the nation had to be defended against British power.[4]

Say quickly became a central point of reference for French political economy, but he rarely used calculation, abjuring the use of statistics collected by the administration as also the use of mathematics, the latter because of the simplifications that this form of reasoning involved and the false sense of certainty that resulted from this: "Behold the mathematician: he never makes a bad calculation, and never has a good idea. He always draws strict conclusions from a false principle. He bases good calculations on bad observations."[5]

All the same, through the different editions of Say's *Traité d'économie politique* that secured Say's reputation, as in the writings of Jean Charles Léonard Simonde de Sismondi devoted to the slave trade[6] and to the abolition of slavery,[7] it is possible to discern continuing interest in the problems raised by Du Pont among those economists in favor of abolition.

THE VIEWPOINT OF BRITISH ECONOMISTS

British economists found the calculation published by James Anderson in 1789 unpersuasive. Those who later took an interest in the slavery question very rarely ventured into calculatory rhetoric.

Henry Brougham only devoted a few pages of his two-volume work on European colonial policy to slave labor. He cited both the Physiocrats and their allies (most notably Turgot) and French defenders of slavery such as Pierre-Victor Malouet and Jean Barré Saint-Venant,[8] and put forward the liberal argument, without using any supporting figures, that slave labor was always more costly than free labor because of the need for white workers to supervise the slaves.[9]

Caught up in the theoretical and practical problems of the political economy of Adam Smith, David Ricardo, and Robert Malthus, the most prominent British writers of the early nineteenth century, there was then little interest among political economists in the issue of slavery. The same applies to some other influential political economists such as James Mill and J. R. McCulloch.[10]

Nonetheless, Adam Smith's comparison of the cost of slave and of free labor sketched in *Wealth of Nations* was examined by several British economists. John Rooke, for example, thought that immediate abolition would be harmful to both slaves and their masters, providing an elementary calculation in justification:

> . . . if we examine the constituent principles of society in England, we find that the natural value of one year's labour is adequate to no more than the maintenance of the labourer and his family during the year. Now, admitting a negro to be worth £50, and that his master is liable to maintain him while he lives, then he is worth £50 more than our English labourers, since their employers pay them no more wages for their labour than what is adequate to their support. If, therefore, we place the final manumission of the slaves in our colonies in a just point of view, the planters alone would be thereby benefited, since they could purchase free labor at as low, or even a lower price, without advancing a sum of money for the value of the slave.[11]

The calculation is simplified by presuming a minimum wage level just adequate for reproduction, since then the cost of maintenance of the wage worker and the slave are the same, and thus the labor cost of the latter is higher given the need to advance the capital for purchase.

In 1830 Nassau William Senior gave three lectures on the rate of wages in which he introduced the idea of the wage fund. He argued that it was not a matter of comparing the labor cost of the free worker, the slave, and the worker subject to the regulations of the established Poor Law, but rather of their respective forms of regulation: the worker received a wage determined by "the fund for the maintenance of labourers compared with the number of labourers to be maintained"; the slave received what his master considered necessary for his reproduction; and the worker subject to the Poor Laws drew a wage that was treated as a right—the worst of all arrangements, because, according to Senior, it combined the liberty of the free worker with the absence of the coercion represented by need or compulsion.[12]

Debate in Britain did not embrace the calculatory élan of French writers who followed on from Du Pont. A moral approach predominated—when the British act of emancipation was being debated Brougham did publish a small pamphlet,[13] in which his abolitionist position was supported with moral arguments only. And, despite its title, Josiah Conder's *The Wage or the Whip: An Essay on the Comparative Cost and Productiveness of Free and Slave Labor* contained arguments in favor of abolition that were, rather paradoxically, organized in terms of moral and political questions.[14] His treatment of the comparative cost of free and slave labor is supported by very undeveloped calculations that are based, as in Rooke, on the idea that there is a basic equivalence in the cost of maintaining a slave and the wage paid to a free worker.[15]

THE PARADOXICAL POSITION OF JEAN-BAPTISTE SAY

Like some Physiocrats, but unlike Scottish economist James Steuart,[16] Adam Smith was opposed to slavery. He argued that the institution was typical of the errors of the "mercantile system" that prevailed in European economic policy of the seventeenth and eighteenth centuries, which had obstructed the natural course of economic development by favoring the interests of merchants over those of landowners, capitalists, and workers. Although he made no calculations in the manner of Du Pont and Steuart, Smith explicitly argued against Steuart that the maintenance costs of the slave and of the free worker were a charge on the master, and that the expenditure made on the first by a negligent owner or overseer was higher than that arising from the employment of a frugal and economic laborer.[17] Smith concluded that free labor cost less than slave labor, and reinforced this by the classic argument that the slave had no interest in working hard. All of these elements form what we could call "the ideology of free labor" shared by Smith and Du Pont.[18] So how does Smith explain the existence and development of colonial slavery, an inefficient economic institution? Unlike Du Pont, who treated it as partly the outcome of an ignorance of the principles of political economy combined with the myopia created by the low direct cost of employing slave labor, Smith argued that the institution had a dual basis. In the first place, the advantages enjoyed by colonial trade made the cultivation of sugar profitable, in spite of the employment of very unproductive workers; and second, there was a "love of domination":

> The pride of man makes him love to domineer, and nothing mortifies him so much as to be obliged to condescend to persuade his inferiors. Wherever the law allows it, and the nature of the work can afford it, therefore, he will generally prefer the service of slaves to that of free men.[19]

Say, however, reacted negatively to the argument that free labor was more economically efficient than slave labor—not what might have been expected from a member of the *Société des amis des noirs et des colonies*, a reader of the Physiocrats, and an economist who appealed to the authority of Smith. As the annotations made in 1789 to his copy of *Wealth of Nations* show,[20] even before the publication of the first edition of his *Traité d'économie politique* he thought that in the colonies *slave labor was more profitable than free labor*.[21] What arguments did he marshal to oppose the "ideology of free labor" embraced by Smith and Du Pont?

Say rejected the argument that slave labor was characterized by poor productivity. A member of the second *Société des amis des noirs*, it is very likely that he had read the book in which Condorcet argued against Du Pont regarding the profitability of slave labor to its owner; but he went further than Condorcet in justifying the idea that slave labor was more productive than free labor. Manual labor depended on the capacity and will of the individual, and Say considered these to be uncertain in the case of the free laborer, who was more easily swayed by idleness than any love of gain.[22] *Say therefore presumed the free worker to be indolent*, as contrasted with the slave aroused by the "infinite needs" of a greedy master. He also adopted the argument advanced by colonists regarding the moderation of owners in the treatment of their slaves, something that was in their interest:

> . . . it can be assumed that planters would be careful to employ their slaves' capacities profitably. . . . in general planters are only too aware of their interests to frequently expose themselves to losses of this kind [the premature death of a slave]; they derive forced labour from the slave in the sense that the slave usually exceeds what he would do if he worked for himself; but they are not at all interested in pushing the slave to the point of destroying his faculties and shortening his days, at least during the time of his virility.[23]

By arguing that slavery was more profitable than free labor Say came back to the position that first Turgot, then Condorcet, had maintained. Turgot's view was, however, only expressed in his private correspondence and so was not a matter of common knowledge, while Condorcet had presented his own in a sufficiently oblique way that admirers of his text took him to be saying the contrary of what he had actually written. By contrast, Say put this argument forward quite openly, and without equivocation. While it was rather paradoxical that a long-time member of the *Société des amis des noirs et des colonies* should adopt some parts of the colonists' arguments, he elaborated an explanation of the superior productivity of slave labor in terms of the "needs" and rationality of the planters, a line of argument that Condorcet had never himself adopted. Hence Say developed an argument that would, much later, be defended by Robert Fogel and Stanley Engerman in their economic history of American slavery, where they maintained that:

> 1. Slavery was not a system irrationally kept in existence by plantation owners who failed to perceive or were indifferent to their best economic interests. The purchase of a slave was generally a highly profitable investment which yielded rates of return that compared favorably with the most outstanding investment opportunities in manufacturing. . . .
>
> 5. The typical slave field hand was not lazy, inept, and unproductive. On average he was harder-working and more productive than his white counterpart.[24]

Hence Fogel and Engerman argued that "From the master's view point, the advantage of force, when *judiciously* applied, was that it produced desired behavior, in certain realms of activity, at a lower cost than could have been achieved through financial inducements."[25]

Say added a calculation of the cost of slave labor to his argument that the output achieved by employing slaves was higher than that using free laborers (see Table 4.1).

The first element of the cost related only to the maintenance of the slave *himself*: food, clothing, and accommodation, which together did not come to much, for they do not cover family needs or the need to provide for old age—an argument put forward by Steuart and rejected by Smith. This second idea is developed by Say in the second part of his book, devoted to the distribution of income, where Say noted that, unlike free workers who had to secure their own reproduction, the maintenance of a slave did not take into account the costs arising from the subsistence of a family. The price of a slave imported from Africa was less than his augmented maintenance "unless they are reproduced on the estates rather than bought from negroes in the slave trade."[26] In this line of argument, like that used to "prove" that the work of a slave is more productive than that of a free laborer, Say makes use of the principle of self-interested calculation to make sense of the behavior of colonists and interpret the numerical data that they advanced. This is a typical way of making a utilitarian economic argument and it is a source of great support for the calculator: by presuming that people are motivated by their interest, it is possible to compensate for the lack of data and rely upon observed behavior. Imputing economic rationality to colonists, it is possible to argue that slave labor is more profitable than free labor.

Table 4.1 SAY'S CALCULATION

Maintenance	300 fr.
Interest and replacement of capital invested	200 fr.

The second element of Say's calculation is the cost of investing 2,000 francs in the purchase of a slave at a rate of 10 percent. Does he take into account the replacement of this capital that disappears on the death of the slave, as did Du Pont? He states that he has "taken account in estimating the maintenance cost of a slave the *annualised* interest of his purchase price,"[27] where this rate of 10 percent can be compared to the rate of return prevailing in European agriculture of between 3 percent and 4 percent. The cost of setting the slave to work through coercion is, on the other hand, left out of the calculation, even if Say mentions the existence of free laborers—the costs of supervision—whose business it is to make the slaves do what their greedy masters wish.

This annual cost of 500 francs is related to the wage paid to a free worker in the colonies, which is 1800 francs per annum, or 6 francs a day.[28] This is a substantial difference, and Say seeks to diminish it by arguing that competition is weak, and that a thrifty worker could save 800 francs a year on this income. The minimum cost of a free worker would therefore be 1000 francs, or double the cost of a slave. "I therefore think myself capable of maintaining that the work of a slave is less costly than that of a free man; I believe myself capable of also maintaining that he is more productive, as long as he is supervised by free men."[29] The stubbornness with which colonists defended slavery therefore demonstrated the error of the opinions held by Steuart, Turgot, and Smith, to the effect that "humanity seems to have been inspired by these respectable men, and they have sought justification in reasoning."[30] Say is, in fact, torn between his calculation and his moral standpoint. As an economist, calculation shows him that slave labor is efficient; as a moralist, he is revolted by the traffic in human beings. While he supports the idea that slavery is economically profitable, he links this with a vigorous moral condemnation of the "most infamous commerce that men have ever known, that in themselves."[31]

Say's argument is surprising, given the way it distances him from Smith whom he regarded as his "master," and also from the views of members of the *Société des amis des noirs et des colonies*, a society of which he was a member. How can we explain the closeness of his argumentation to that of colonists, their adversaries, to whom he attributes economic rationality? His position can be explained, at least in part, by his adherence to a pessimistic view of the human being who, he thought, often lacked foresight, failed to appreciate his or her best interest, or, even worse, did not possess sufficient firmness of character to conform to this interest even when it was clearly recognized. In his text on morality he wrote that "You complain that everyone only listens to their own interests, but what grieves me is the opposite. To know one's own interests is the beginning of wisdom; having the courage to follow them is its complement."[32] Two manuscript notes highlight the negative view that Say held regarding the economic behavior of the lower classes that he witnessed when he managed a cotton manufactory in the Pas de Calais from 1806 to 1811:

> In a manufactory. I realise that it is more difficult to support three hundred men than to have them killed. . . . I was often disgusted, I admit, to see the lack of cooperation that they showed with what I did for their good and to their advantage, so that if I had done it for the sake of goodness in itself I would have had no reward; I even experienced from them not only vexation in what I did for their good, not only opposition, but also hatred; and yet I do not think that I was harsh in the way I did good.[33]

Individuals, therefore, are themselves blind to their interests and are diverted from following them by their ignorance and their passions—here through hatred, there through vanity. This explains his curious assertion that violence is more effective than self-interest in making slaves work on plantations. What is not explained here is why this reasoning does not apply to colonists. Why do their own passions not cloud their supposedly rational behavior, including the appropriate use of force? Without saying so explicitly, Say's analysis of the use of slave labor is based on the idea that *the passions and interests of the colonist are aligned.*

Always firm in his moral condemnation of slavery, Say would be led by the reactions of his contemporaries, but also by developments in the data he used, to shift his position on the profitability of slavery in the sugar colonies. His hesitations on the issue can be traced through his *Traité d'économie politique* and his *Cours complet d'économie politique pratique.*

THE REPLIES

The argument presented by Say in the first edition of his *Traité* was disputed by Ganilh, one of his old colleagues from the Tribunate and who was astonished to find such views in a work in which "liberal and philosophical sentiments were expressed."[34] Ganilh was certain that free labor was superior to slave labor; he countered Say with the argument that fear, far from galvanizing the slave to work, was more likely to induce sloth. However, Ganilh was careful to make no generalizations on this point; while maintaining that the nature of men and women was everywhere the same, he admitted that the habits instilled by slavery or liberty could alter behavior, and that fear could work more powerfully on a slave than

Table 4.2 GANILH'S CALCULATION

Land	500 m. *livres*
Negroes	1,000 m. *livres*
Buildings and tools	250 m. *livres*
Total fixed capital (Kf)	1,750 m. *livres*
Maintenance of negroes	15 m. *livres*
Wages of overseers	32 m. *livres*
Depreciation on slaves and materials	55 m. *livres*
Total capital (ΣK)	1,861 m. *livres*
Gross product (P)	225 m. *livres*
Annual expenditure	111 m. *livres*
Tax	9 m. *livres*
Net product or gain (NP)	114 m. *livres*

self-interest on a free man.[35] If it had been demonstrated that free labor was more advantageous than slave labor it was perhaps true that, in the colonial system as it then existed, the second would be more productive that the first. The enlightened administrator should therefore undo little by little that which education had slowly instilled: he deserved greater recognition the way in which he formed a general rule "without shaking too violently the opinions, the tastes and the habits of peoples subject to its administration."[36] Coming back to the question a few years later, Ganilh reasserted the idea that free labor was generally superior to slave labor, from antiquity up to the present.[37] Given his ambition of evaluating various theories according to their ability to take into account available statistical data, he sought to present the most complete calculation of all products in this period to determine the profitability of the economy of the French sugar colonies (see Table 4.2).[38]

Ganilh then compared these figures, cast up to measure the return on capital invested in colonial plantations with respect both to gross and net product, with the relevant figures for metropolitan France, and came to the conclusion presented in Table 4.3.

Placing the emphasis on capital, especially the capital invested in slaves (57 percent of fixed capital), and using the concepts of gross and net product, this calculation has clear filiation with physiocratic procedures. Following Say, Ganilh includes in his account the cost of setting slaves to work, which is represented by the wages of the overseers—although Ganilh estimates the maintenance cost for the slave at 1.5 percent of his price, as opposed to 8.3 percent in Du Pont's calculations. The bottom line shows that colonies have the advantage, in terms of both gross and net

Table 4.3 GANILH ON THE RATE OF RETURN

	Colonies	Metropole
Rate of return on fixed capital (NP/Kf)	7%	3%
Apparent capital productivity (P/ΣK)	12%	8%

profit. Ganilh notes that the difference between colonies and metropole is modest, at 4 percent in both cases, if one takes into account the real advantages enjoyed by the former: exceptionally fertile soil, abundant capital, and products that were sought after in many parts of the world. He considered that the limited scope of this differential proved that free labor was superior to slave labor.[39] Ganilh did, however, obscure the conclusions that could be drawn from his calculations; he introduced new, unquantified, and disputed variables that made the argument much more complex. The argument that the differential was small turned out to be problematic given that his calculation showed that the rate of return on fixed capital is more than twice that prevailing in the metropole, whereas the apparent productivity of capital is 50 percent higher!

In an open letter to Say published in 1822, English abolitionist Adam Hodgson expressed his uneasiness about an analysis that provided legitimation to those defending slavery:

> It is with much concern that I observe, in your excellent and popular work on Political Economy, the sentiments you express on the subject of the comparative expense of free and slave labour. Accustomed to respect you highly, as an enlightened advocate of liberal principles, and to admire the philanthropic spirit which pervades your writings, I cannot but regret deeply, that opinions so much calculated to perpetuate slavery should have the sanction of your authority; and that, while you denounce the slave system as unjustifiable, you admit that in a pecuniary point of view it may be the most profitable.[40]

Hodgson's pamphlet was formed mainly of quotations from economists, colonists, and abolitionists whose views were in opposition to Say; it appears to have made some impression, since it was republished in 1823 and lengthy extracts from it were translated into French and published in the *Revue Britannique*.[41] The second edition included a letter by Say, included in the *Revue Britannique* version, in which he defended himself by stating that he had changed his mind:

> You have probably read only the first editions of my *Traité d'économie politique*; since in the more recent editions I have greatly amended what I said on the labor of slaves; and in so doing come a little closer to the same conclusion as you; but not being restricted to one single question and not wanting to make the book any longer I was only able to touch on the subject. I come much closer to your opinion in the works on which I am working.[42]

SAY'S LENGTHY AND INCOMPLETE ADJUSTMENT OF HIS POSITION

Say made significant changes to his *Traité* in successive editions, and at the time he wrote to Hodgson the fourth edition of 1819 was the current version. However, as far as the slavery question was concerned, the changes were here quite limited. In all editions Say retained the calculation presented previously, and consistently interpreted it in terms of the economic rationality of planters.[43] The most striking change was that he no longer compared free and slave labor in such a way that the latter was said to be more productive than the former.

The more significant changes were yet to come. In 1825, in the fifth and final edition of the *Traité*, Say made very significant changes to the chapter on colonies and on slavery in relation to the international context:

> Everything has changed; and to deal here only with the French West Indies, with its dubious institutions and the mode of cultivation; where the regime of slavery has depraved, in two different senses, the master as well as the slave, altering the qualities that make true industry, that is to say intelligence, activity and economy; the fact is that Martinique and Guadeloupe can no longer compete with a number of countries that can supply Europe with much cheaper sugar.[44]

Colonists could only sell their sugar to France because of the existence of the rights given to them by protectionism, which still did not prevent them from becoming even more indebted every day, and so ruining themselves. It did not seem likely that the abolition of slavery would solve the problem: no European can work the land in the torrid climate of the West Indies; freed, the black man, who had little ambition and few needs, would refuse to devote himself to the very hard work of cultivating cane. The experience of free labor in the British islands had not achieved the desired result. In Haiti the production of sugar was more expensive than in the neighboring slave islands (Jamaica, Cuba) despite the introduction of forced labor; it would probably have to be abandoned in favor of growing coffee, cotton, and indigo. The cost of labor, however, should not be the sole criterion for the system of production:

> Moreover, it is not only a matter of knowing for what price a man can be made to work, but at what price we can make him work without injuring justice and humanity. Poor calculators are they who rely entirely on brute force, and rely on equity for nothing. . . . There is no lasting and sure way of producing other than that which is legitimate, and there is only one way in which the advantages of the one are not acquired at the expense of the other.[45]

Finally, calculation and morality go together. Liberal principles were gaining ground, and "this consideration [would] soon render superfluous all controversy over the labor of slaves compared with that of free laborers."[46]

Say did come back to the question in his *Cours complet d'économie politique pratique*, his last great work. He did not here reproduce the comparison he had made in the *Traité*, but presented an alternative that was not numerical. As before, he took account of the costs associated with the conversion of fixed capital into an annuity, the costs associated with the death of slaves, the care costs associated with sickness and old age, the cost of overseers, and the costs arising from the sumptuous lifestyle of masters. All of these factors led him to reverse his previous view concerning the profitability of slavery:

> All of these costs represent the wage paid to the free worker, and would represent a high wage. But these costs would still seem too great if one took into account the lack of interest on the part of the slave in working very hard, or very well.[47]

While he recognized this, it did not lead him to abandon his pessimistic vision of the foreseeable effects of abolition on the production of sugar, effects that he outlined by extending the examples already presented (regarding the British West Indies and Haiti) in the final edition of the *Traité*. And he repeated in identical terms the position taken in his earlier work: it was not entirely a question of pecuniary interest—the calculator could not disregard the issue of equity.

Say's thinking changed significantly from the mid-1820s. It is possible that Charles Comte, his son-in-law, had communicated to him in private the argument that he developed in the fourth volume of his *Traité de législation*, published in 1827. Comte's position is robust: the comparison of free and slave labor is a question that Smith posed badly, the error of which ran through virtually everything that had been written since on the matter.[48] Smith had posed the question badly because *the question related to masters*:

> . . . the question posed at the beginning of the chapter involves knowing if the labor that one man gains from a large number of others driven on by the free use of the whip costs more than that which he would obtain from those paid a fair wage. It is plain from the way in which the question is posed that the first writers who addressed the issue belonged to the race of masters, and the question was primarily approached in relation to the interests of the strongest. The enslaved would never think of raising the issue of whether the hardships and sufferings through which they gained their meagre subsistence were less than the labor and suffering with which free workers gain their wage. The question is however the same as the preceding one; there is no difference between the two, other than that the first are masters who consider whether slavery is in conformity with, or contrary to, their interests; while the second are slaves who make a similar evaluation.[49]

This comment is quite justified, since the calculations of economists and abolitionists were made from the standpoint of masters, who were shown that their interest lay with the employment of free workers. Comte provided an alternative perspective: in exposing the impact of slavery on the production of wealth, economists needed to guard against forgetting that this was only a means, and that it should be assessed less in terms of sheer quantity and more in terms of the welfare with which they endowed people. The production of wealth should not be detached from its distribution. Hence Comte placed himself, as had Du Pont in the conclusion of his first article in 1771, within the logic of a hyperbolic calculation that sought to determine "what a product costs not to this or that person, but to the human race as a whole."[50] To make this calculation he asked after the effects of slavery on the three human resources underlying the creation of wealth: the development of intelligence, which permitted understanding of the laws of nature and how one might serve them; physical skill; and, lastly, moral habits. The negative impact of slavery on all three of these elements, for both master and slave, fostered the mediocrity of production both in quality and in quantity, and the retardation of farming techniques and cultivation—he noted that the plough was not used in the Antilles. The expense of free labor also ran counter to the development of production, since it led to the increased import of consumer goods rather than their local production by artisans. The impact of slavery on distribution was also quite pernicious: the concentration of wealth in a few hands was associated with the poverty of the majority. Hyperbolic calculation led to a political judgment that bore down heavily on slavery as a social system:

> From the foregoing, it follows firstly that slavery is an unconquerable obstacle to the formation and accumulation of wealth, because it robs the working class of all means of working intelligently and making economies; and endows the masters class with vices that lead them to consume unproductively the fruit of the labour of the enslaved population. The second outcome is that in regions exploited by slaves work is infinitely less productive for the worker as well as the master as compared with those regions where all work is done by free men; finally, it follows that, in the state of slavery, the small amount of wealth that can be produced is distributed in a manner most contrary to equality, morality and justice.[51]

Hyperbolic calculation is ultimately nothing but a moral discourse.

The same logic dominated the writings that Sismondi devoted to the abolition of slavery. He adopted Smith's approach at two separate levels: he explained the perpetuation of the system of slavery by the mass of capital that the islands swallowed up and which could only be valorized by colonial monopoly;[52] and he related, more strongly than Say ever had, the maintenance of this inefficient mode of production to the pleasure of domination that it lent the master.[53]

Sismondi did not calculate in the way that Du Pont, Frossard, Say, Ganilh, and the colonists sought to do. He limited himself to the assertion that "slavery is the most expensive of all the ways to get work done; it is the one which, with the greatest investment, gives the least profit. . . . Even discounting the purchase price of the negro, his maintenance is not worth the work he does, compared with the maintenance and the work of a free man."[54] He also explained his refusal to engage in calculation by the answer colonists gave to those who committed themselves to it: "The planters respond to this comparison between the cost of free and servile labor by overwhelming you with the details of a sugarcane plantation, and asserting that such a plantation could not be cultivated without slavery."[55]

The stance of Turgot, appealing more to principles than to quantified calculations, is here justified. The political and intellectual context in which Sismondi developed his argument was quite novel; after the abolition of slavery in the British colonies the debate in the French colonies turned to the conditions for emancipation, and the compensation to which planters might have a claim, an important point that French economists discussed during the early 1840s in the Commission de

Broglie.[56] The aim of Sismondi was therefore to demonstrate that since slave labor was more expensive than free labor and also less productive, "it must be concluded that the owner has no right to compensation when slavery is abolished. He has, indeed, no useful property in the work of his slave."[57]

* * *

Early nineteenth-century economists who sought to reveal the comparative costs of slave and free labor were no more successful than Du Pont in providing convincing calculations. They were no more able to provide proofs than the abolitionists of the eighteenth century had been, and had the same difficulty in establishing a definitive frame of reference for their calculatory speculations. The development of Say's position is the best illustration of this. These economists did not, however, assign to calculation the weight that their predecessors had given it. While Du Pont and the Physiocrats saw it as an essential source for public debate, they instead gradually abandoned it. While Say based his approach on the observation of social life, he gave political economy, as a science capable of defining causal relations, precedence over statistics that were treated as ancillary knowledge, a collection of more or less reliable observations whose links could not be understood without the aid of economic theory.[58] Sismondi did not express the same reservations about the use of statistics, of which he makes intensive use, using data drawn from the *Statistique des préfets* in his *De la richesse commerciale*, his first book on political economy published the same year as Say's *Traité*. However, in his later works and generally in his writings on slavery he changed his approach, to the point of refusing, as we saw earlier, to take into account the "calculations" with which settlers drenched the subject. No doubt he became entangled in the same difficulties as those who, according to Seymour Drescher,[59] attacked English anti-slavers and economists during the 1840s and 1850s; although slavery had been abolished in British colonies, there was now evidence that cast doubt on the idea that free labor was superior to slave labor. The British abolition of 1833 modified the French political agenda: reviving the debate over the emancipation of slaves, it prompted a new series of calculations intended to demonstrate the validity of the arguments already advanced by Du Pont. Calculation was therefore revived as a rhetoric capable of convincing, if not a French public opinion not overly concerned with the issue,[60] then at least those likely to intervene publicly in favor of the abolition of slavery, especially in those debates taking place in Parliament. Calculation became part of the institutional fabric of French political life.

NOTES

1. Yves Benot, *La démence coloniale sous Napoléon*, La Découverte, Paris 1992.
2. For an account of the diffusion of the work of Smith in France, see Gilbert Faccarello and Philippe Steiner, "The Diffusion of the Work of Adam Smith in the French Language: An Outline History," in Keith Tribe (ed.) *A Critical Bibliography of Adam Smith*, Pickering and Chatto, London 2002.
3. Jean-Claude Perrot, *L'âge d'or de la statistique régionale française (an IV-1804)*, Société des études robespierristes, Paris 1977.
4. David Todd, "La liberté, la nation et les colonies dans la pensée de Charles Dupin," in Carole Christen and François Vatin (eds.) *Charles Dupin (1784–1873). Ingénieur, savant, économiste, pédagogue et parlementaire du Premier au Second Empire*, Presses universitaires de Rennes, Rennes 2009.
5. Jean-Baptiste Say, *Petit volume contenant quelques aperçus des hommes et de la société*, Déterville, Paris 1817, p. 47.
6. Jean Charles Léonard Simonde de Sismondi, *De l'intérêt de la France à l'égard de la traite des nègres* (1814) and "Nouvelles réflexions sur la traite des nègres," 1814, in Sismondi, *Écrits d'économie politique, 1799–1815, Œuvres économiques complètes*, vol. 3, Économica, Paris 2012.
7. Mainly in the eighth and ninth essays of his *Études sur l'économie politique (1837–1838)*, Slatkine, Geneva 1980.
8. Henry Brougham, *Inquiry into the Colonial Policy of the European Powers*, Balfour, Manners & Miller, Archibald Constable 1803, vol. 1, pp. 141–147; vol. 2, pp. 478–489, 490.
9. Ibid., vol. 1, p. 157.
10. See Seymour Drescher, *The Mighty Experiment. Free Labor versus Slavery in British Emancipation*, Oxford University Press, New York 2002, pp. 55–59.
11. John Rooke, *An Inquiry into the Principles of National Wealth: Illustrated by the Political Economy of the British Empire*, A Balfour & Co., Edinburgh 1824, pp. 374–375.
12. Nassau William Senior, *Three Lectures on the Rate of Wages, with a Preface on the Causes and Remedies of the Present Disturbances*, John Murray, London 1831, pp. vi–ix.
13. Henry Brougham, *Opinion of Henry Brougham, Esquire, on Negro Slavery*, H. J. McClary, London 1830.
14. Josiah Conder, *The Wage or the Whip. An Essay on the Comparative Cost and Productiveness of Free and Slave Labor*, Hatchard and Son, London 1833.
15. "The actual expense of slave labor resolves itself into the annual sum which, in the average term of the productive years of the slave's life, will liquidate the cost of purchase or rearing, and of support in old age, if he survive the capacity for labor, together with interest and the sum annually expended in his maintenance. Now, although the expense of free labor really includes the same elements, (since the wages of labor must be such as will enable the laborer to bring up his family so as to perpetuate the supply,) the West Indian planters are, at this moment, complaining of part of this necessary cost of slave labor as their particular burden, and one cause of the admitted depression and distress." Ibid., p. 3; see also p. 19.
16. James Steuart, *An Inquiry into the Principles of Political Œconomy: Being an Essay on the Science of Domestic Policy in Free Nations*, 2 vols., London 1767. Steuart

here compared free and slave labor and maintained that the latter was superior for agriculture, recommending that governments should profit from this kind of labor without concerning themselves about the winds of liberty blowing through Europe.

17. Adam Smith, *The Wealth of Nations*, in *The Glasgow Edition of the Works and Correspondanve of Adam Smith*, vol. 1, Liberty Classics, Indianapolis 1981, p. 98.
18. Drescher, *The Mighty Experiment*, chap. II.
19. Smith, *Wealth of Nations*, vol. 1, p. 364. This aspect of Smith's argument is examined in detail by André Lapidus, "Le profit ou la domination: figure de l'esclave dans l'économie d'Adam Smith," in Fred Célimène and André Legris (eds.) *L'économie de l'esclavage colonial. Enquête et bilan du XVIIe au XIXe siècle*, CNRS éditions, Paris 2002.
20. See Hitoshi Hashimoto, "Notes inédites de J.-B. Say qui couvrent les marges de la *Richesse des nations* et qui la critiquent," *Kyoto Sangyo University: Economics and Business Review* 7, pp. 71, 78.
21. Jean-Baptiste Say, *Traité d'économie politique ou simple exposition de la manière dont se forment, se distribuent et se consomment les richesses*, Déterville, Paris 1803. Say had worked for Clavière and then for the comte de Mirabeau in 1789, and had become acquainted with the group of Genevan opponents of slavery that surrounded Clavière; he also knew Frossard, the pastor who signed his baptismal certificate in Lyon in 1767, as correspondence between the two from 1809 shows. There was also his brother Louis Say, who in 1812 had taken over a sugar refinery in Nantes and made a success of it. The two brothers were opposed on economic matters, but Louis confirmed that his brother had consulted him on the subject before the first edition of the *Traité d'économie politique* appeared in 1802—Louis Say, *Etudes sur la richesse des nations et réfutation des principales erreurs en économie politique*, Renard, Paris 1836, p. ii. If at this time Louis had been able to influence his brother, his interest in the sugar beet industry could not have been of prime relevance since he also was an entrepreneur in the cotton industry.
22. Say, *Traité*, vol. I, p. 216.
23. Ibid., pp. 221–222.
24. Robert W. Fogel and Stanley L. Engerman, *Time on the Cross. The Economics of American Negro Slavery*, Little, Brown & Co, Boston 1974, pp. 4–5.
25. Ibid., p. 237.
26. Say, *Traité*, vol. II, p. 248. Say does no more here than make explicit the nature of the rational "horrible calculation" of colonists seeking to optimize the duration of a slave's life, who is fed for as long as his productive effort allows the level of profit sought to be achieved. Failing that, there was an advantage in disposing of one slave and buying a new one.
27. Ibid., vol. I, p. 222.
28. Ibid., vol. I, p. 218.
29. Ibid., vol. I, p. 224.
30. Ibid., p. 224. By placing Turgot together with Steuart and Smith, Say reveals that he read Turgot's *Réflexions* in the version that Du Pont had modified. His comparison does, in fact, adopt the position that Turgot had defended in his private correspondence with Du Pont, and it also agrees with the argumentation in which Turgot and Condorcet detached the interest of the colonist from that of the nation.
31. Ibid.

32. Say, *Petit volume*, p. 84.
33. Say Papers, Bibliothèque nationale de France, Box F, ff. 376.28 and 376.36.
34. Charles Ganilh, *Des systèmes d'économie politique, de leurs inconvénients, de leurs avantages, et de la doctrine la plus favorable aux progrès et à la richesse des nations*, vol. 1, Xhrouet, Déterville, Lenormand et Petit, Paris 1809, p. 216. This text is presented as an attempt to elucidate the range of systems of political economy; it saw itself as a defense of the administration, which he thought was too often criticized by economists.
35. Ibid., p. 223.
36. Ibid., p. 227.
37. Charles Ganilh, *La théorie de l'économie politique, fondée sur les faits résultans des statistiques de la France et de l'Angleterre; sur l'expérience de tous les peuples célèbres par leurs richesses; et sur les lumières de la raison*, vol. 1, Déterville, Paris 1815, p. 280.
38. Ibid., pp. 279–289.
39. Ibid., p. 289.
40. Adam Hodgson, *A Letter to M. Jean-Baptiste Say on the Comparative Expense of Free and Slave Labour*, Hatchard and Son, 2nd edition, London 1823, p. 1. Hodgson was the son of a Liverpool merchant active in the slave trade, who became an activist in the British abolition movement.
41. *Revue Britannique ou choix d'articles traduits des meilleurs écrits périodiques de la Grande-Bretagne sur la littérature, les beaux arts, les arts industriels, l'agriculture, la géographie, le commerce, l'économie politique, les finances, la législation, etc., etc.*, vol. 1, Méline, Brussels 1826, pp. 175–183.
42. Say, letter to Hodgson April 23, 1823 (in French), in Hodgson, *A Letter*, p. 59.
43. To follow the complex changes made to the text see the *variorum* edition of the *Traité d'économie politique* created by Claude Mouchot, *Œuvres Complètes de Jean-Baptiste Say*, vol. 1, t. 1, Économica, Paris 2006, pp. 404–421.
44. Say, *Traité d'économie politique*, ibid., p. 409.
45. Ibid., p. 413.
46. Ibid., p. 415.
47. Jean-Baptiste Say, *Cours complet d'économie politique pratique. Ouvrage destiné à mettre sous les yeux des hommes d'État, des propriétaires fonciers et des capitalistes, des savans, des agriculteurs, des manufacturiers, des négocians, et en général de tous les citoyens, l'économie des sociétés*, 1828–1830, in *Œuvres complètes de Jean-Baptiste Say*, vol. 2, t. 1, Économica, Paris 2010, p. 254.
48. Charles Comte, *Traité de législation ou exposition des lois générales suivant lesquelles les peuples prospèrent, dépérissent ou restent stationnaires*, vol. 4, A. Sautelet et Cie, Paris 1827, p. 238.
49. Ibid., p. 239. Sismondi very much valued the work and summarised it at length in his essay "des effets de l'esclavage sur la race humaine." This passage was quoted by Sismondi in its entirety, and expanded on the topic of the high level of net product being related to a low level of gross product: "One could calculate for the masters to demonstrate to them their advantage in the abolition of slavery; but the national accounts, as used by our author, is still more important. It demonstrates that the system of slavery creates, distributes and accumulates much less wealth than any other system through which the labour of society might be executed." Jean Charles Léonard Simonde de Sismondi, *Études sur l'économie politique, (1837–1838)*, t. 1, Slatkine, Geneva 1980, pp. 281–282.
50. Comte, *Traité de législation*, vol. 4, p. 242.

51. Ibid., p. 282.
52. Sismondi, *De l'intérêt de la France à l'égard de la traite des nègres*, pp. 283–285. He presented the same argument in his first great work as an economist, *De la richesse commerciale* (1803), *Œuvres économiques complètes de Sismondi*, vol. 2, Economica, Paris 2012, pp. 319ff.
53. "It has to be said that the power that a master has over his slave cannot be measured solely in money. It is a pleasure to command as a despot and be immediately obeyed; and a pleasure to make others tremble, to be able to reward or punish according to caprice, to be above the rules of justice, to believe oneself superior to all other races of men. . . ," Sismondi, *Études sur l'économie politique*, p. 296.
54. Ibid., p. 291.
55. Ibid., p. 292.
56. Steiner, "Les économistes libéraux et l'esclavage (1815–1880): limites et ambiguïtés d'un engagement," in Pétré-Grenouilleau (ed.) *Abolir l'esclavage, Un réformisme à l'épreuve (France, Portugal, Suisse, XVIIIe-XIXe siècle)*, Presses universitaires de Rennes, Rennes 2008.
57. Sismondi, *Études sur l'économie politique*, p. 291.
58. "Statistics reveals the condition of production and consumption in one or several nations during a particular epoch, or during several successive epochs, in the same way that it deals with population, its properties, the common actions that occurred and which could be submitted to calculative assessment. There is the same difference between political economy and statistics as there is between politics and history"; Say, *Traité d'économie politique*, vol. I, p. v.
59. Drescher, *The Mighty Experiment*, ch. II.
60. Lawrence Jennings, *La France et l'abolition de l'esclavage: 1802–1848*, French translation, André Versailles édition, Paris 2010, pp. 52, 54.

CHAPTER 5
The Institutional Inscription of Calculation

Despite the suspicion with which several early nineteenth-century economists viewed the use of numbers and calculation, this did not mean that numerical calculation played no part in the ongoing debate over the abolition of slavery. As evidence of this, in 1830 the abolitionist Pierre-Armand Dufau published a book in which numbers played a decisive part:

> Let us present some calculations that will succeed in demonstrating the veracity of this all: reduced to the terminology of money, the sum that a slave costs is generally put at 500 francs a year, including the interest on capital; this sum, divided into 300 days, produces 33 or 34 sous a day, which will no doubt seem rather high compared with the average daily wage of the European agricultural worker; but which then becomes exorbitant if a comparison is made with the vile and cheap articles of subsistence and primary consumption in the colonies.[1]

The work of free blacks would therefore cost the planter half that of slave labor; the planter would therefore benefit from the emancipation of his slaves. Sixty years after Du Pont's article, in the eyes of some people calculatory rhetoric retained its force.

Despite the lack of urgency with which the July Monarchy approached the issue of slavery, abolition became a fixture on the French political agenda in the creation of a series of commissions, through which calculatory rhetoric became an established part of political institutions. Having been partially eclipsed, the comparison of free and slave labor became a live issue once more during the last fifteen years of slavery.

THE DEVELOPING POLITICAL CONJUNCTURE

The July Monarchy was proclaimed on August 9, 1830, following the "three glorious days" of disturbances in late July, succeeding the Restoration Monarchy of Charles X. Louis-Philippe, a member of the Orleanist branch of the French royal line, was crowned King of the French. Many of the new ruling elite had belonged to the former liberal opposition that favored the abolition of the slave trade and of slavery. A law of March 4, 1831, provided for the effective suppression of the illegal trade in black slaves that had flourished under the Restoration, establishing significant penalties for all those engaged in the trade (the seizure of boats; forced labor for boat-owners, the captain, supercargo, and officers; imprisonment for sailors, investors, and insurers). Parallel to this an ordinance of February 24, 1831, abolished all colonial statutes limiting the ability of free persons of color from enjoying full civil rights; but it would not be until the law of April 24, 1833, that they acquired political rights as defined by law.[2] At the end of August 1833 the British Parliament debated and approved the Act for the Abolition of Slavery, to apply to all British colonies from August 1, 1834, onward. While Parliament thought it "just and expedient" to emancipate slaves, they also considered that "a reasonable Compensation should be made to the Persons hitherto entitled to the Services of such Slaves for the Loss which they will incur by being deprived of the Right to such Services." They also added that

> Whereas it is also expedient that Provision should be made for promoting the Industry and securing the good Conduct of the Persons to be manumitted, for a limited Period after such their Manumission: And whereas it is necessary that the Laws now in force in the said several Colonies should forthwith be adapted to the new State and Relations of Society therein which will follow upon such general Manumission as aforesaid of the said Slaves; and that, in order to afford the necessary Time for such Adaptation of the said Laws, a short Interval should elapse before such Manumission should take effect.

Every slave of six years or older would then become an apprenticed laborer, and these were divided into three classes: praedial apprenticed laborers attached to the soil; praedial apprenticed laborers not attached to the soil; and non-praedial apprenticed laborers. The apprenticeship of the two last categories was to end at the latest on August 1, 1838, while for those in the first group the termination date would be August 1, 1840. The number of hours an apprentice laborer was permitted to work for a former master was limited to forty-five hours a week. However, given serious social tensions in the colonies and the denunciation by abolitionists of apprenticeship as a new form of slavery, the Colonial Office decided to bring forward the date of termination for the transitional regime: all categories of apprentices would be emancipated on January 1, 1838.

The French Ministry of the Navy and Colonies made an effort to collect material that could inform the French administration on the impact of emancipation in the British colonies.[3] It also collected together articles appearing in the French and British press, and from 1837 included newspapers from Jamaica, Barbados, and Antigua where freedom of the press permitted information from a range of sources to be published. However, the Ministry gradually came to rely more and more on observers sent to report directly on conditions—French Colonial Archives record thirty-nine such reports between 1833 and 1841. However, the objectivity of many, if not all, observers was questionable, since they were selected by colonial governors and were mostly drawn from colonial administrators and French naval officers and so came from a social stratum known for its sympathy to the established colonial order. They were instructed by the Ministry to pay especial attention to the prospects for the export of food crops from the colonies. As Jennings emphasized, "Injunctions of this kind tended to stress a negative aspect of British emancipation—declining production—rather than positive or ethical ones, such as the preservation of order, the improvement in freedmen's living standard, or the recovery of human dignity."[4] These reports emphasized the decline in production of colonial goods and often predicted their ruin, and so tended to support the colonial position and a desire on the part of the July Monarchy to procrastinate. The Ministry of the Navy and of the Colonies published five volumes between 1840 and 1843 dealing with the abolition of slavery in the British colonies, bringing together British materials (acts of legislation, ministerial instructions regarding their application, local statutes, and the observations of British governors and "special magistrates") but also including the reports of French observers. The intention was to inform deputies, the press, and all interested parties who in France sought deeper understanding of "this very serious question."[5] The abolitionist movement did not, however, wait for ministerial publications to provide information about the course of the abolition of slavery in the British colonies. Encouraged by the initiation of the July Monarchy and by British emancipation, a group of prominent liberals had at the end of 1834 formed the Société française pour l'abolition de l'esclavage (French society for the abolition of slavery), its high profile being assured by the appointment of the duc de Broglie as its president.[6] The presence at the first major meeting of a party of British abolitionists suggests that they had played a direct part in the formation of the new society.[7] Zachary Macaulay, who had collaborated with William Wilberforce in the struggle against the slave trade, was also made honorary president. In 1835 and 1836 he published, in Paris and in French, five works dealing with the emancipation of slaves. Two of them[8] presented to French readers a compilation of official documents published on the order of the House of Commons. Macaulay notably included evidence from special magistrates who confirmed that the production of various colonies had remained stable or had fallen only slightly and that the productivity of free labor was higher than that of slave labor, in conformity with the expectations of many abolitionists. He did, however, condemn apprenticeship unequivocally:

> If the character of the colonists had been well-known and duly appreciated, the British government would never have proposed, nor the British parliament sanctioned, a system (repudiated, it is true, by the nation in general) which, by leaving in place grim passions, blind prejudice, and immoral habits on the part of men long accustomed to the exercise of untrammelled power, confronts serious obstacles to the complete and speedy success of this ordeal.[9]

He explained in a conclusion that the purpose of these texts was to explain to the French public that "the emancipation of slaves in the French colonies presents no greater difficulties, nor real dangers, than those which are altering the condition of slaves in British colonies."[10] The connection between the French and the British abolitionist movements also made personal communication possible. Alexis de Tocqueville was close to British intellectual circles, and the economist Nassau Senior sent him documents relating to the situation in British colonies, supporting him in his role as secretary of a parliamentary commission.[11] When sending these documents Senior emphasized the very poor quality of the great mass of documents: "yesterday evening post took a large packet of documents to you under the cover to the President of the Chamber—& more to follow. But they are so voluminous, & the proportion of chaff to wheat is so great that I doubt your commission being able to make much use of them."[12] Senior advised Tocqueville to contact his friend Sir James Stephen, Undersecretary for the Colonies, directly. It is not known whether Tocqueville followed this advice; although his report does include several references to *Parliamentary Papers*,[13] and repeats extensively the comments that Senior had made to him concerning the conditions for the success of emancipation in the British colonies.[14] He noted that freed slaves were forced to work for a moderate price when the population was numerous in relation to cultivable land, and where the fertility of the land did not allow the freed slaves to contribute to their own maintenance, since they were in no position to demand "extravagant" wages. The slogans of French colonists were for their part based selectively on reports regarding the abolition of slavery in British colonies, taking from them those elements that supported their argument. They argued that the reduction in labor and the consequent fall in colonial production were ruining British colonies. They therefore urged the French government to avoid making any hasty decision regarding slave emancipation, repeatedly emphasizing the dangerous economic consequences of the measure.[15]The rising pressure of Anglophobia in France following the Egyptian crisis of 1840 and the polemics between Great Britain and France over the "right-of-search" controversy that blew up between early 1841 and 1842 helped the colonial position. The boarding of French merchant vessels off the African coast by the Royal Navy stirred up considerable resentment in the French press, accusations being made that the British government was seeking to destroy French trade while claiming to be acting from philanthropic interests. Defenders of slavery used this to discredit abolitionists as unpatriotic, as puppets of Britain. Some parts of the press favorable to abolition (*Le Constitionnel, Le National, Le Siècle*) cast doubt on British humanitarian intentions by suggesting that Britain had an interest in ruining American slave plantations so that its own possessions in India might benefit. Criticized on all sides, the abolitionist movement was very much weakened.[16] Some liberals with the reputation of being partisans of abolition had been given high office under the July Monarchy. In March 1835 the duc de Broglie was named prime minister, a post which he held until February 1836, and this seemed to augur well for the abolitionist cause. Careful to avoid appearing to oppose the will of King Louis-Philippe, the president of the Société française pour l'abolition de l'esclavage adopted a carefully pragmatic position, like his predecessors.[17] Far from providing a model to be followed, the abolition of slavery in the British colonies was used as an argument favorable to the status quo. Following the July Revolution successive governments were unsettled by the economic effects of emancipation—the fall in output and consequent drop in metropolitan trade, but also the high cost of compensation to planters. Combined with the prevailing Anglophobia after 1840, they became pragmatic, and refrained from applying their liberal principles to contemporary policy.

ADMINISTRATION, STATISTICS, AND THE RETURN OF CALCULATION

By the later 1830s there was a new "sugar question." The production of sugar from sugar beet in metropolitan France introduced a new element into the discussion of slavery, much of colonial slave labor being engaged in the cultivation of sugar cane in colonies that were increasingly facing pressure from foreign competition. The French government sought to inform itself on the economic situation: on the way that the viability of slave economies was becoming increasingly dependent upon protectionist policy.[18] Paul Lavollée was an inspector of finances sent by the government to review sugar production in Guadeloupe and Martinique, and much of his report was taken up with numerical data—area devoted to sugar production and other plantation foodstuffs together with quantity produced, the condition and number of livestock and fixed capital, the cost price of sugar, extent of planter indebtedness, the return on capital employed in cultivation, and so forth. His report was published in 1841 on the order of the Ministry of the Navy and the Colonies and at the demand of the President of the Royal Commission, Victor de Broglie; however, the text, and especially the abundant data, had been previously mobilized in the debate over abolition conducted in the press and within a series of commissions. Lavollée was not asked to compare the relative cost of slave and free labor, but he did shed light on the cost price of sugar, which was itself a crucial question for the survival of sugar production in the Antilles. Drawing on his experience as an inspector of finance, he took figures from estate accounts relating to the direct cost of sugar that also, of course, included evidence of the cost of slave labor (see Table 5.1).

Using figures provided by the local agricultural society, Lavollée examined the case of a much smaller and much less well-situated estate worked by ninety slaves. The summary results of the figures collected relating to the cost of slave labor led to the calculation shown in Table 5.2.[19]

Lavollée does not take into account any capital costs entering into the cost price of sugar. Hence the cost of slave labor finally established by his data does not include the capital represented by the slaves, an element of calculation employed by economists, abolitionists, and, most frequently, by colonists. Lavollée obviously did not ignore the existence of this capital, and integrated it into another part of his report: in a political context that was reducing the value of slaves, he estimated the value of a black worker to be 1,000 francs, for old men and children between 200 and 600 francs. He therefore put the capital value of a slave collective of

Table 5.1 RESULTS OF THE EXTRACTION OF THE PRICE OF SLAVE LABOR FROM THE BALANCE SHEET OF AN ESTATE ON MARTINIQUE IN 1838 WITH 250 SLAVES

Expense	Amount (in francs)
Salt cod	5,609
Manioc and maize flour	9,329
Hospital, costs of medicines	1,970
New Year Tips as per custom	300
Shrouds	10
Baptism—14 at 5 francs each	70
Gratification to 14 mothers	280
Expenses for one marriage	20
Gratification to workers	67
Pay for overseers	120
Total	17,775

Source: Paul Lavollée, *Notes sur les cultures et la production de la Martinique et de la Guadeloupe*, Imprimerie royale, Paris 1841, pp. 86–87.

Table 5.2 RESULTS OF THE EXTRACTION OF THE PRICE OF SLAVE LABOR FROM THE BALANCE SHEET OF AN ESTATE ON MARTINIQUE IN 1838 WITH NINETY SLAVES

Expense	Amount (in francs)	
Salt cod	2,500	
Manioc and maize flour	5,000	Reduced to 4,320
Medicaments and medicines	900	
Clothing	1,400	Reduced to 900
Total	9,800	8,620

two hundred persons at 162,000 francs.[20] Taking into account only current expenditures in his calculation of the cost of sugar, he estimated in the same way as the most extreme eighteenth-century defenders of slavery, who presumed that the price of slave labor was limited to the provision of food and clothing to slaves. Moreover, he did not include in his report the cost of replacing dead slaves, an element that was generally taken into account by calculators. The explanation for this is that, with the cessation of the slave trade, the slave market was limited to the sale of creoles, and was almost moribund. This was reflected in the way that estate accounts were cast up.[21] By contrast, and unlike previous calculations, the costs arising from births were noted explicitly in the accounts of the first estate, marking the new interest that colonists took in the natural and indispensable reproduction of the creole slaves. Expenditures under this heading were certainly very small (2 percent of the total), but it is significant that they were present. In addition to spending on food, clothing, and reproduction, like other economists and abolitionists Lavollée noted the direct costs of coercion (the overseers' pay), but did not take into account the indirect costs that it generated (general domestic security) as Du Pont had done. He also introduced into his calculation the costs related to another form of incentive to work: gratuities paid to laborers; this element was a real innovation compared to previous calculations, even if it was a small amount—at just more than half of the pay for overseers, the implication is that this form of incentive was marginal. Lavollée does not calculate the cost of slave labor; by applying to his data the usual methods of calculation used by contemporary commentators (250 working days per year, 70 percent of slaves active, and including the cost of capital embedded in slaves), the price of slave labor came out very low: 73 centimes per day on the large estate, and 94 centimes for the smaller, very low figures compared to those previously advanced and not favorable for settlers whose interest, at that time, was to show that production costs were sufficiently important to justify the protection and subsidy. The "Observations on the Administration of Guadeloupe" annexed to Lavollée's report did, moreover, state that "in order to establish the cost of dwellings, it is first necessary to determine the capital employed and annual expenditure."[22] Colonists also reacted to the Lavollée report by resuming their eighteenth-century approach. Jacques Sully-Brunet, a colonist from Réunion, used Lavollée's data (which he thought to be an under-estimate) to show that the wage bill for free workers—each receiving 20 francs a month, a little less than one franc per working day—"would absorb, and more, the income of the colonist; although he [would] still have to provide for all other operating costs and personal expenses."[23]

According to the appendices of the Lavollée report, the economist André Cochut, who was very active in the contemporary periodical *Revue des Deux Mondes*, relied on figures supplied by the administration of Guadeloupe for the budget of an estate of two hundred slaves, calculating the cost of slave labor and hoping that "in such a matter he will be pardoned for the dryness of an argument bristling with figures."[24]

The calculation was innovative in that it added to the usual capital cost (the purchase of slaves) the costs incurred for the construction of slave dwellings and a hospital. Current expenditures included health costs, which among the settlers only Barré Saint-Venant had previously taken

Table 5.3 COCHUT'S CALCULATION

Capital Invested (annual cost at a rate of 10%, in francs)	
Purchase of 200 negroes	22,650
80 huts	2,800
Hospital	400
Current Expenditure	
Medicine and medicaments	2,500
Food (allowance made for Saturday and garden being left out)	10,800
Clothing	3,800
Total	42,950
Total per slave	214

into account; the costs associated with the use of force on slaves are, however, passed over in silence, since Cochut did not think it worthwhile to add them to the data presented by planters. Considering that only 135 slaves out of the 200 present on the estate were active, and with 250 days worked a year, Cochut obtained a daily cost of 1.27 francs per slave. This result is very different from the very low figure obtained using the data provided by Lavollée, a result which would not suit a calculator convinced of the economic superiority of free labor.

On the basis of this calculation Cochut embarked on the comparative logic first articulated by Du Pont and the abolitionists of the eighteenth century. Unlike his predecessors, however, he had a solid empirical basis for the task he had set himself, thanks to the British experience. From the hearings of colonists and others familiar with the situation in the British colonies following the 1833 abolition, it appeared that the wages of emancipated slaves ranged from 1.25 to 1.5 francs, and at a yet level lower in some islands, as with Barbados, Antigua, and Dominica. Comparison of costs between bonded and free labor showed that emancipation was becoming economically efficient, a process that was accelerating because it then made possible the introduction of more productive techniques.[25] Cochut concluded by quoting from evidence given to the Broglie Commission:

> A very distinguished man, Mr. Burnley, stated to the Colonial Commission: "The abolition of serfdom in Europe has succeeded precisely because of the fact that the price and quality of free labor, at the time when this revolution was accomplished, had become preferable to those of slave labor." If we do not deceive ourselves, emancipation is not far from the same chances of success in the French Antilles.[26]

THE INSTITUTIONAL PRACTICE OF CALCULATORY RHETORIC

The activity of abolitionist parliamentarians during the July Monarchy led to the creation of various commissions of inquiry, whose reports then prompted publications that sustained debate over the question of slave emancipation. In February 1838 Hippolyte Passy put forward a project for gradual emancipation based on two elements: the freedom of every child born in the colonies after the law came into effect; and the right of slaves to purchase their liberty at a price fixed by arbitrators appointed by metropolitan authorities. This proposal was examined by a commission whose report was written and presented to the Chamber of Deputies by Charles de Rémusat in June of the same year.[27] He suggested that various measures designed to prepare the slave population for liberty be associated with his project: the introduction of religious and primary education, civil recognition of marriage between unfree persons, the right for a slave to purchase his or her liberty, and the establishment of an inspectorate to review the application of the law. One year later Victor de Tracy presented the Passy proposition to the Chamber,[28] proposing that the matter be examined by a new commission headed by Tocqueville. Tocqueville's report of July 1839 consisted largely of a review of statistical information.[29] The question was also raised of how quickly a functioning labor market could be created following emancipation, the impossibility of immediately creating such a market upon emancipation having been foreseen by the commission; a period of "state tutelage" was anticipated to resolve this issue. Accordingly, the comparative cost of slave and free labor was still an important element of his report. Rémusat was a member of the Thiers government, and this seems to have played a part in the subsequent creation of another commission "to examine questions relating to slavery and the political constitution of the colonies," established by royal command and headed by the duc de Broglie. This did, however, remove parliamentary authority from the issue, and so allowed the government to postpone any decision indefinitely under the pretext of making careful preparation for abolition.[30] Nonetheless, this marked an important point at which calculation re-entered institutional debate over slavery. The commission's hearings showed clearly the degree to which its members were aware of the issue regarding the relative price of free and slave labor, related to the way in which the demand for labor could be organized after emancipation in 1853, the date that most if its members had in mind.[31] However, no decision was made, and it was only with the 1848 Revolution that the abolition of slavery was finally decreed by a commission headed by Schœlcher;

which rendered any further discussion of the comparative costs of free and slave labor redundant.[32]

How were the calculations made on this issue incorporated politically into the discussions of these various commissions?

The majority of the nine members of the commission established to examine Passy's proposal, and that sat between the beginning of February and the end of April 1838 under the presidency of Guizot, were opposed to slavery—five of them were members of the Société française pour l'abolition de l'esclavage, and only two represented colonial opinion. Its report included extensive summaries of the evolving legislative framework, while its author, Rémusat, explained that the commission had conducted a "kind of inquiry" aimed primarily at investigating how social order was maintained and work continued in the British West Indies after the Abolition Act. The cost of slave labor and of wage labor prevailing in the colonies was nowhere addressed in the text. Calculation only entered into discussion on the sole occasion where the impact of the slave trade on the fate of slaves was raised. When the trade was legal, or when it was operated illegally, the relationship between master and slave was dominated by *commercial calculation.* Rémusat stated that

> Colonial slavery realised more completely than ancient slavery the brutal fiction of Roman Law that made the slave a chattel, a thing. Given that the man was of necessity acquired through the market, he became in reality a commodity, a property. And since the market renewed itself unceasingly, the right of property became in fact the right to use or abuse; too often, calculation alone determined how the possessor used his thing.[33]

The prohibition of the slave trade altered everything, henceforth creating "an irrevocable need for economy and foresight to manage this capital [the slave]."[34] The calculation of the colonist changed into an *industrial calculation* that impelled him to manage his slave, who had now become a capital that was hard to replace. The idea was not new: this was already in the eighteenth century a major argument against trading in African slaves.[35] The novelty was that now Rémusat set about seeking to prove its validity using numbers, showing that since the cessation of the slave trade the number of births in the slave population was slightly more than the number of deaths.

The subsequent parliamentary commission that took up Tracy's revision of Passy's proposal was likewise dominated by those opposed to slavery: six out of nine members belonged to the Société française pour l'abolition de l'esclavage. The commission rejected the Passy-Tracy proposal for gradual and progressive emancipation and instead opted for general abolition. Tocqueville was a leading figure in French political and intellectual life, and his report both summarized the problem and advanced an emancipation plan that kept this process in view, while not provoking any specific measures. In the first part of his report Tocqueville explained why the gradualist approach of Passy and Tracy had been rejected. While the metropolitan government could free all slaves at the same time, it could easily subject them to a transitory regime in which they gradually become accustomed to making good use of their liberty. A gradualist process, however, would require the administration to introduce legislation applicable to only one kind of worker, which would not fail to provoke social tensions. A government apparatus that sought to suppress vagabondage and idleness among free workers could give rise to substantial social costs.

The success of complete and simultaneous liberation of all slaves would, however, require that a number of conditions be fulfilled. The most critical of these was the indemnity to be given to planters. Its amount was directly linked to the question of the cost relationship for the colonist between free and slave labor.

In place of the slave who no longer existed, the law would offer him a free worker. The free worker only works for a wage; but the slave could only work on condition of being bought, fed, cared for, and clothed; that would simply be a wage in a different form.[36]

The productivity of freed slaves would in any case be higher than that of slaves:

> Science shows, and much experience already gained in the tropical hinterland seems to prove that cultivation by freed black must become easier, more productive and less onerous than cultivation as practised by black slaves. It is therefore permissible to believe that the revolution brought about in our islands would be as fortunate for the colonists as it would be for the blacks, once this revolution had been completed, it would cost less to the landowner to cultivate his fields with a small number of workers whom he paid according to the work they had actually done, whereas today he is obliged to purchase and maintain the whole year round a large number of slaves, of whom a substantial part always remained unproductive.[37]

While holding to the view that the possession of slaves always had been, and remained, illegitimate, the commission considered it equitable and prudent to forcibly compensate colonists, the prosperity of the colonies being a factor determining the success of the transition from slavery to liberty.

The British experience was examined to understand the difficulties arising from the establishment of free labor in their colonies. Tocqueville distinguished the situations in the different colonies according to two criteria: the chance of emancipated slaves having access to the land, and the quality of the soil. When access to land was difficult, the supply of labor was sustained and wages were low; conversely, colonists could continue to cultivate the land profitably if it was fertile, but met with great difficulty if the land was exhausted. In this last case, it was hard to secure a well-functioning labor market; Tocqueville wrote that this disagreeable situation could be attributed to

> . . . the bad relationships that became established between masters and freed slaves during the period of apprenticeship in the majority of colonies. The defiance and hatred that then arose made it very difficult to arrive at a fair settlement for wages. It is plain that the colonist always seeks to employ the negro at a very low price, and that the latter always demands a price that is too high. Since the two men not only have opposed interests, but are secretly enemies, it is almost impossible that they ever arrive at a good arrangement.[38]

In the last part of his report Tocqueville outlined the commission's proposal regarding a tutelary stance of the state toward freed slaves: The state would, according to its will and its conditions, offer the services of blacks to the colonists, while retaining the use of disciplinary means. The determination of wages and working conditions by the state would have the advantage of avoiding the development of relationships marked by defiance and animosity between freed slaves and landowners, but would undermine the prospects for the emergence of a normal labor market. The moderate wage paid by the planters would be partially allocated to pay off the interest on the capital that paid compensation to the former owner, while another part would go to black workers who retained a plot of land and the free Saturday that had been conceded to them during their time of slavery.[39] The level of the wage paid depended implicitly upon a comparison of the costs of free and slave labor. Tocqueville published a series of articles in late 1843 in *Le Siècle*, using elements from the report to the Broglie Commission to elaborate his proposal. Set at 300 million francs for the 250,000 slaves of the French colonies (the average price per head being fixed at the very high level of 1,200 francs), compensation would be paid half in the form of a pension of 4 percent on 6 million francs. The metropolis would thereby acquire the right to withdraw from colonists half of the work of the emancipated slaves; in place of which the state would leave colonists free to enjoy their services in full for ten years. Since the daily cost of a former slave's work was estimated to be 50 centimes, the state in fact granted the master 25 cents a day; this benefit over ten years being equivalent to the 150 million francs that had not been given to them. All in all, "the costs of emancipation are distributed in a manner that seems fair to all those who have an interest in the success of the measure: half of the compensation is provided by the mother country, the other by the work of the blacks, and the rise in the price of labor is borne by the colonists."[40] The interests involved are reconciled, if they are not completely identical: Tocqueville explained in his report that

> The commission, gentlemen, is therefore convinced that an apprenticeship system based on the foundations noted could also reconcile the rights of the Treasury and the interests of the colonists. Above all, it is the happiest combination that could be adopted in favour of the blacks, of that race oppressed and degraded by slavery, whose situation it is France's honour to regulate, enlighten, and render moral, as well as to emancipate.[41]

Comparisons of the price of labor were also central to the concerns of the members of the Broglie Commission. Unlike those commissions established by Parliament, this commission was composed half of persons favorable to abolition, and half of representatives of the interests of port cities and of the administration. It was responsible for examining various colonial issues—including the political representation of colonies—which qualified the importance it attached to slavery. It sat for a very long time. A first series of meetings in June 1840 was followed by a second between December 1840 and May 1841, then a third from January to May 1842. The political tactic of procrastination worked very well.

Examination of the minutes of the commission testifies to the importance it gave to the cost of labor. The question of determining wages after abolition was raised in several hearings.[42] The Attorney General of Guadeloupe emphasized the need to set the wage level in relation to the sale and cost price of sugar, a statement that gave Passy the opportunity to explain that it was difficult to calculate a cost price, conditions varying from one estate to another; but that it was possible to establish a "necessary price"—covering all operating costs—from which it might be possible to establish "a certain estimate of the cost of labor" from elements like "the food and the maintenance of the blacks, and even the land transferred to them in Martinique and Guadeloupe. There is already data on the basis of which this can be done."[43]

What part did the comparison of the cost of slave labor and free labor play in these debates? In this respect the report of the Broglie Commission made use of a strange formulation, repeatedly contrasting "obligatory and free work to free work at an agreed price."[44] This terminology departs radically from the approach initiated by Du Pont in 1771 which is based on the idea that servile labor is only apparently for free. Despite this astonishing way of posing the problem, the report did, during its treatment of settler compensation, consider the comparative costs of slave and free labor. While he was being questioned Jules Lechevalier, who was developing a Guyanan colonization project that we will discuss later, declared his belief in the greater profitability of free labor:

> Mr. President. Do you believe that free labour is more productive than slave labour?—Mr. Lechevalier. I have no doubt about it. The real difference that should be made between free and slave labour is that the latter is extorted labour, and the other is paid labour. The work of the slave is extorted labour; and, if I were able to enter into some detail on this subject, I would show that the economy with which the planters think they are working has degenerated into real expense.[45]

Lechevalier added that the low productivity of the slave was explained by the fact that the slave ensured his subsistence thanks to the concession of a plot of land, which prevented a connection being made between his means of subsistence and cane cultivation.

According to the report of the commission, abolition could not be treated as expropriation for reasons of public utility: property in slaves was no ordinary or natural form of property guaranteed by the rules of universal morality, but only a legal property resulting from an excessive privilege that the state had granted to colonists, which it could therefore likewise withdraw. Compensation did not consequently relate to a repurchase of slaves; it was only compensation for the damage that the loss of this privilege inflicted upon settlers, compensation that the state agreed to pay for reasons of equity and the maintenance of economic activity. To determine the amount of compensation it would be necessary to "determine the extent of the appreciable direct damage which will fall exclusively on the settlers, in other words, . . . to estimate in money the privilege that emancipation removes from them, an advantage that they lose with the return to common law."[46] To achieve this, the commission compared the wages of the free laborer to the cost of the slave. In countries where labor was free the wealth produced was distributed between the capitalist and the worker according to the proportion of supply to demand on the market; slavery, on the other hand,

> sets, *a priori* and at a flat rate, the payment made to the worker at the minimum possible; it is invariably reduced to the most strictly necessary, to the

quantity indispensable to the worker for subsistence. The remainder accrues to the master; that is his privilege; this is the advantage he derives from his position; that is the *quantum* of his benefit. This advantage is worth, in money, precisely what it costs: it is the venal value of the black slave; it is this advantage that one buys in buying this slave.[47]

This passage is an exercise in applied liberal economic theory. It can be presented as follows: the benefit of slave labor to the master is defined by the difference between the wage fixed according to the rules of competition (W) and the minimum remuneration granted to the slave (W_{min}). The *quantum* of profit received by the slave-owning colonist can be determined by equating the sum of the gains generated by the slave during his productive life to his market price, because a rational colonist would not buy a slave at this price if he were not able to derive a benefit at least equal to this sum.

The benefit derived from owning the slave = the sum of gains made by setting him to work = the price of the slave.[48]

Based on this elementary calculation of the choice of a technique of production by a rational colonist, the commission would have been able to make economic calculations aimed at estimating the amount of compensation as a function of the difference between the costs of free and of slave labor, the length of a working life and the market price of slaves. But this was not what they actually did. Instead, they used the data gathered by the government-appointed investigators in the four colonies to assess the average value of a slave at 1,200 francs; and then fixed compensation at this level to indemnify the master in respect of the loss of the privilege of possessing slaves with which he had originally been endowed by the state.

Published in three volumes, the work of the Broglie Commission was taken into account by the abolitionists. As already noted, Tocqueville repeated—sometimes verbatim—parts of the Broglie report in the series of articles he published in *Le Siècle*. Cochut seized on the report to argue in favor of Lechevalier's colonization project for Guyana, founding a company that would exploit the colony by employing a free workforce:

The fundamental point is the regulation of free labor. The slave costs much more than liberty; this is a fact proved a long time ago by political economy, and the planters, in spite of their prejudices, would have been the first to emancipate their slaves if they had not feared that the slaves, left to themselves, would have abandoned colonial cultivation.[49]

An enthusiastic supporter of Lechevalier's proposals regarding the organization of labor in such a way as to preserve colonial cultivation in Guyana (including ceding to the company a monopoly of the production and sale of food, and the fixing of wages by the authorities), he appealed to calculation to prove that this project of slave emancipation was well founded:

> Fearful of being dazzled by a seductive illusion, we have translated the facts into figures, supplementing the documents provided officially with our own investigations. It appears to us to have been demonstrated that the expenditures made by colonists today suffice to improve considerably the lot of the former slaves by gaining a greater amount of work from them. Let the numbers talk.[50]

Making a distinction in terms of the rate of interest between an economy based on free labor and the slave system—the former being half that of the latter—Cochut also stated that the annual number of days worked in a system of free labor (300 days) would be greater than that observed in slavery (250 days, due to the concession of free Saturdays made to slaves by their masters). Assuming that only two-thirds of the 15,000 blacks were active, he derived a total of 3 million working days in the first case, against 2.5 million in the second.

Using these figures, the daily cost of slave and free labor are, respectively, 1.03 francs and 1.33 francs. This one-third increase in the price of

Table 5.4 COCHUT'S CALCULATION ON LECHEVALIER'S PROPOSAL

Interest on Capital Invested (in francs)			
Slavery (rate of 8%)		Free Labor (rate of 4%)	
15,000 black slaves	1,440,000	Repurchase of 15,000	720,000
5,000 huts & gardens	160,000	Repurchase of huts	80,000
Hospitals	24,000	Hospitals	12,000
Current Expenditure (in francs)			
Food	600,000	Wages	3,000,000
Clothing	150,000		
Medicine	187,500	Medicine	187,500
Various costs	38,500		
Total	2,600,000	Total	4,000,000

labor would not be a true additional cost for the estate: about 90 percent of the salary of the freed slave would flow back into the landowner's hands in the form of the rent paid by the slave for his hut and for the expenditure on food, clothing, and medical care that the slave will have to make. The *real wage* will actually be lower than the labor cost of the slave: *Quod erat demonstrandum*!

Cochut goes on:

> The important thing is that the emancipated black, living on his own, gains in the present a noticeable improvement in his condition, and acquires for the future the chance of improving his in the absence of which freedom is only a lie.[51]

To demonstrate the possibility of initiating such a process Cochut outlined a hypothetical budget for a family of emancipated slaves made up of three persons, two of whom work for three hundred days a year for the modest daily wage of 1 franc, assuring to the household an annual income of 600 francs. The first items of expenditure—as would be the case for statistical studies of consumption made during the second half of the nineteenth century[52]—are food, clothing, and housing (see Table 5.5).

Cochut argued that this showed that workers would find a real improvement in their conditions, given that the family would have available a sum of money greater than "the available portion of military pay," to which could be added dividends from sharing in the profit of the estate (a measure envisaged by Lechevalier's project).

Table 5.5 COCHUT'S HYPOTHETICAL BUDGET FOR A FAMILY OF EMANCIPATED SLAVES

Annual Expenditure (in francs)	
Housing	30
Clothing	60
Food	365
Medicine	20
Tobacco, salt	55
Various payments (church, school, assistance, tax, savings	10
Total	540
Left to the family	60
Sum equal to wage	600

THE SCHŒLCHER COMMISSION AND THE END OF COMPARATIVE CALCULATION

During the 1848 revolution Schœlcher traveled to Senegal, and on his return had a meeting with François Arago, the Minister of the Navy and Colonies, persuading him that the government should adopt the principle of emancipating French colonial slaves. He was subsequently appointed Under-Secretary of State, and appointed president of a commission charged with the preparation of decrees regarding the emancipation of slaves. The commission of seven members, all abolitionists, sat from March 12 to July 21, 1848. In addition to drafting the decree for abolition that was then ratified by the provisional government on April 27, the commission prepared fifteen further decrees on various aspects of social, political, and economic life in the colonies.[53]

The aims of the commission naturally affected the nature of its work. While seeking to support decisions with accurate knowledge of the economic situation in the colonies—Lavollée was heard during the sessions of March 30 and April 15 and it took into account the wage rates of free workers in the French colonies[54]—it showed no interest in the relative costs of free and slave labor. *Once the decision to abolish slavery had been taken, this form of calculation became irrelevant.*

On the other hand, the question of how work on the plantations might be sustained was central to its concerns. Schœlcher's report was reassuring in this respect: the day after emancipation the former black slaves would no doubt abandon the hoe, a symbol of servitude, "but one might believe that after devoting some time to leisure they will return to work, now free from coercion and the whip, regenerated by liberty, transformed by a fair wage into a source of well-being."[55] The commission established a framework for work in the colonies in line with prevailing contemporary conceptions. The basic principle was clearly stated: *the organization of work should not be understood to involve coercion.* The freed slave would work hard if his work provided him with a suitable return; society would benefit from competition between various forms of wage labor (payment by piece or by day without a fixed minimum or maximum), free association, and sharecropping. Having stated this principle, the commission sought to assure everyone of the *right to work*, opening national workshops where everyone could find work and "a wage calculated according to a just measure of everyday needs. . . . By providing a wage below the general level the state provides for the worker without actively attracting him; the state gives him the necessary, leaving the worker with the desire to seek better pay in private industry."[56] This wage—the commission in fact setting a minimum wage for free labor—would vary, according to strength and age, between 25 centimes and 1.25 francs for a working day of nine hours. While respecting the right of everyone to choose for themselves, the government also had to *protect public order*; this was the objective of the law against begging and vagrancy which governed the creation of disciplinary workshops where the freed slaves were detained, fed, housed in common, and given uniform dress, receiving only a modest sum of 20 to 35 centimes a day. While the national workshop was the free refuge of the man looking for work, the disciplinary workshop involved the forcible detention of a worker who did not want to look for work.

* * *

After the passing of the British Abolition Act in 1833 French abolitionists renewed debate within political institutions. The work of the various committees, first parliamentary, then royal, generated new calculations seeking to prove the validity of arguments that Du Pont had already made. Calculatory rhetoric was now seen as a way of convincing those with decision-making power in Parliament and government.

The developing political situation itself transformed calculation. The capital cost of replacing dead slaves lost its importance with the decline of a slave market once the slave trade was suppressed. The gratuities offered for the birth of children to slaves, a new element in the calculations, showed the new significance of the natural reproduction of the slave population for the colonists. It was now less a question of enlightening planters who were blind to their true economic interest than proving to them that abolition would not lead to a rise in the price of labor and/or a shortage of labor likely to ruin their estates. It was still necessary to demonstrate to the authorities that the emancipation of slaves would allow the colonial economy to avoid being trapped by the indebtedness of owners—a major theme of the Lavollée report then taken up by the Broglie commission; this would be effected through a restructuring of the sugar sector, thus upgrading production techniques and making colonial sugar competitive on the international market.

Reviewing the data on which surveys, committee reports, and committee minutes were based, we can appreciate the difficulty that they encountered in forming a clear consensus on the comparative costs of slave and free labor. From various sources—the Lavollée report, information from the slave-owning planters in the French colonies, or from the administration and the owners of the English islands—the contradictory figures available to them did not allow them to develop unambiguous and reliable calculations. In 1861 Augustin Cochin commented on the method of calculating the compensation as proposed by the Broglie Commission:

> In short, the colonists received only about 500 francs per slave. This compensation was really inadequate. The most suitable basis would have been the calculation made by the government, if it had been possible to determine exactly the difference between the price of slave labor and the price of free labor. But what did slave labor cost? What would free labor cost? Nobody knew: the formula was ingenious, but the elements of calculation were pure hypothesis.[57]

Moreover, the profitability of estates depended not only upon the price of labor, but also upon its *productivity*, a central element of the abolitionist argument that must now be analyzed.

NOTES

1. Pierre-Armand Dufau, *De l'abolition graduelle de l'esclavage dans les colonies européennes et notamment dans les colonies françaises, considérée à la fois dans l'intérêt des esclaves, des maîtres, des colonies et de la métropole*, Bureau central de la Revue Encyclopédique, Paris 1830, pp. 106–107.
2. The franchise was restricted to males, and inclusion was conditional upon the payment of a tax so high that it effectively excluded the majority of persons of colour.
3. The following remarks are based upon Lawrence C. Jennings, *French Reaction to British Slave Emancipation*, Louisiana State University Press, Baton Rouge 1988, Ch. 2, pp. 27–59.
4. Ibid., p. 34.
5. *Précis de l'abolition d'esclavage dans les colonies anglaises*, Preface to Vol. I, Imprimerie royale, Paris 1840. The three subsequent volumes were published in 1841, and the last in 1843.
6. The vice-presidents were Hippolyte Passy and Odilon Barrot, with Alexandre de Laborde and François-André Isambert as secretaries.
7. Jennings, *French Reaction*, p. 93.
8. Zachary Macaulay, *Détails sur l'émancipation des esclaves pendant les années 1834 et 1835*, Hachette, Paris 1836; and *Suite des détails sur l'émancipation des esclaves pendant les années 1835 et 1836*, Hachette, Paris 1836. His other three works were *Faits et renseignements prouvant les avantages du travail libre sur le travail forcé, et indiquent les moyens les plus propres à hâter l'abolition de l'esclavage dans les colonies européennes*, Hachette, Paris 1835; *Haïti, ou renseignements authentiques sur l'abolition de l'esclavage et de ses résultats, à Saint-Domingue et à Guadaloupe*, Hachette, Paris 1835; and *Tableau de l'esclavage tel qu'il existe dans les colonies françaises*, Hachette, Paris 1835.
9. Macaulay, *Détails sur l'émancipation des esclaves*, p. xiv.
10. Macaulay, *Suite des détails sur l'émancipation des esclaves*, p. 81.
11. See the letters of Senior to Tocqueville of June and July 1839 in Alexis de Tocqueville, *Correspondance anglaise, Œuvres complètes d'Alexis de Tocqueville*, t. 6, vol. 2, Gallimard, Paris 1991, pp. 83–89.
12. Senior to Tocqueville, letter of June 22, 1839, ibid., p. 84.

13. Alexis de Tocqueville, "Rapport fait au nom de la commission chargée d'examiner la proposition de M. de Tracy, relative aux esclaves des colonies," 1839, in *Œuvres complètes d'Alexis de Tocqueville*, t. 3, vol. 1, Gallimard, Paris 1962, pp. 63–69.
14. The comparison made by Senior at the end of his letter to Tocqueville of June 22, 1839, and sections of the latter's report make this quite plain—Tocqueville, "Rapport,"ibid., pp. 70–71.
15. See Jennings, *French Reaction*, ch. 3.
16. Ibid., ch. 6.
17. Lawrence C. Jennings, "Abolitionnisme, jeux politique et réforme: France 1814–1848," in Pétré-Grenouilleau (ed.) *Abolir l'esclavage. Un réformisme à l'épreuve (France, Portugal, Suisse, XVIIIe–XIXe siècle)*, Presses universitaires de Rennes, Rennes 2008.
18. David Todd, *L'identité économique de la France. Libre-échange et protectionnisme 1814–1851*, Grasset, Paris 2008, ch. 15.
19. Ibid., pp. 89–90. Lavollée criticized the estimates given by the agricultural society as being too high in respect of the amount of food supplied to slaves and the total of payments made, hence the adjustment downward in the second column.
20. Ibid., p. 218.
21. This approach can be found in the critiques of British and American estate accounting practices for the slave era: David Oldroyd, Richard Fleischman, Thomas Tyson, "The Culpability of Accounting Practice in Promoting Slavery in the British Empire and antebellum United States," *Critical Perspectives on Accounting*, vol. 19 (2008), pp. 764–784.
22. Lavollée, *Notes sur les cultures et la production de la Martinique et de la Guadeloupe*, Imprimerie nationale, Paris 1844, p. 92.
23. Jacques Sully-Brunet, *Considérations sur le système colonial et plan d'abolition de l'esclavage*, Félix Locquin et Cie, Paris 1840, p. 44—he took his figures from Lavollée, *Notes*, pp. 128–129.
24. André Cochut, "La société coloniale—Abolition de l'esclavage," *Revue des deux mondes*, t. 3 (1843), p. 222. The figures used came from Lavollée's report, *Notes*, pp. 93–95.
25. Following Lavollée, Cochut noted that cultivation techniques in the Antilles were stuck at the level they had reached at the beginning of the eighteenth century: "Cultivation and manufacture are in the Antilles in the same condition as they were one hundred and fifty years ago. The soil yields half as much as it could do if it were adequately fertilised; the tardiness with which processing is conducted creates a great deal of waste, such that the sugar yield from the cane is barely 7%, instead of the 18% that it contains." Cochut, "La société coloniale," p. 225.
26. Ibid., p. 222. Burnley was a planter from Trinity, Martinique, who was heard by the Broglie commission.
27. Charles de Rémusat, *Rapport fait au nom de la commission chargée de l'examen de la proposition de M. Passy sur le sort des esclaves dans les colonies françaises*, Société française pour l'abolition de l'esclavage, no. 9, 1838.
28. *Développements de la proposition relative au sort des esclaves dans les colonies*, M. de Tracy, Deputy for the Orne, Chamber of Deputies, Second Session, sitting of June 12, 1839.
29. Alexis de Tocqueville, "Rapport fait au nom de la commission chargée d'examiner la proposition de M. de Tracy, relative aux colonies," 1839, in *Ecrits et discours politiques, Œuvres complètes d'Alexis de Tocqueville*, t. 3, vol. 1, Gallimard, Paris 1962.

30. Jennings, *French Reaction*, pp. 150–151.
31. [Commission de Broglie], *Commission instituée, par décision royale du 24 mai 1840, pour l'examen des questions relatives à l'esclavage et à la constitution politique des colonies, Procès-verbaux, Ire partie—du 4 au 18 juin 1840*, Imprimerie royale, Paris 1840; *Procès-verbaux, IIe partie—du 22 décembre 1840 au 12 mai 1841*, Imprimerie royale, Paris 1841; *Rapport fait au ministre secrétaire d'Etat de la marine et des colonies*, Imprimerie royale, Paris 1843.
32. *Procès-verbaux, rapports et projets de décrets de la commission instituée pour préparer l'acte d'abolition immédiate de l'esclavage*, Imprimerie nationale, Paris 1848.
33. Rémusat, *Rapport fait au nom de la commission chargée de l'examen de la proposition de M. Passy*, p. 6.
34. Ibid.
35. Caroline Oudin-Bastide, "Discours colonial et discours abolitionniste: entre passions et intérêts," in Pétré-Grenouilleau (ed.) *Abolir l'esclavage. Un réformisme à l'épreuve (France, Portugal, Suisse, XVIIIe–XIXe siècle)*, Presses universitaires de Rennes, Rennes 2008.
36. Tocqueville, "Rapport fait au nom de la commission," p. 54.
37. Ibid., p. 55.
38. Ibid., p. 71.
39. Ibid., p. 74.
40. Tocqueville, articles published in *Le Siècle* December 14, 1843, in *Ecrits et discours politiques, Œuvres complètes d'Alexis de Tocqueville*, t. 3, vol. 1, Gallimard, Paris 1962, p. 108.
41. Tocqueville, *Rapport fait au nom de la commission*, p. 76.
42. *Commission instituée, par décision royale du 24 mai 1840, Procès-verbaux, Ire partie*, pp. 23–25, 28, 41, 44–45.
43. Ibid., p. 92.
44. *Commission instituée, par décision royale du 24 mai 1840, Rapport fait au ministre secrétaire d'Etat de la marine et des colonies*, p. 262; see also pp. 278, 280.
45. *Commission instituée, par décision royale du 24 mai 1840, Procès-verbaux, Ire partie*, p. 45.
46. *Commission instituée, par décision royale du 24 mai 1840, Rapport fait au ministre secrétaire d'Etat de la marine et des colonies*, p. 274.
47. Ibid.
48. If the idea of present value is added to the flow of income obtained from the employment of slave labor, the final phrase in the preceding text can be written as the elementary formula expressing the fundamental value of a financial asset, with an interest rate (i) that is given and constant over the period: Price of a slave = $\Sigma(w - W_{min})_t/(1 + i)^t$. Both practical men of the time and economists were familiar with the procedures for calculating rates of interest, as can be seen from *Manuel du capitaliste ou comptes faits des intérêts*, Garnier Frères, Paris n.d. (first edition 1815).
49. André Cochut, "De la colonisation de la Guyane française," *Revue des deux mondes*, t. 11 (1845), p. 539.
50. Ibid., p. 540.
51. Ibid., p. 543.
52. The study of workers' budgets only really began to develop with the work of Frédéric Le Play, following the publication of his *Les ouvriers européens* in 1855. Cochut was therefore being innovative in presenting the advantages of the introduction of free labor in the form of numerical budgets. We should note that,

unlike Le Play and his collaborators and followers, Cochut cast up a hypothetical budget for a family of free workers, while Le Play built his own on observations of expenditures made by households that were part of his study. The distribution of expenditure between these three broad categories underlies the result that became known as "Engel's Law," the name of the German statistician who first published his findings in 1857.

53. *Procès verbaux, rapports et projets de décrets de la commission instituée pour préparer l'acte d'abolition immédiate de l'esclavage*, Imprimerie noyale, Paris 1848.
54. The report mentioned that free black workers in Guyana were paid 1 franc per day—women received half—but emancipated slaves paid 65 centimes per days enjoyed the use of a hut, an allotment, and a free Saturday, so that their pay was equivalent to a daily wage of 1.50 francs—ibid., p. 84.
55. Ibid., p. 304.
56. Ibid., p. 309.
57. Augustin Cochin, *L'abolition de l'esclavage, I*[re] *partie—Résultats de l'abolition de l'esclavage*, Jacques Lecoffre & Guillaumin et Cie, Paris 1861, p. 159.

CHAPTER 6
Another Form of Calculation
Productivity

The productivity differential between slave and free labor reinforces Du Pont's demonstration that the first is less efficient than the second. Since it was not based upon any numerical data, Du Pont's contention that the productivity of a free worker was *double* that of a slave was really nothing more than the kind of proposition that Petty had described, ". . . at worst . . . sufficient as Suppositions to show the way to that Knowledge I aim at." While abolitionist discourse from the later eighteenth century and the first half of the nineteenth largely accepted that free labor was more productive than slave labor, the quantitative validation of this idea proved more difficult. Concerned to demonstrate the rigor of their analysis, some sought to support their assertions using calculations drawn from the reports made on colonial society, or by using available statistical sources.

To talk of productivity in this context might seem anachronistic, since none of the writers studied here used the term. While it is absent from eighteenth-century dictionaries—it does not even appear in the sixth edition of the *Dictionnaire de l'Académie* (1832–1835)—the adjective *productif, -ive* was, however, a key term used by the Physiocrats; consciously derived from the verb *produire*, and an antonym to *stérile*, for Quesnay it signified creative activity producing a new value.[1] His purpose was to mark the difference between agriculture (productive) and commerce and industry (sterile). In his "Dialogue de Mr. H et Mr. N," published in 1766 in the *Journal d'agriculture, du commerce et des finances*, he did use the term *productibilité* to signify the capacity to produce value, but this was a neologism that he would quickly abandon.[2] It is difficult to determine exactly when the word *productivité* did appear, and it seems to have taken some time to become established. It is ignored in the eight editions of the *Dictionnaire de l'Académie* (the last edition being published between 1932 and 1935); it is missing from the Littré's first edition of the *Dictionnaire de la langue française* (1872), while it does have an entry in the *Grand dictionnaire universel* published by Pierre Athanase Larousse in 1875: "Faculty of producing, condition of that which is productive" is the vague definition that it is given. It would not be until the twentieth century that economists would begin to attach a new sense to it, as the (measurable) relationship between *product* and *factors of production*, in which terms it became a central element in public debate.[3]

CALCULATIONS OF LABOR PRODUCTIVITY IN THE EIGHTEENTH CENTURY

The absence of a word does not signify the absence of an idea. The distinction that Quesnay established in his early economic writings between *petite culture* and *grande culture* rests on the relationship, differing in each case, between revenues created and capital invested ("*avances*" in his terminology). This is, in fact, a calculation of the apparent productivity of capital employed (income ÷ capital invested), and he sets this for *grande culture* at 250 percent for gross productivity, and 100 percent for net.[4] This rate is of great practical importance since it allows options for economic policy to be evaluated, for example the impact of the introduction of an indirect tax.[5] But Quesnay never did make a calculation of labor productivity; in his view only nature was productive, and he consequently thought that the key element in economic development was capital, not labor.

Du Pont did use a notion of labor productivity in his study of road construction and maintenance published in 1767 in the *Éphémérides du citoyen*. His treatment is indirectly relevant to our discussion of slavery, in that he sought to demonstrate the economic irrationality of the *corvée*, the regime of forced labor still prevailing in France. Du Pont opposed this practice as a violation of a person's right of self-determination, suggesting that the work could be done by soldiers or, failing that, by wage laborers. He proposed a ratio between free and *corvée* labor that went far beyond the 1:2 relationship that he would employ a few years later when discussing slavery:

> Time is lost, men and animals wear themselves out, and carriages suffer a thousand accidents from the impassable roads before reaching the place of work. One needs to leave home early to be able to get back there again. And during the brief interval remaining, work is carried on with the lassitude and lack of

> enthusiasm inevitable among men who expect no payment. A man paid for his work can do in an hour what otherwise takes two days, working hard for fear that someone will steal the bread from his mouth; and a soldier working with his comrades under the eyes of his superior, eager to mark himself off, would do the same in half an hour.[6]

These assertions are quite obviously excessive, and that do not meet the standard of calculatory rigor of which he so often proud! He did, however, estimate the proportion between the work done and the cost of the corvée as being 1:2: "It is a tax that in reality costs those who perform the work, in terms of money, in days for men and animals, in damage to carriages, etc. at least double the value of the resulting work."[7]

All abolitionist writers who put numbers on the superiority of free over slave labor based their positions—explicitly when they made a calculation, or implicitly when they invoked figures supposedly known to everyone—on placing two things in relation to each other. First, the relation between a given output and the number of slaves employed to obtain it; second, between this same output (or an output thought to be similar) and the number of free laborers required to produce it after abolition. In relating a *product* (measured, of course, in a different way to that of modern economists) to a *factor of production* (*labor* measured by the number of workers employed), it can be said that, even if they did not use the terminology, they made a calculation of labor productivity.

In 1788 André-Daniel Laffon de Ladebat claimed to compare the "product of the annual labor" of the slave with that of the free worker.[8] He stated that all his calculations were made in terms of the "absolute" product of labor (the gross product), and not in terms of the net product "that many other causes [other than the productive effort of the worker] can increase or decrease." According to the figures put forward by Arthur Young, it was impossible to value the annual product of a slave in the prime of life at any more than 1,200 livres, while that of a good English farmer was 2,400 livres; so this ends up as a ratio of 1:2. But it does not end there. Seeking to shore up his remarks with data that were more detailed, Ladebat made a complex calculation relating to the output from slaves in several colonies of the Antilles (Saint Domingo, Jamaica, Guadeloupe, and Martinique; see Table 6.1).

He added to the output of the export crop the value of food grown by black slaves (60 million *livres*), arriving at a total product of 240 million *livres*. Using these data, he estimates an annual product per slave of about 353 *livres*, placing this in relation to the average product of an individual working on the land in France (3,164 million livres/ 6 million people = 527

Table 6.1 WORKERS AND OUTPUT IN THE CARIBBEAN ACCORDING TO LADEBAT

	Number of Black Workers	Output (in m. *livres*)
Santo Domingo	300,000	100
Jamaica	200,000	35
Guadeloupe	100,000	18
Martinique	80,000	18
Total	680,000	171

livres). He then points out that the difference between these two magnitudes (240 and 527 *livres*) must then be re-evaluated according to the difference in soil fertility (800 annual *livres* per arpent of land in the colonies against 108 *livres* in Britain); hence in a land as fertile as that of the Antilles[9] a European worker would produce about 3,851 *livres*. However, this could be reduced by a third "because of the advantage that the European cultivator has in using machinery that the slave cultivator does not have." If the land were of equal fertility the result is that the output would be 1,283 *livres* per European worker versus 353 *livres* per slave, a ratio of 3.6 to 1. Taking into account variables other than that of the worker's activity does not, however, guarantee the rigor of the calculation, which as its author admits is based in no small part on very rough estimates, or even assertions that are entirely unsupported.

To reinforce his argument Ladebat finally outlines, although in a very confusing way, the results of the comparison he has made between the work in vineyards in metropolitan France and that done on sugar plantations in the Antilles. The output of the free laborer and that of the slave are then, respectively, 4,000 and 1,200 *livres* a year, a ratio of 3.3 to 1: he concludes that "This is how it can be proved that the slave does not produce even a third of the output of a free man."[10] Although his text had a degree of exposure—it was presented at a general meeting of the Société des amis des noirs on December 2, 1788, an organization of which he was a member[11]—Ladebat's calculations do not seem to have convinced abolitionist thinkers.

Very shortly after the printing of Ladebat's pamphlet, Frossard in 1789 published another text in which he claimed that the "proportion" between slave and free labor was about one to two, this figure being supported by the fact that the right of representation in the United States was based on the observation that the ratio of the free man's labor to that of the slave was 4 to 7.[12] However, he thought it necessary to support this statement with some quantitative data. He first referred to the very detailed observations made by the Rev. James Ramsey published in 1784.[13] According to Ramsey, who had lived for twenty years in St. Kitts, thirty slaves took one day to hoe 40.5 *ares* (100 square metres) with holes 150 cm long by 120 wide and 20 to 30 cm deep, leaving between the strips space for the earth removed equal to half that of the holes. One slave therefore worked on average an area of about 150 cm by 90, something that a free laborer of ordinary strength could do in half a day. In St. Kitts, Ramsey continued, 16,000 slaves cultivated 44,551 ares, or 1 slave for 27.6 ares, a proportion that would fall if the work were to be carried out by free men.[14] The precision of these examples is only superficial; while the calculation of the output of the slave is made using precise numerical data—the extreme detail in describing the task carried out is clearly intended to suggest that these are exact observations—the statement that it could be done by a much smaller number of free laborers is pure speculation.

Frossard wanted to demonstrate that the destruction of slavery would bring about neither the abandonment of the colonies nor the ruin of the colonists; and a little further on he presented a new illustration of his proposal. While a slave might tend 1,000 coffee bushes a year, which would bring in about 667 *livres*, a free worker would easily tend 1,500, with an annual product of 1,000 *livres*. The wage of the latter would, according to his estimate, be 390 *livres*, and so taking account of interest on land, tools, and so forth, the profit for the planter would again be significant. We might note that here the difference in productivity between free and servile labor is here put not at 1 to 2 but at 1 to 1.5.[15]

While the idea that slave labor had low productivity was a common assumption in abolitionist writings published during the period of the French Revolution and the early nineteenth century, these authors did not seem especially convinced by the calculations of Ladebat and Frossard, and did not usually present this idea numerically.[16] This would not be the case for writers after the Restoration period.

THE PRODUCTIVITY GAP BETWEEN SLAVE LABOR AND FREE LABOR: A KEY ELEMENT IN THE ABOLITIONIST DISCOURSE OF THE NINETEENTH CENTURY

In 1827 Comte reported that a traveler observing slaves in Martinique estimated that, for the same price, they did one-tenth of the work of French workers.[17] Dufau in 1830 maintained that, even if one assumed that following emancipation various factors would double the cost of labor, planters would still benefit. Free and intelligent workers would work better and more quickly than slaves—a fact that had been demonstrated and which was generally recognized—so that the work of ten day laborers would, during an equal period of work, be *double* that done by ten slaves.[18] In a book published in 1833 Schœlcher maintained that "it is known that the work of a free man, black or white, is equal to that of five slaves"—and so putting the productivity gap between free and slave labor at 5 to 1.[19] In 1835 François Mongin de Montrol claimed that the superiority of the work of a free man over that of a slave was "a truth that some who are either blind or prejudiced by interest deny in vain,"[20] the evidence for this being provided by economic science. Adam Smith, Thomas Clarkson, William Wilberforce, Edmund Burke, and Benjamin Franklin; Henry Koster in his *Travels in Brazil* (1816); William Marsden in his *History of Sumatra* (1784); Lord Brougham in his *Colonial Policy* (1803); all of these had put this question beyond doubt. In France Alexandre Moreau de Jonnès,[21] Pierre-Armand Dufau, and many economists were in agreement about the many proofs that could be adduced—Say, "who was at first of the old and false opinion that negroes were the only ones capable of working the scorching soil of the Antilles, had announced his error after being convinced by the facts contained in a letter from Mr. Hodgson."[22] Fortified by his illustrious predecessors, Montrol stated that it had been calculated that forty thousand ordinary cultivators produced more than the three hundred thousand slaves in French colonies (and so a ratio of 7.5 to 1).

The productivity gap between free and slave labor identified by these authors seems fanciful; it depends on a simple assertion, or a pseudo-consensus for which there is no serious support. However, the experience of abolition in the British colonies provided an opportunity to test the liberal principle that free labor is always superior to slave labor.

Taking advantage of this opportunity was a different matter, however. In 1837 the *Revue Britannique* published a "quick overview" of the "excellent pamphlet" by Hodgson, *A Letter to M. Jean-Baptiste Say on the Comparative Expense of Free and Slave Labor* (1823) reminding French readers that, contrary to Say's assertions, many economists and observers of slave societies[23] had maintained that free labor was less expensive than slave labor, and this was owed especially to the greater productivity of the former, as the article repeatedly emphasized. The author recapitulated Hodgson's position by alluding to recent events in the British colonies.

In 1836 the abolitionist Zachary Macaulay published *Détails sur l'émancipation des esclaves pendant les années 1834 et 1835* (Details on the Emancipation of Slaves in the Years 1834 and 1835) in which he cited evidence that the principle of the superior productivity of free labor had proved itself during the period of apprenticeship.[24] Among the materials included was a memorandum dated April 13, 1835, by Sir J. Carmichael Smyth, the governor of British Guyana, in which the governor made an interesting calculation. Taking account of the quantity of sugar produced on average during the last three quarters of 1831, 1832, and 1833, which was 16,716 hogsheads, the quantity produced by the apprentices in the last quarter of 1834 (the first three months of the apprenticeship system) was 16,930 hogsheads. Since the apprentices only worked 7.5 hours a day, one-sixth less than they had done as slaves, the planters could reasonably anticipate that production would be only five-sixths of that realized during slavery (which would be 13,930 hogsheads). And so they had actually gained 2,657 hogsheads more than the quantity they "had a right to calculate on." He then compared the output during the first quarter of 1835 (11,986 hogsheads of sugar) with the average output of the first quarters of 1832, 1833, and 1834 (12,088 hogsheads of sugar). Given the reduction in working hours, plantation owners could only reasonably expect an output of 10,074 hogsheads, but instead the output had been 1,912 hogsheads greater than the quantity the planter had "a right to expect." It therefore appeared that altogether 4,569 more hogsheads of sugar than had been anticipated had been shipped along the Demerara River, despite the reduction of one-sixth in working time.[25] Rather than drawing attention to the fall in production, the governor's calculation emphasized the fact that labor productivity had increased.

Macaulay also included for his French readers several messages addressed to the Marquess of Sligo, Governor of Jamaica, from special magistrates who confirmed with enthusiasm the increases in productivity evident in the British colonies since the initiation of the apprenticeship system. For example, in a letter dated July 1, 1835, the special magistrate Edmund B. Lyon expressed his satisfaction with the "contentment and industry" that he saw in his district:

> I hesitate not to say that the quantity of labour performed of the apprentices, on particular estates around me quite equals the average of slave-labour, and that the labour of the apprentices, on particular estates, is in all kind of work much greater than ever performed or expected to be by them. As a proof of the correctness of my assertion, I have only to refer to the Blue Mountain apprentices, who, in the absence of the overseer from the property, turned trash and moulded canes at the rate of five people to the acre, where eight to nine would have formerly been considered good work, and on another piece, extremely foul, performed the same kind of work at six the acre.[26]

The magistrate multiplied the examples of estates where apprentices showed a level of labor productivity very superior to that which had existed during the period of slavery. On July 14, 1835, an other special magistrate Alex N. Macleod wrote that

> The amount of produce furnishes, in my humble apprehension, sufficient proof to satisfy any candid man that the negroes here, since the commencement of the apprenticeship, have done more work than they were ever in the habit of accomplishing in the same given time before the 1st of August; I say this advisedly, and with a pretty full knowledge of the various points to be considered in the estimate of slave and apprentice labor.[27]

French abolitionists did not take up these writings to support their arguments, perhaps because the coercive nature of the apprenticeship system quickly came under criticism from British abolitionists, and so was not thought to supply a model of free labor. The British documents and evidence from French observers published by the Ministry of the Navy and the Colonies between 1840 and 1843 in the five volumes of the *Précis de l'abolition de l'esclavage dans les colonies anglaises* left the matter open. The administrators of some British colonies were optimistic during the period of apprenticeship—the Marquess of Sligo, the Governor of Jamaica, maintained that the hourly product of labor had doubled in sugar production;[28] the Governor of Guyana claimed that production had increased while the hours worked had fallen by one-sixth[29]—but the economic outcome of abolition was a burden for planters by the early 1840s, when emancipation became fully effective. The Report of the Committee of the House of Commons appointed to inquire into the State of the West Indian Colonies (July 25, 1842), while registering the physical and moral improvement of the black population, complained of the fact that the output of large-scale cultivation had declined to the point where estate owners were suffering considerably, some of them being completely ruined. If the harm was less obvious in the smaller islands where the shortage of land compelled emancipated slaves to offer their labor for low wages, it was very marked in the larger colonies where old slaves abandoned work on the estates for other, more lucrative, employment. Permitted to grow food on land for which they either did not have to pay, or which they could rent, often able to buy land at a low price, emancipated slaves refused to work on a continuous basis, and demanded very high wages for so doing.[30] During hearings the colonists constantly complained of the collapse in work and in output, arguing that planters were headed into ruin and the former slaves were reverting to barbarism. The overviews written by French observers were no more positive. In a report on the situation in Jamaica dated July 1, 1840, Marie Jean-François Layrle, the captain of a corvette, wrote that:

> We can no longer deceive ourselves about the consequence of free labour in as Brougham, Wilberforce, O'Connell, Seaford, Sligo and others did when they forecast to the British Parliament that the work of a free black worker would be equal to that of three slaves. Since then the facts have spoken; they have overturned all the theories of the abolitionists, and destroyed all the arguments in favour of production and wealth.[31]

He explained his position in his study of British Guyana:

> In Europe, where daily needs are pressing, do workers do as much work as they can, as they should do, in the interests of their own welfare and that of their family? No. How then can one hope that under a sky which is always propitious, on land that freely produces the necessities of life, that labour will remain at the level it was when coercion was the rule? In no part of the world does voluntary work produce as much as forced labour. The blacks of Guyana have not proved this principle wrong.[32]

Layrle, echoing Say, attributed the lower productivity of freed slaves to the propensity of the free worker to idleness, whatever the race. Since this view had the advantage of not resting upon racist arguments it confirmed the government in its policy of wait-and-see.[33]

But this was not the stance of many French abolitionists. Without reference to the British example, Moreau de Jonnès, a noted statistician, published some calculations in 1842 that were aimed at proving, once more, that the productivity of free labor was higher than that of slave labor.[34] To begin with, he based his demonstration on data relating to the cultivation of sugar cane, which he considered the sole serious object of toil in the colonies. The work of each slave cultivated no more than half a hectare, "an amount so limited that one will not find any comparable task in the agricultural of any other country in the world" (see Table 6.2).[35]

Following these figures he gave those for other colonial plantations producing coffee, cotton, cocoa, and vegetables. He stated that

> . . . it is essential to remark that if the task for a slave rises to nearly one hectare when working on crops other than sugar cane, this is mainly because a large part of this cultivation is made up of the negroes' own allotments, so that the products belong to the slaves. Hence work that is stimulated by the interest of property is nearly double that performed for the master, of which the quantity, estimated on average and taking proper account of everything, most certainly does not exceed half a hectare.[36]

Table 6.2 WORKERS AND CANE PRODUCTION ACCORDING TO MOREAU DE JONNÈS

	Hectares Devoted to Sugar Cane	Number of Slaves on Plantations	Cultivated Area per Slave (in *Ares*)
Martinique	21,179	35,735	60
Guadeloupe	24,810	44,615	60
Guyana	1,571	4,932	32
Bourbon	14,530	24,066	61
All together	62,090	109,348	57

Table 6.3 WORKERS AND CULTIVATED AREA FOR PRODUCTS OTHER THAN CANE ACCORDING TO MOREAU DE JONNÈS

	Hectares Cultivated	Number of Slaves Attached	Cultivated Area per Slave (in *ares*)
Martinique	17,141	22,059	78
Guadeloupe	19,935	39,966	50[45]
Guyana	10,255	9,281	110
Bourbon	51,172	33,280	154
All together	98,503	104,586	94

There is an important caveat here, since the way in which slave and free labor are compared involves some rather heroic assumptions.[37] Crops other than cane sugar were in large measure produced by slaves on their allotments or gardens,[38] and so the second table (see Table 6.3) reflects the production of slaves who *worked for themselves*; whereas the first table, relating to the sugar plantations, provides information on *work done for the master*, who derived all the benefit from this work. By "working for oneself" we mean here all work organized by an individual or a family group for themselves; the product of this work is either consumed by those who have produced it, or exchanged in the market with the aim of acquiring other goods. In the majority of cases—since at least on Guadeloupe and Martinique the master provided either no food, or very little—the slave met his needs by *working for himself*, working on his plot or plots of land in his "free time," which meant on Sunday, or also on Saturday as well if the master had made this concession for the purpose.[39] Insofar as the product of this labor was his in its entirety (being able to consume it as his subsistence and exchange any surplus in the market), the *self-interest* of the slave was a powerful incentive to make the best of the garden or allotment. The productivity gap between the two forms of cultivation, amounting to almost 1:2, does show that the black slave was capable, when his own interests were at stake, of shedding the idleness that was characteristic of slavery.

Moreau de Jonnès also made an attempt to estimate the total productivity of labor in the colonies. Taking the total cultivated area as 160,598 hectares (62,090 devoted to cane sugar, 98,508 to other crops); with the number of rural slaves being 213,934 (109,348 attached to the sugar plantations, 104,586 to other forms of cultivation), and the number of urban slaves 46,352, this gave a total number of slaves as 260,286. From this he derived a cultivated area of 75 *ares* per rural slave, and only 65 *ares* for all slaves taken together.[40]

This finding was compared with the situation in Great Britain, where an agricultural population of 4.3 million persons cultivated 7.2 million hectares, hence 167 *ares* per head and so around *three times as much as that of a slave in the colonies*. If this latter result were transferred to France, he went on, then the 20.7 million hectares that were under cultivation there would require a population of 41.5 million to work all the land.

Objections can of course be raised against the way in which Moreau de Jonnès drew up his calculations: differences between various islands are not clarified; variations in the amount of work needed for different crops are not examined; the urban slave population is simply added to the rural slave population, whereas in Great Britain only the agricultural population is taken into account. All the same, his calculations are more rigorous than those of all his predecessors on the issue, and this shows his interest in comparing the productive effort of slave workers with those of free European workers, resulting in a demonstration—and here he was quite original—that an important productivity gap existed between slave labor *performed for the master*, and *working for oneself*, where the slave reaped the direct benefits of his work.

Arguing in favor of applying Lechevalier's project to Guyana, Cochut laid emphasis on the impact of investment on labor productivity, suggesting that a company with a large amount of capital at its disposal could reap large rewards in a backward country, whether investing in agriculture or manufacture: "It is recognised that *forty negroes* scratching the land with hoes do less work than *one single man* with a plough and three horses."[41]

Cochut favored European immigration to Guyana, although he did view this as secondary to the success of the project, and gave two examples to illustrate his proposal. Fifteen soldiers of the Guyana battalion who had quarried the stone necessary for the construction of a courthouse did more work than would have been done in the same time by sixty good black slaves; during other quarrying works where French soldiers and blacks from Gambia were employed together, the former did twice the amount of work of the latter. The productivity differential seems to have been attributed more to race than to the status of the workers. The relationship between the work of slaves and soldiers, for a task of the same type, is quite different (1 to 4 in the first case, 1 to 2 in the second).

In 1847 Gustave Du Puynode first noted the conclusions of Moreau de Jonnès,[42] and then went on to summarize a report from Henry George Ward, a British envoy to Mexico.[43] One hundred fifty free workers employed on an estate near Vera Cruz each produced three tons of sugar, while in Martinique, where the land was infinitely more fertile, a slave produced at most two tons. He concluded that "In general, *a free man accomplishes in one day what a slave can only do in three*,"[44] this being a somewhat rushed conclusion since the ratio between free and slave labor is here 1 to 1.5. This ratio, he added, had already been established by Dr. James Anderson in his *Observations on Slavery* published in 1788, where he compared the work of indentured laborers employed in Scottish coal mines to that of free miners paid by the day. But although Moreau de Jonnès's careful calculations were not forgotten, they never became authoritative.

* * *

If the numerical estimates made in the eighteenth and nineteenth centuries differed in the assessment of the scale of the productivity gap between free and slave labor, they did all come to the same conclusion: the productivity of the slave was lower than that of the free worker.

Modern economists calculate labor productivity per hand by dividing gross output by the number of workers contributing to that output. The writers about whom we have been writing had no such indicator. Some simply asserted that there was "proof" of a difference between slave and free labor. Others supported their statements by using microeconomic data where generalization was, at the very least, troublesome: this is what Frossard did in referring to the example given by Ramsay, what Cochut did when he repeated the views of Guyanese administrators, or Du Puynode when he summarized Ward's observations. Some did, however, try to argue in terms of macro-economic factors, such as when Ladebat took into account the "absolute product" of labor, while Moreau de Jonnès argued in terms of the cultivated area.

Efforts on the part of abolitionists to calculate the gap in productivity between free and slave labor were balked by their inability to assess the number of free workers who could do the work currently performed by slaves. Ladebat and Moreau de Jonnès sought to resolve the problem by comparing the productivity of slaves with that of European rural workers. The abolition of slavery in the British West Indian colonies did not ease the problem; neither Moreau de Jonnés, nor Cochut, nor Du Puynode tried to compare the productivity of emancipated slaves with that of slaves in those colonies. The data available were difficult to interpret in terms of labor productivity given the diversity of economic circumstances (a greater or lesser amount of land in cultivation) and the manner in which emancipation was effected (the transition to apprenticeship being a special factor in the British colonies). Both of these factors had major consequences for the availability of labor and the amount produced on the plantations.

Du Pont had himself introduced the issue of labor productivity to the controversy between abolitionists and colonists; but the introduction of this element marked the transition from a *static* approach—asking what, here and now, slave labor cost as opposed to what free labor would cost—to a more *dynamic* one, estimating what the worker would produce if he were free. The special place occupied here by productivity introduced a *temporal dislocation*: it engaged with the future, and opened up the possibility of action. It was in this space of temporal dislocation that the reforming activity of abolitionists and economists occurred, both convinced of the inefficiency of slavery in the colonies and of the benefits to be realized from the employment of free labor. This activity was based on the certainty that free workers (both Europeans and freed blacks) would increase output simply because of their zest for work, for the same number of workers.

There was one major question here: what would the work incentive be for newly freed workers who had yesterday been supervised in the fields by drivers wielding whips, or for poor white workers introduced to replace them? To lend force to the link that was established between the growth of labor productivity and the abolition of slavery, reformers invoked self-interest, which then became the axis around which morality and calculation turned.

NOTES

1. Marie-France Piguet, *Classe, histoire du mot et genèse du concept des Physiocrates aux historiens de la Restauration*, Presses universitaires de Lyon, Lyon 1996.

2. The term can be found in the subtitle and in the advertisement that precedes the dialogue. It does not, however, appear in the second edition of the text published by Du Pont in the collection of texts by Quesnay published under the title *Physiocratie* in 1767–1768 (*Œuvres économiques complètes*, t. 2, pp. 883 and 903).
3. Anon, "Concepts et terminologie de la productivité (note communiquée par le Centre d'Etudes et de Mesures de la Productivité)," *Revue de statistique appliquée*, t. 2, no. 1, 1954, p. 89. There are many meanings of this term and the problem of interpreting them is examined in François Schaller, *Essai critique sur la notion de productivité*, Droz, Geneva 1966.
4. "According to this hypothesis, the annual advances reproduce 250 per cent. The income of proprietors can therefore be equal to the annual advances." François Quesnay, "Analyse de la formule arithmétique du Tableau économique" (1767) in *Œuvres économiques complètes*, t. 1, p. 548.
5. In this way Quesnay lists "the different relationships between advances and revenue": "If therefore total reproduction is 5 billion, produced by 2 billion of annual advances, there will remain . . . 2 billion for revenue. This revenue is therefore rated at 100% of the advances. If total reproduction is only 4 billion . . . the revenue will only be one billion. This will be at the rate of 50% of the advances. If it were 6 billions, the revenue would find itself equal to 3 billion . . . , rated at 150% of advances." François Quesnay, "Second problème économique" (1767) in *Œuvres économiques complètes*, t. 1, pp. 621–622.
6. Du Pont, "De l'administration des Chemins," p. 158.
7. Ibid., p. 157.
8. André Daniel Laffon de Ladebat, *Discours sur la nécessité et les moyens de détruire l'esclavage dans les colonies*, Imprimerie Michel Racle, Bordeaux 1788, p. 18.
9. We should note here that Du Pont maintained that the fertility of the soil in colonial cane plantations was more or less exhausted, a view endorsed by many observers; Ladebat, and also Ganilh, by contrast, maintained that the soil was more fertile than that in Europe.
10. Ladebat, *Discours*, pp. 18–19, and especially note 13, pp. 36–38.
11. Marcel Dorigny and Bernard Gainot (eds.), *La Société des amis des noirs*, Éditions de l'UNESCO/EDICEF, Paris 1998, pp. 186–187. Ladebat's text would also have been well received coming as it did from a Bourdeaux merchant and shipowner whose family, of Protestant faith, was involved in the slave trade. A letter of thanks addressed to the author asked for copies of his book so that they could be sent to societies in London and the United States.
12. According to the first article of the 1786 Constitution of the United States, the number of representatives of a state in the House of Representatives was based on the population of that state. Included in this figure were all "free persons" and three-fifths of slaves (non-citizens), with Native Americans paying no tax and therefore being entirely excluded. The ratio of 7 to 4 that Frossard used is roughly equal to that of 5 to 3 included in the American Constitution (around 1.7). Frossard probably took this estimate from Condorcet who in 1788 added to the second edition of his text a note concerning this. See Schwartz [Condorcet], *Réflexions sur l'ésclavage des Nègres*, 2nd edition [1788], Harmattan, Paris 2003, p. 19.
13. In note 1, p. 180, he included an almost literal translation of two paragraphs from Ramsay's text, *An Essay on the Treatment and Conversion of African Slaves in the British Sugar Colonies*, London 1784, pp. 119–120.
14. Ramsay employs acres, feet, and inches, which have here been converted to a metric scale.

15. Benjamin-Sigismond Frossard, *La Cause des esclaves Nègres et des habitans de la Guinée, portée au tribunal de la justice, de la religion, de la politique ou Histoire de la traite et de l'esclavage des nègres, preuves de leur illégitimité, moyens de les abolir sans nuire ni aux colonies, ni aux colons*, Lyon 1789, p. 189.
16. The ratio of 1 to 2 can, however, be found in a text published by Antoine-Jean-Thomas Bonnemain in 1792; he maintained, without any substantiation, that "two free servants did more work than four slave servants"—a servant being anyone providing services for another. Antoine-Jean-Thomas Bonnemain, *Régénération des colonies ou moyens de restituer graduellement aux hommes leur état politique et d'assurer la prospérité des Nations; et Moyens pour rétablir promptement l'ordre dans les colonies françaises*, impr. du Cercle Social, Paris 1792, p. 52.
17. Charles Comte, *Traité de législation ou exposition des lois générales suivant lesquelles les peuples prospèrent, dépérissent ou restent stationnaires*, vol. 4, A. Sautelet et Cie, Paris 1827, p. 257.
18. Pierre-Armand Dufau, *De l'abolition graduelle de l'esclavage dans les colonies européennes et notamment dans les colonies françaises, considérée à la fois dans l'intérêt des esclaves, des maîtres, des colonies et de la métropole*, Bureau central de la *Revue encyclopédique*, Paris 1830, p. 109.
19. Victor Schœlcher, *De l'esclavage des noirs et de la législation coloniale*, Paulin, Paris 1833, p. 85.
20. François Mongin de Montrol, *Des colonies anglaises depuis l'émancipation des esclaves et de l'influence de cette émancipation sur les colonies françaises*, Imprimerie Paul Dupont et Cie, Paris 1835, p. 3.
21. Before publishing a book on the subject in 1842, Moreau de Jonnès had written extensively on the colonies, some of this remaining unpublished. Montrol showed that Moreau de Jonnès' calculations of productivity had circulated before 1842, but he did not provide their results.
22. Montrol, *Des colonies anglaises*, p. 3.
23. He cited in particular Adam Smith, Henri-Frédérick Storch, the Russian author of a *Cours d'économie politique*, Henry Brougham, Edmund Burke, Benjamin Franklin, and Henry Koster.
24. Macaulay drew his evidence from *Papers in Explanation of the Measures Adopted by His Majesty's Government for giving effect to the Act for the Abolition of Slavery Throughout the British Colonies*, Part I, Jamaica, 1833–1835.
25. Zachary Macaulay, *Détails sur l'émancipation des esclaves pendant les années 1834 et 1835*, Hachette, Paris 1836, pp. 73–74. The document comes from *Papers in Explanation of the Measures Adopted by His Majesty's Government for giving effect to the Act for the Abolition of Slavery Throughout the British Colonies*, published April 16, 1835, pp. 174–175.
26. Macaulay, *Détails sur l'émancipation des esclaves*, p. 127; the document comes from *Papers in Explanation of the Measures Adopted*, p. 102.
27. Ibid., p. 268.
28. *Précis de l'abolition de l'esclavage dans les colonies anglaises*, Imprimerie Royale, Paris 1840, vol. 1, p. 90.
29. Ibid., vol. 1, pp. 119–120.
30. Ibid., vol. 5, pp. 155–157.
31. Ibid., vol. 4, p. 71.
32. Ibid., vol. 5, p. 21.
33. The reports of Layrle were very much appreciated by the Ministry of the Navy and of the Colonies, which secured their wide diffusion in various

publications: See on this Lawrence C. Jennings, *French Reaction to British Slave Emancipation*, Louisiana State University Press, Baton Rouge 1988, Ch. 2, pp. 42–46.

34. Alexandre Moreau de Jonnès, *Recherches statistiques sur l'esclavage coloniale et sur les moyen de le supprimer*, Paris 1842, pp. 231–232.
35. Ibid., p. 232.
36. Ibid., p. 233.
37. Coffee, cocoa, and cotton were secondary export goods cultivated by slaves for the benefit of small estates, or even for large sugarcane plantations whose owners sought to diversify away from sugar. Their cultivation accounted for at least the same extent of land that was used for the production of foodstuffs, and this came not only from slave gardens or allotments, but also from smallholdings devoted to this kind of crop belonging to whites or free colored workers.
38. The slaves of Guadeloupe and of Martinique (and to a lesser extent those of Bourbon) tended to possess gardens of three types: small gardens surrounding their huts in which they planted fruit trees, banana trees, and cotton plants, sometimes growing root crops and raising poultry and small livestock; plots of land sometimes placed in rather inaccessible places and where they mostly grew foodstuffs; and temporary gardens on plantation land that was not being used at the time for sugar cane during the rotation cycle.
39. On "working for oneself" and "working for the master" see Caroline Oudin-Bastide, *Travail, capitalisme et société esclavagiste*, La Découverte, Paris 2005, chap. 4.
40. The figure 65 *ares* is wrong; according to his own figures, the area cultivated by slaves was around 61 *ares*, the correction actually reinforcing his conclusion.
41. André Cochut, "De la colonisation de la Guyane française," *Revue des deux mondes*, t. 11 (1845), p. 545—our emphasis.
42. Gustave Du Puynode, *De l'esclavage et des colonies*, Joubert, Paris 1847, pp. 18–19.
43. Henry George Wood was an envoy to the Mexican empress from 1825 to 1827. He published *Mexico in 1827*, Henry Colburn, London 1828.
44. Du Puynode, *De l'esclavage et des colonies*, p. 19.
45. Moreau de Jonnès' text has 90 *ares* for Guadeloupe, where the true number is 50.

CHAPTER 7
Self-Interest and Needs

While maintaining a position of honor and sensitivity to the misfortune of others, abolitionist calculators considered it essential to show the economic interest—understood as "utility"—involved in the replacement of slave labor by free labor. This was continuous with the logic of the Physiocrats, for whom greed or the desire for enjoyment was the foundation of competition, the keystone of the economic order. Le Mercier de la Rivière wrote:

> As Pope said, behold the Author of Nature has grafted a wild tree that bears excellent fruits: the greed that divides the seller and the buyer in their projects is precisely that which brings them together and reconciles them in practice: this greed, this desire to enjoy, that becomes the spirit of competition.[1]

This interest is, however, combined with the desire to improve one's condition, a desire that Adam Smith thought was shared by most men: "The most common and obvious way" to achieve this goal was to increase their wealth, which also involves saving.[2]

Can the black slave for whom the only incentive to work is the whip be transformed into a free worker driven by self-interest? This question was central to the debate during the eighteenth and the early nineteenth centuries over the calculation of the respective costs of slave and free labor.

BLACK SLAVES CANNOT ENTER INTO THE LOGIC OF INTEREST

In his response to the first text published by Du Pont during 1771 in the *Éphémérides du citoyen* Petit sought to undermine the arguments put forward in favor of white immigration.[3] Was he not aware of, or did he just choose to ignore, the text published a few months later by Du Pont in which he abandoned this position, but without saying so explicitly? This we do not know. All the same, while worried about the future of the black population if such a substitution were made, he never imagined that freed slaves could work on the plantations as day laborers.

A decade later Duval de Sanadon explained why black labor could not escape servitude.[4] It was too much to expect man in general, and the black slave in particular, he wrote, to be willing to submit to wage labor in a country where, almost without effort, there is an abundance of rice, corn, millet, and bananas. Man was everywhere born idle; only need compelled him to work; whenever nature provided for his needs or satisfied them for little effort, he remained idle. Those who in Europe did not confine themselves to the work indispensable to the satisfaction of their "prime needs" belonged to a class superior to those of the sort that the colonies needed: they were the producers of luxuries—tailors, embroiderers, hairdressers, shoemakers, locksmiths, and so forth. European day laborers, meanwhile, had no more than the necessary, a condition that gave rise to the shortage of hands in French agriculture, laborers looking for more lucrative jobs in the towns and cities. If it were a question of introducing the industrious arts into the colonies, there would certainly be among the black slaves some whose taste and skill would suit them for such work. But these artisans were of no use to planters who needed carters, workers for indigo and sugar, but especially slaves who could work in the fields and plantations, a position presently occupied by black slaves but in which they would refuse to remain once free. Peopled by freed black slaves, the colonies would become uncultivated deserts; this would be unwelcome in the metropolis, and so the colonies would soon be soaked with the blood of Europeans. To overcome the laziness of the freed black slaves they would need to be paid such high wages that the planters would soon be forced to abandon their plantations, the price of labor destroying all profitability. This approach, in which the behavior of the former black slave is not related to a particular nature but is on the contrary assimilated to that of all men, is quite clever. Duval de Sanadon does not deny the ability of the freed slave to be really productive nor, implicitly, his ability to act according to his self-interest; but he expresses bluntly the view that the planters have no interest in such a development. Posing as an enlightened man, he does not venture on to the terrain of racial inequality, but stands on that of economic necessity.

At about the same time a small pamphlet titled *Principes sur l'esclavage des Noirs dans les colonies à sucre, café. etc.* (*Principles of Negroes Slavery in*

Colonies for Sugar, Coffee, etc.)[5] put forward an essentialist explanation of the black slave's idleness. God had placed strong and robust men in the high latitudes where the temperature was cold, and in the tropics had put indolent men who were enemies to work. Two factors explained the idleness of the second: on the one hand excessive perspiration which, by relaxing and drying their fibres, "blunt[s] the faculty of the soul which leads to thinking, to calculating, to making plans, to feeding oneself," and which prevents them from experiencing "that animated hope that work fosters in satisfying it even before its enjoyment"; and secondly, that abundance of nature that makes it possible to reduce cultivation to a few crops that are sown and collected with almost no effort. Since men act only because of their "real or imagined needs," it is absurd to expect inhabitants of the warm regions to do the hard work that the cultivation of tropical export products requires. "The Negro works to live, and not to enrich himself. . . . He can live well with some fish, rice or some roots that cost him but the slightest work. Nature brings it to him at rest. . . . Offer him wages, offer him all the fruits of labour; he will work to live from day to day; nothing more; and you must agree that it would be a great mistake to expect him to perform work as painful and continual as that of the cultivation of sugar, from a person who can with hardly any effort satisfy all his tastes."[6] Interest—in the sense of the desire to improve one's material condition—cannot therefore replace the stimulation of the whip.

The author of *Principes sur l'esclavage des Noirs* distinguished real from imaginary needs and related this to the theory of climate. While he never quoted Montesquieu, he had quite probably read him, like many of those who wrote on behalf of colonists' spokespersons. [7] He used two arguments developed in *L'Esprit des lois*: climate acts on the length of the fibres, limiting them in cold countries and increasing them in hot countries, making men vigorous in the first and indolent in the second; and the sterility of the land makes men industrious, sober, courageous, while the fertility of a country easily leads, through material comfort, to indolence. However, the way in which colonial thought appropriated the theory of climates differed markedly from Montesquieu's approach. He had argued in terms of non-hereditary characteristics; so that "the northern peoples, transported to the countries of the south, have not done as well as their compatriots who, engaged with their own climate, enjoyed all the fruits of their courage."[8] Hence the children of Europeans born in the Indies lose the courage that was characteristic of their fathers. Most colonists thought the indolence of black slaves to be quite irreversible, and something that could only be dealt with by force.

Until the end of slavery colonists would use the climatic and racial argument to show that the black slave, taking no care for improvement in his material well-being, could not, if free, be motivated by self-interest. The examples given to support this assertion vary according to author and period. In 1790 Saint-Cyran argued that the native Caribbeans had always refused to work for whites, refusing to exchange their leisure for new pleasures.[9] The following year Moreau de Saint-Méry noted that the black Caribbeans of Saint Vincent, who were descendants of captives from an English slave ship wrecked about 110 years previously, had a little tobacco that was cultivated by their wives, lived on cassava, went naked, and procured from occasional bartering with the whites what they needed to get drunk. He added that the blacks of the Jamaican Blue Mountains got their wives and children to do agricultural work, reducing them to the status of slaves, but satisfying their needs which were "as limited as their intelligence."[10] These examples were included in 1802 by Barré Saint-Venant, adding to them those who had revolted in Dutch Guyana, the Bahoraco from the Spanish part of Santo Domingo, and finally the colored and black population following emancipation from the French part of the same island.[11] In 1810 Richard de Tussac noted the behavior of the Haitians. They had become owners of the island, had abandoned the cultivation of sugar cane and indigo, were happy to pick coffee from the trees that they had not been able to destroy, and only grew food when compelled to do so by the government which, despite the use of force, had failed to restore export crops.[12] Taking a different viewpoint, A. de Lacharrière explained in 1831 that Haiti had escaped the ruin of its agriculture and trade only because the authors of the rural code had had the wisdom to attach the black cultivators to the glebe by introducing a compulsory work system little different from that established in Guadeloupe and Martinique.[13] Using the British data following the Abolition Act, Pelletier Duclary stated in 1839 that freedmen had fled the plantations of English islands since emancipation and that Antigua, the model colony, was threatened with depopulation. The former slaves, confronted with the alternative of working or dying of hunger, had chosen to migrate to other colonies where they lived in the forests, indulging themselves in idleness and raiding, living quite like an African tribe.[14] These allegations were renewed three years later by Maynard, who maintained that the situation of the British colonies proved the absurdity of emancipation: the climate, the soil, the nature of the black race all meant that work ended the first day that it could.[15]

The behavior of free colored workers in the French islands, already mentioned by Saint-Cyran and Barré de Saint-Venant, strikingly highlighted the native idleness of the blacks. The author of the introduction to the

Manifeste des habitans de Saint-Domingue emphasized in 1802 that they only worked when they had to: "dancing, horse-riding, surrendering to voluptuousness: there is the supreme happiness of the man of colour and his exclusive preoccupation."[16] This was a view already present in the eighteenth century, and continuously reassessed until the abolition of slavery.[17]

And, as M. Dejean de la Batie, delegate of colonists from the island of Bourbon during the final days of slavery, exclaimed: "If you can show me a people of negroes, free or emancipated, working the land voluntarily, then the cause of abolition is won."[18] The same formula was repeated for more than sixty years.

Some commentators did, however, impute a degree of calculative capacity to blacks.

Saint-Cyran maintained that the needs of a black slave were half those of a (more sober) European peasant, and that once he was freed he would be able to gain his subsistence with just two hours of work; and to induce him to work for twelve hours it would be necessary to pay him six times as much, or 48 *sols*, a level of pay that would not allow planters to hold their own against foreign competition.[19] While admitting that the black worker might be interested in an increase in wages (which itself sat badly with the idea of climatic determinism) Saint-Cyran claimed that the supply of labor would only rise if his remuneration reached a level incompatible with the maintenance of colonial cultivation.

During the early years of the French Revolution a text was published anonymously that retained its allegiance to the climatic theory, and presented a sophisticated argument of the way that freed slaves would deal with working for wages. It was argued that liberty would favor the natural idleness of blacks who were really only interested in their "prime needs"; they would benefit by working less, and this would bring about a reduction in the cultivated area. Since they were hardier than the whites, less interested in an active life and, above all, less concerned to anticipate the future than whites, surrounded by the prodigies of nature blacks "would always know how to exactly match their work and wage for the day to the needs of the day."[20] This situation can be represented by an inverse labor curve: the needs of the worker being finite, increasing the wage does not result in a rise in the supply of labor, but a fall, once the point has been passed at which income reaches a level sufficient to satisfy the needs of the worker.

In 1843 M. de Bovis, a colonist, was given the task of drawing up the advice of the Guadeloupe Colonial Council on the proposals of the Broglie Commission, and what he outlined came close to Saint-Cyran's proposal. Having stated that the African, "left to himself, will vegetate on a soil where he is hardly the most perfect animal," he concluded that, on balance, emancipation in the British islands had gone badly, the society descending into licence and the newly freed demanding usurious wages so that they might devote themselves to unrestrained consumption.[21] This is a view that departed from the more general view that former slaves had relatively small needs, a view of which abolitionists had to take account.

The anonymous author of *Principes sur l'esclavage des Noirs* made a distinction between *real* and *imaginary* needs, otherwise understood by various colonists and abolitionists as a distinction between *prime* and *artificial* needs or, more often, *factitious* needs. The first category included those necessaries of subsistence such as proper food, a minimum of clothing, and a roof for shelter from the elements—food, clothing, and accommodation were the standard headings for the budgets of the mass of the population right up to the early twentieth century.[22] The second category of needs included those items not indispensable for life, such as jewelry, home improvements, new furniture, and the like. The dividing line between the *factitious* and what was *needed* was always hard to draw: how, for example, to tell the difference between those which were a physical necessity and those arising from social pressure? Within the debate between slavers and abolitionists the distinction made between *real needs* and *factitious needs* was one arising from economic and moral relationships that actors had with the market. When colonists excoriated the petty needs of the blacks and their propensity to do little or nothing they were condemning the prospect that the latter, once emancipated, would focus their efforts upon their own plots of land, engaging in economic activity whose products played only a very marginal part in the market. Adopting a life of routine, emancipated slaves would position themselves with respect to what historian Fernand Braudel called a "material civilization," a vast platform from which emerged, during the period between the fifteenth and the eighteenth century, the market economy and capitalism: "A past that is obstinately present, voracious, swallows up through monotony the fragile time of men. And this layer of stagnant history is enormous: rural life, which means 80% to 90% of the global population, for the great majority this is their fate."[23] Beyond its temporal permanence and the mass of humans that it includes, material civilization is defined by the weakness of its relationship to the market:

> Between "material life" (in a very elementary economic sense) and economic life a discontinuous surface of contact materialises at thousands of small points: markets, shops, stalls. . . . These points of contact are as much points of rupture: on the one hand, economic life with exchange, money, nodal points and higher media, places of trade, *bourses* or fairs; on the other, "material life", the

> non-economy, characterised by obsessive self-sufficiency. The economy begins at the threshold of the *value in exchange*.[24]

The masters of the plantation economy and of the slave order ultimately feared that newly freed slaves would confine their activity to subsistence agriculture, representing the foundation of their "material civilization" as described by Braudel, placing themselves outside market relationships. They expressed no solicitude, no "interest" in the sense of a sensitivity to the prejudice that free blacks might suffer. It is not the risk that the blacks will descend into poverty that worries them, but the fact that the limitations of their needs will lead them to absent themselves from the labor market. It is this *situation of self-sufficiency*, of *non-market production* and therefore of *the non-existence of the labor market that* the settlers consider to be a return to barbarism, the risk they call upon in seeking to delay the moment of abolition. The Baron Dupin, a member of the Chamber of Peers and delegate of Martinique, published a memorandum in 1844 that summarized in one sentence the colonial point of view: "Well, if the products that are today the wealth of our colonies were abandoned, if the blacks were reduced to cultivating only food, and for them alone, they would be purely and simply what the blacks of Santo Domingo are today: they would return, by stupidity and poverty, into barbarism."[25] The influence of this economic and moral vision of the world was strong: for the most part the anti-slavers also shared it. Their approach to the future of the former black slave differed, however, from that of the settlers. Whereas these were convinced that the return of freed slaves to material civilization, to non-economy, was inevitable, the abolitionists were convinced that their self-interest, properly stimulated, would save them from barbarism and make it possible for them to be retained within the economy.

LIBERTY IS THE MOTHER OF SELF-INTEREST

Du Pont had shown in his calculations that slave labor was relatively more expensive than free, and he supported this argument by maintaining that it would be easy to move free laborers from Europe, where twenty-five million laborers barely earned 30 *livres* a year, since on the plantations they might earn 420 *livres* a year. The hope of improving their condition and enjoying a much higher level of welfare would lead the most impoverished to leave the metropole for the colonies. Some months later he modified his analysis; he hypothesized that the wages paid to freed black slaves would multiply their material comfort by a factor of 2.5 if they were paid 17 *sols* per day, and by a factor of 4 if they were paid at the higher rate of 28 *sols*. Black or white, the labor force was driven by self-interest.

The idea was not new. Montesquieu had observed in *L'Esprit des lois* that the work of those who worked in mines—an occupation that in Europe was reserved for slaves and criminals—could be done by free workers after the abolition of slavery:

> This occupation has been encouraged by the granting of small privileges; the increase of work has been linked to a greater gain; and it has been possible to make them happier in their condition than they would have been in any other.[26]

Twenty years later Pierre Poivre, a colonial administrator close to physiocratic circles, declared that liberty and property were the foundations of abundance and a flourishing agriculture; his experience in Cochin China allowed him to confirm that free agricultural workers, to whom the land of America was being given, would produce double the amount that slaves could.[27]

Ten years after the publication of Du Pont's article, Diderot proclaimed the unity of human nature:

> You have among you beings made like you who have consented to enter mountains to furnish you with metals, copper that poisons you probably; why do you seek to maintain that negroes are less credulous, less foolish than Europeans? While granting these unfortunates their liberty, take care to subordinate them to your laws and your customs, to give them your own superfluities. Give them a country, interests to harmonise, natural products to grow, consumption matching their taste; and your colonies will not want for hands which, relieved of their chains, will become more active and more robust.[28]

The same idea was expressed that year by Condorcet when he stated that men, after they have worked to provide for their subsistence, work for their comfort if they are able to secure it; and that there were no truly idle people in civilized nations besides those who were so badly governed that they had nothing to gain by working more. In 1792 Antoine-Jean-Thomas Bonnemain, an abolitionist who boasted that he had visited French, Spanish, and British colonies, added to these sentiments by demonstrating that the needs of black slaves would inevitably increase after emancipation: working on their own account, the free blacks would discover a taste for the "luxury of comfort," a powerful stimulant that would redouble their efforts.

Colonists argued that the limited nature of the needs of black slaves was the key to their lack of effort. Eighteenth-century abolitionists did admit, following Montesquieu, that a warm climate had a deleterious impact upon labor;[29] but they argued that needs were not a *given*, determined by nature, but instead a *construct* capable of changing in step with the social system. The desire for well-being was invoked as a more effective spur to labor than the whip. They substituted a sociological perspective for the essentialist approach of the colonists. This line of thought led to the ways in which artificial needs might be awakened in blacks, but also an interest in the future that would be an even more effective stimulant to an interest in labor.

These ideas were elaborated by nineteenth-century abolitionists. Comte argued in 1827 that a man motivated by the hope of reward works with much greater skill and energy than one stimulated only by the fear of punishment. While the work of the slave has no influence over the fate and the future of his children, the free man is stimulated by the desire to have a family and the need to make it flourish. Hence liberty fosters more energetic and continuous activity than punishments inflicted by masters.[30] Six years later Sismondi argued that a system allowing emancipated slaves to share in the wealth that they created, providing a right to the land and the guarantee of a stable future, was the only way in which they could be persuaded to work with enthusiasm.[31] Not only does the slave have no interest at all in doing the task he has been given well, according to Sismondi, but

> . . . he has an interest in doing it badly, he has an interest in giving the master the least that he can physically do, to tire himself as little as possible, of not doing more one day, however pressing the task, for fear of being asked to do more the following day; to avoid gaining a reputation as a good worker, for fear of raising the price of his ransom [the price of his liberty], if ever the moment came when he might be able to pay it.[32]

In 1840 Victor Schœlcher added his voice to the view that one should not worry about the consequences of abolition for the plantation economy. The emancipated slave would fall neither into lassitude nor into barbarism, he said; in continual contact with civilization, he would quickly discover needs that would make him work harder. There was, ultimately, an unfailing coincidence between labor and liberty.[33] Two years later he explained that the success of emancipation would depend on the ability of planters to encourage work in a way that neither justice nor public law could condemn:

> Negroes are men; if one should still doubt it, their vanity, their pride is sufficient to prove it; life will create for them artificial needs in the same way it does for

> us, and these needs will multiply the means for their satisfaction, as also with us. Education, the enjoyment of their rights, marriage, the development of their faculties will not delaying in endowing them. Association with civilised men will initiate artificial necessities that will support industry. . . . With their disposition to imitate the whites we would be very surprised if the negroes did delay in assuming our habits.[34]

This assertion was, moreover, confirmed by changes in consumption in the British islands, where it could already be seen that emancipated slaves owned cabriolets. To make work attractive planters should not seek to obtain labor at the lowest price, but should on the contrary set the wage at an honorable level at which workers would gain a taste for profitable exertion.[35] The growth of needs in a colonial society in which free labor prevailed was not simple speculation: the British experience was proof enough.

Some eighteenth- and nineteenth-century abolitionists also detected self-interest at work even within slavery. Working for himself enabled the slave to acquire money that was spent to satisfy not only subsistence needs, but also artificial needs such as his love of play or for jewelry, but which was often enough set aside for a nest-egg that could improve his future condition—in the best of circumstances, he could purchase his own liberty or that of his children by making such economies. In 1838 Agénor de Gasparin, future member of the parliament, wrote that, thanks to these small savings, the slave had made a major step toward the intelligent life of a responsible adult, working on his own account and providing for his own needs.[36] The calculations of productivity published in 1842 by Moreau de Jonnès led to a similar conclusion: stimulated by an interest in owning the fruits of his own activity, the slave showed himself to be twice as productive when working for himself as when working for the profit of the master.[37] From the eighteenth century the extension of working for oneself seemed to be a means of preparing the black slave for liberty; in 1789 the abbé Sibire suggested that colonists should allow their slaves two or three days a week.[38] Jean-Baptiste Rouvellat de Cussac, a magistrate, thought the concession of free Saturdays ungenerous, and in 1845 proposed that legislation be drawn up providing for a second free day in the week, a measure by which the colonist would not incur any loss: better dressed, better housed, better fed, the slave would be less susceptible to sickness, stronger and more vigorous, working more on the remaining days.[39] None thought that the development of self-interest while working for a master an impossibility; piecework would show this. Frossard declared himself in favor of this new distribution of agrarian tasks which would work in favor of both master and slave, the latter having a direct interest in redoubling his efforts.[40] Comte argued that a master could get the most work from a slave by leaving him to organize his own time, but requiring a certain amount for each of his working days. The slave would be stimulated by the hope of making economies, and would first of all work to pay of the master's "tax" that had been imposed upon him to subsidise his maintenance, and then eventually purchase his freedom, as had been done in many cases.[41] This is an idea that can also be found in the Broglie report:

> Work by task or the piece is the work of a free man; he completes it on his own; every worker begins work more or less when it suits him, and how it suits him; the result of his work is the sole object of examination, at the point when it is done; the worker who completes two tasks, three tasks, in his day is paid twice or three times as much as he who does only one. That is the real stimulus to activity; that is the true germ of independence.[42]

The idea that the free worker is stimulated by a desire to increase his gain, and through that his welfare, was in fact only seriously contested by one abolitionist writer: Jean-Baptiste Say who, as discussed previously, attributed to slaves a higher level of productivity than free workers. In 1803 he wrote that

> The free man often has few needs in the present and little regard for the future, and he does not think it necessary to work beyond that which he can foresee and these needs. The slave works for an unlimited need, which is the greed of his master; and his master's indolence, his love of pleasure, only aggravates his needs.[43]

All the productive output from the slave colonies results from the labor that the master can extract from his slaves by the use of a whip, labor which is necessary to satisfy his own, unbounded, needs. With emancipation the former slave will simply revert to the innate indolence of the free worker. This was a perspective that shocked his friends among the abolitionists, a reaction that led him to revise, with some qualifications, his original position.

According to the dominant abolitionist discourse, the growth of needs on the part of workers who had become free would in essence have two beneficial results: production would be increased, and the former slaves would be integrated in a civilizing process.

The first point was often emphasized by those opposed to slavery. Condorcet was sure that the emancipation of slaves would allow the gross output to increase and so benefit the country, rather than increase the net product gained by planters; the colonies would flourish and trade would increase.[44] Antoine-Jean-Thomas Bonnemain wrote in 1792 that from the augmentation of the labor supply rivalry would necessarily develop between cultivators, workers, and servants, a rivalry that would be to the profit of rich proprietors and merchants who would be able to conduct their affairs with greater facility and less expenditure. The growth of the population, of ease, and of luxury would create new needs and, as a consequence, an increase in trade between the metropole and the colonies, the development of European factories, the prosperity of nations. If this line of argument is not without ambiguity—the growth of the supply of labor would tend to reduce wages, and this would in turn restrict expenditure on "luxuries" by the laboring classes—this writer did not hesitate to argue that the interests of all were conjoined: the interests of humanity, of governments, of colonists, or merchants, and all would come together to express their wish that slaves be emancipated.[45] Comte, for his part, heavily criticized the evil consequences of the limited nature of slave consumption for the industry and commerce of France; limited to the sale of clothing, the export of consumption goods from the metropole to the colonies brought little reward, while farmers and free workers, who had much more extensive needs than those of slaves, would acquire a much greater portion of manufactured products.[46] Ten years later Sismondi himself emphasized the pernicious impact of slavery on consumption: while slaves, for lack of income, consumed nothing, indebted owners were in financial difficulties. The legislator had to act to secure sufficient affluence for emancipated slaves and plantation owners so that their consumption fostered a prosperity favorable to the industrial class, whether through a rise in local exports flowing to the metropole or (and this was a novel perspective) through the formation in the colonies of a class of men capable to provide for needs that agriculture did not satisfy.[47] Tocqueville followed Schœlcher in maintaining that the British experience reinforced the abolitionist position: the value of exports from Britain to its colonies went from £75 million before emancipation to £100 million in 1840, increasing by almost a third in ten years. Such figures, he concluded, are unanswerable.[48]

The development of artificial needs was not solely conceived as an economic issue. It also furthered axiological investigation.[49]

Agénor de Gasparin had studied the impact of emancipation in the British colonies and concluded that work on St. Lucia would continue after the end of the apprenticeship period for an apparently frivolous reason: in this otherwise French colony slaves had retained an excessive taste for jewelry and baubles. They therefore had needs unknown to slaves in other colonies, needs whose satisfaction called for greater effort than that which would be necessary for their subsistence only.[50] This led him to a formulation of whose importance he was certain:

> I would be able to involve our colonists in creating among their slaves such artificial needs that are one of the strongest guarantees against their dispersion: some additions to their dress; suitable grooming materials capable of developing a taste among the black race that could not be satisfied after emancipation without continuing to work at cultivation and which would nullify any project of desertion. But there is in this appeal to vanity, in this provocation addressed to the most frivolous instincts, in this voluntary and premeditated corruption of a native simplicity of a whole people, there is something immoral in this that makes it inevitably alien to me. I do not believe that good will ever be able to emerge from the bad, and I spurn guarantees that might one day become risks.[51]

Besides the curious ambiguity of his proposal—he advances the remedy while at the same time condemning it—Gasparin poses an unexpected question: far from raising the former black slave into civilization, might not the growth of needs risk degrading him morally, debasing him?

Louis Vitalis, a slaveowner on Martinique who declared himself to be a resolute abolitionist, did not allow such scruples to worry him. The vanity of the black slave benefited the wider society, being a powerful force of attachment to labor without a need for the chain and the whip, while also expanding consumption, and so favoring the development of commerce and industry. Vitalis was quite blunt about the matter: it was of little importance whether the freed slaves worked for their subsistence or to adorn themselves with ornaments and trinkets, dress in fine clothes and so forth; as long as these needs put them at the service of the planters, the aim was met.[52]

In 1839 the colonial delegates who were members of the commission investigating Tracy's proposal for the abolition of slavery adopted a similar logic: how had it come about, asked one of them, that on the one hand one despaired of inducing black workers to work through the spur of their own needs, while on the other it was said that as slaves they were more interested in acquiring objects of luxury, and even that some of them preferred to spend their money in this way instead of negotiating with their master to purchase their freedom, something which demonstrated a very developed taste for spending money?[53]

Schœlcher dismissed the uneasiness expressed by Gasparin. He might be persuaded that some black slaves of a philosophical bent might regard with irony and pity those whites who had transformed artificial needs into necessities;[54] but he had himself no hesitation in basing the way in which emancipated slaves were set to work on their vanity. The development of artificial needs was not only an economic necessity, but also the leavening agent of civilization. The observations he made regarding free Haitian peasants were clear on this point:

> They still have not felt the need to create in themselves the needs that nurture industry, obliging them to work, and, in developing our nervous sensibility, refine our enjoyments. . . . As a philosophical stance it is naturally very nice not to have more needs, but this is not a matter for any regret since such a life would distance us from all spiritual sense and lead us into a state of bestiality.[55]

This was a view also expressed by the abbé Grégoire, who had thirty-five years earlier explained that the lack of development of the arts and civilization in Africa was due to the scant needs of its inhabitants—the need for clothing and shelter being more or less non-existent because of the warmth of the climate, and the need for food being very easily satisfied given the prodigality of nature.[56]

The expansion of artificial needs, assuring the motivation to work through self-interest, did not therefore only secure the growth of production and the prosperity of all; it also provided a route out of bestiality for black Africans by allowing them access to "arts." Far from morally corrupting them, it developed their spirituality and entered them into "civilization." We can detect behind this discourse a particular ideal: that of the free worker motivated by his own self-interest and of the consumer in the grip of what we might call the endless dynamic of needs. This was well described by Say, a republican who favored a society made up essentially of the middle classes. He was just as hostile to luxury as he was to poverty, since the two often went together, something that in his eyes was proof of their equally malign character. Instead, he hoped that "material comfort" would develop the enjoyment of "the sensible commodities of life."[57] The essential nature of this comfort was to be based on increasing needs:

> Needs multiply to the degree that they are satisfied. The man wearing a jacket wants a coat; he who has a coat wants a frock coat. The worker who has a room to live in wants another one; he who has two shirts thinks of having a dozen, so that he might change his linen more often; someone who has never had one does not think about procuring one. Having gained one thing does not mean one will refuse another.[58]

Acquiring things means spending, and this fosters the desire for a higher income so that one might be able to buy rather more extravagantly. The dynamic of need and of acquisition are mutually connected, and at the same time ensure that those on the lowest rung of the social ladder will want to work their way out of poverty, but also fosters the ambition of the artisan to acquire some of the wealth that he produces.

All the same, Say hits a snag when he comes to the way in which workers can be included in this dynamic. Symptomatically, he cites the savage, the image of material poverty that allows the process developing in Europe to be understood:

> If destitution were a motivation for working the savage would be the most hard-working of men, since he is the most destitute. But we know how indolent he is, and that all the savages put to work died of sorrow. In our Europe the most lazy workers are those who are most like savages in their habits: the amount of work done by an uncouth manual worker in a wretched district is not comparable with the amount of work done by a well-off worker in Paris or London.[59]

If poverty, or in other words the compulsion to work because of need, strikes Say as a maxim "as false in principle as it is barbarous in its consequences," and if comfort seems to him a more certain and morally preferable economic motivation, he does not know how he might show the way in which one can move from an indolence rooted in poverty and a lack of will to consume to regular work and the dynamic of needs.

WHITE WORKERS AS A STIMULUS TO WORK THROUGH SELF-INTEREST IN THE COLONIES

Initially Du Pont suggested that slaves be replaced with European workers. His reversal on this was justified by a second calculation in which he showed that in gaining their liberty slaves would experience a great increase in their welfare, although their demands for pay would be limited by the existence of a reserve army of agricultural labor made up of metropolitan indigents who were always likely to emigrate to the colonies if the wages offered were sufficiently attractive.

In 1781 Condorcet had the idea of reorganizing cultivation in the colonies under the direction of new European colonists. This involved settling white families on the estates through an arrangement similar to that practiced in the British colonies and North America: the concession of hitherto uncultivated smallholdings by the government to immigrants, the harvests then being processed by indigo manufactories or mills established by merchants; combined with permission given to Jews and Protestants to acquire estates in the colonies and to freely practice their religion. This form of recolonization would have many advantages: the colonies were the only region where Jews had the right to acquire real territorial property, this proposal would be very attractive to them, and since very many of them were poor, hard-working, naturally sober, and parsimonious, the condition that they only employ free workers would not worry them. Furthermore, it would not be difficult for rich Jews to establish settlers on land divided between families to whom they advanced the initial costs of cultivation and transport in return for a share of the harvest. In order to promote such emigration it would be prudent to limit the number of slaves freed by the new settlers to no more than one-sixth of the "permanent slaves" who they found already living on the estates. It was not, therefore, a matter of replacing black slaves with white workers. Emancipated slaves, who would be granted a plot of their own land, would hire themselves out cheaply, most of them not being capable of any work other than agricultural labor; and since not all of them could be employed, they would find themselves in the situation of simple wage laborers whose salary, thanks to competition, would not rise beyond a level sufficient to supply the bare necessities. To begin with, the two populations, whose food, habits, and customs differed, would co-exist; subsequently the black workers would adopt the way of life of the whites, the difference in color being the only remaining distinction; and eventually the mingling of the races would eliminate all differences.[60]

This proposal made only a very limited impact during the last quarter of the eighteenth century,[61] a period during which the majority of abolitionist writers sought to elaborate plans for the gradual abolition of slavery intended to enlighten former slaves as to their interest in becoming regular and enthusiastic workers.

The loss of Saint Domingo did, however, renew discussion of a suitable settlement policy for the colonies.

In 1807 Charles-César Robin, a writer who abolitionists included in their ranks,[62] put forward a project that was drastically remote from any colonial reality. He proposed that the French state should adopt a colonial emigration policy similar to that which had allowed the United States to increase its population and prosperity through emigration from Ireland and Scotland. Rather than buying for a high price restive black Africans for a regular working life, those living in the French colonies should attract from metropolitan France indentured workers who had become accustomed to work in Europe, providing the colonies with more productive workers than unskilled slaves. Treated properly, unlike "ruthlessly left naked" slaves, they would provide a market for metropolitan manufactures. The implementation of such a policy would make it possible to absorb the surplus of population that disfigured the French countryside:

> Of what use [to France] are impoverished peasants who dress only in coarse cloth for which they collected the hemp themselves, who feed only on bad bread which they also made from what they had grown, and who for want of work languish in idleness for part of the year? If their consumption were balanced against the product of their work, it will be plain that their existence produces nothing, and is possibly costly to the state. But transported to a colony, their labour would multiply annually the foodstuffs whose local value would exceed, without any exaggeration, two million francs, quite independently of the many families that they could support in comfort.[63]

This proposal, whose prime aim was the prosperity of the nation, would allow in addition very many of the rural poor to become better off. Encouraged by the "immunities" related to their hiring of these indentured workers, colonists would see the advantage in doing without black slaves, and emancipation would happen of itself and without crisis, without any violation of property. This was a plan that could save Saint Domingo: indentured workers, ready for work and acclimatized, would be able to defend the colony by exterminating the remnants of the former black slaves. If, however, one wished to negotiate with them, they could be given remote parts of the island where they would cultivate crops that they would exchange for European goods, creating a lucrative colony, but one which could never be "powerful, because it would have neither the intelligence nor the activity nor the resources" of the white population. This is a racist dream of abolition in which European labor is *substituted for* the mass of slave workers, including the associated cost of "exterminating" the latter.

If the issue of a complete substitution of black workers by white was never raised by abolitionists, the question of how a proper French emigration policy could be made to work remained open. Supporters of this idea argued that this would augment the active population, but also compensate for the possible defection of newly liberated slaves, a risk whose occurrence was, however, always denied on the grounds that self-interest would lead them to work on the plantations, but which was a recurring fear.

In 1827 Comte canvassed the sending of European workers to the slave colonies in order to boost the level of activity of the established population:

> It will necessarily happen that the established population will become active and hard-working, or they will cease to increase and the land will be peopled by individuals of a European race; for everywhere it is the most industrious section of the population that increases with the greatest rapidity.[64]

The alternative was simple: either emancipated slaves adopted the way of life of Europeans—an eagerness to work and a taste for well-being—or they were doomed to disappear. His proposal was, however, moderated by the idea that emigration could bring with it an important benefit: having no prejudice relating to color or birth, the new arrivals would form alliances with those persons in the colonies whose class corresponded to their own. Echoing Condorcet, Comte wrote that "*this fusion of races*, which creates great advantages for all, is supported by nature herself, for it can be observed that cross-breeding brings improvement."[65]

Three years later Dufau enumerated the benefits that both metropole and colonies could draw from the emigration of European workers: the absorption of the surplus from the French population; a much better life for emigrants in the colonies than in their country of origin; the mixing of races that would break down color prejudice; the extension of cultivation to previously unused land; and the advancement of technical progress in the colonies. In this way one would gain both an increase in production for the owners and an increase in welfare for the producers.[66]

At the end of the 1830s Gasparin adopted a novel perspective on the question of immigration. He excluded any idea of fusion between races that prejudice had made incompatible, as Tocqueville had shown in his *Democracy in America*. He thought that replacing blacks by whites was impractical; while he did not regret the Liberian experiment in which three or four thousand blacks had escaped the moral and physical torture that Anglo-Saxon prejudice had inflicted upon them, he thought that this had had no detectable impact upon American society. He added that the proposal from the Algiers Commission to transport black slaves from the French colonies to the African coast would require too much in the way of resources to be practical on a large scale. He also prophesied, with conviction and without regret, the peaceful substitution of black for white populations after abolition, through the process of buying and selling land.[67] While he emphasized that colonists had no interest in attracting at great cost workers who were less accustomed to the climate when they had at their disposal more than enough blacks, he did nevertheless approve of the importation of white immigrants since they would provide an example of eager and regular labor to free black workers.[68]

Schœlcher's position on this changed over time. Having stated that emancipated black slaves would hire themselves out voluntarily to planters and that the black population would increase considerably under a regime of liberty, in 1833 he suggested—when he was still in favor of the gradual abolition of slavery—both that freed slaves should be sent to form colonies in Africa, as had happened with Liberia and Sierra Leone created by the Americans and British, respectively, and that European emigration to French possessions should be encouraged. Having broken away from the prejudiced idea that whites could not withstand the climate, he saw the extinction of slavery as a means to find employment for the surplus European population that was pauperized. Suffering from poverty and the cold climate, the poorest of them, whose "strong hands were only waiting for work so that they might cease being a threat," were ready to leave. The idea of *substitution* shines through his argument, French emigration seeming to be the means of reducing pauperism in metropolitan France and, as a consequence, blocking the development of dangerous classes. Taking their "active industry" to overseas possessions, emigrants would revivify them, their knowledge re-animating both agriculture and manufacturing.[69] Following their self-interest in leaving metropolitan France for the colonies where they would discover their well-being, the poor would initiate a process as beneficial to the former as to the latter. The proposal, close to that which Du Pont had initially developed, did however pose more problems than it claimed to resolve: how would the blacks that the whites would quickly displace in agriculture find a living?[70] How would individuals who had long been deprived of employment and were simply vegetating in France bring "active industry" to the colonies?

In the introduction to his book published in 1842 Schœlcher reaffirmed the necessity of organizing French emigration to the colonies by establishing a contracting system.[71] While the surplus European population created disorder and suffering, the colonies only had a quarter of the population that it could support, only one third of cultivable soil being exploited. They could therefore gather up the children of the mother country who aspired to establish themselves there.[72] It was not a question of encouraging the immigration of celibate adventurers but of poor families, sad victims of the social anarchy prevailing in France:

> It is no longer a matter of playing double or quits on the islands' green baize, to stake an existence begun badly in Paris against a fortune quickly accumulated in America. No, it is a question of giving up the old homeland for the sake of the new, of exchanging inadequately paid work, an empty crib, an icy hearth where shivering children cry from cold wearing scraps and rags, a miserable life and as

> painful as that of a great number of European workers, even the most honest ones; it is a question of exchanging all this, not for the riches lavished on an idler by the work of negroes, but for work that brings in a fair wage, a perpetual abundance guaranteed to the hard-working man, a warm and easy life in the midst of the world's most generous nature, where healthy children grow happily under a bright sky.[73]

Through European immigration the colonies could thus be provided with a population that was already civilized, having the habit of work and a taste for well-being, and therefore perfectly fit to produce and consume. Together with the abolition of slavery, this abundant infusion of young immigrant blood into the veins of the sick body of the colonies would bring effective assistance to their regeneration.[74]

Moreau de Jonnès' project to develop a "culture of emancipation," published in 1842,[75] also gave a significant role to white labor. Prompted by the public works carried out by the military in the colonies, often on the estates themselves, he suggested soldiers might be detached from their garrisons to work in agriculture. They would provide a role model for slaves: free men doing the same work voluntarily and cheerfully, while producing in twice the time[76] four times the quantity. It was important to make their real interests clear to colonial populations, and to get them to recognize that without work there would be no future for them. Otherwise the employment of European labor in agriculture after abolition would be inevitable; the slave population had shrunk since the abolition of the slave trade, and emancipation would probably result in the removal of some former slaves from the estates, and to maintain production it would be necessary to introduce new workers.[77]

Two years later Lechevalier developed the idea of a colony populated by whites.[78] His recommendations were not intended for the colonies as a whole, but were directed to Guyana, where the population was relatively sparse. Lechevalier did admit that the labor force could be increased by purchasing slaves from Cayenne or Brazil who would already be acclimatized, and liberating them; or by employing blacks captured from ships illegally continuing to trade in slaves; or by employing free colored workers from other colonies. However, he maintained that if a real break were to be made with the old colonial routines, competition from a white European population was vital if regular and skilled work was to be organized.[79] Deploring the fact that Martinique and Guadeloupe each had at least twenty-five thousand free workers who lived in a condition of near vagabondage, he did not attribute their inactivity to an idleness inherent in blacks and those of mixed blood, recognizing that they were as capable as Europeans if they were stimulated by needs and a wage.[80] His proposal was founded upon racial solidarity:

> It is good to be a friend to black and yellow men, but above all, one has to be a friend to one's own skin, and I swear that I have a great and active interest in the lot of those who live in the *fauborgs* of Lyon, Rouen and Mulhouse, victims of the enthusiasm of hands and of machines, of declining wages and the irregular availability of work. It is the European race that suffers the most, for that is the race that has the greatest need to work; and it is this race that knows best how to work.[81]

To encourage movement it would be necessary to provide immigrants (drawing only on those who have a trade and some savings) with credit equal to three times the amount they would pay before leaving, and to distribute to workers one part of their benefits in shares of certificates in the company created for the exploitation of the colony. While Schœlcher presumed in his 1842 project that the self-interest of emancipated slaves and of immigrants would converge and promote the social and economic progress of both colony and metropole, Lechevalier treated them as in conflict, opting like Robin to choose in favor of the whites. He considered this choice to be not only fair but also rational, since they belonged to the race that best knew how to work, and which had a greater need than any other to gain work.[82]

Abolitionists did not develop a consensus on the question of white emigration to the colonies. While some thought in terms of *racial fusion* though not entirely excluding the forcible *substitution* of whites for blacks, others vigorously defended this second solution. During the final years of slavery another idea emerged: that white labor in the colonies was *exemplary*. Placing white workers at the side of blacks would make it possible for the blacks to understand their own interests, to understanding that they had to work hard so that they might increase their earnings, and so therefore their welfare. All the projects of white emigration also presupposed that the European population was already in possession of a work ethic—including, paradoxically, among those classes who lived in poverty and destitution in France. By contrast, the work ethic had to be inculcated among the slave population.

How did colonists respond to these proposals?

As we have already seen, in 1777 Petit put forward two politico-economic arguments: of costs created by the introduction of a new labor force, and of the absence of interest among Europeans in emigration, since a wage laborer could not improve his conditions by emigrating to the colonies.

These arguments were taken up again nine years later by Duval de Sanadon who rejected the climatic argument. He considered exaggerated the malign nature of the local climate, since immigrants also have the advantage of escaping the European winter that contributed greatly to their indigence. Nonetheless, he argued that there was a lack of any powerful spur, in the form of any certainty of a better life or a brighter future, capable of making Europeans decide to emigrate, and he was aware of the high cost of their transportation and subsequent wages. He concluded that the wage that would have to be paid to them, which could not be any lower that that generally prevailing for free colored workers (three *livres* a day), would be unaffordable, taking up the owner's income.[83]

However, most of those arguing for slavery objected to the idea of importing European labor on the grounds that whites would find it impossible to work in the tropics—an argument already rebutted by Du Pont. An anonymous author wrote in 1797:

> Do we not know that [the climate] is a mortal danger for some of the Europeans who look to make a fortune in foreign countries? And that others languish inside trying to breathe and are in no respect able to stand the sun and do any work that might fatigue them?[84]

What Robin contemptuously called the "climatic dogma" was justified, according to colonists, by the failed colonization of Kourou in Guyana during 1763-64 in which twelve thousand men and thirty million *livres* were lost in eighteen months.[85] This dogma would be repeated right up to the end of slavery;[86] white workers had no interest in moving to a colony where they could expect almost certain death.

* * *

To read the arguments exchanged between colonists and abolitionists *the black does not calculate*. While most of the former attributed this deficiency to his nature, the latter mostly explained it by circumstance: the violence experienced by the slave related to his personal identity, his environment, and his body; he was denied access to the faculty of calculating his interest, in the process being treated as a universal anthropological datum. Paradoxically, however, his laziness proves to the abolitionists that this capacity is not entirely absent. The low productivity of the black slave is the outcome of a fair estimation of the costs that greater eagerness for work would create (great fatigue and even, as Sismondi pointed out, an increase in the price that would have to be paid to purchase freedom), even though the profit he could make would remain zero.

What would happen once freed? Would the freed slave then recognize his self-interest? Abolitionists thought that a desire to better themselves could be implanted in the mass of newly freed slaves through the increase of their needs, a connection that European workers already understood. While arguing that the newly freed would be eager to work by virtue of their own self-interest, they often implicitly put forward what Hirschman has called the "principle of compensatory passion," according to which "the passions oppose the passions, and can serve as counterbalances."[87] They argued that the vanity of the black, especially his immoderate love of adornment, would overcome his laziness. Only subsequently, when the former slave has acquired a concern for the future, thanks in particular to family life, will that reason lead the worker to calculate, and to save,[88] and will the slave understand that renunciation of the immediate satisfaction of his passions will permit him to guarantee lasting welfare and continually extended for himself and his family. The remuneration for free labor is not only a cost, as Condorcet pointed out from 1781 onward. It stimulated production in the colonies, permitting increasing consumption for black workers, a condition of their access to civilization; but it was also a factor in the development of trade, maritime transport, and the activity of European manufactures.

The proposals for European emigration to the colonies that abolitionists made did, all the same, betray their fear that free blacks would not easily engage with this process, and sought in this respect to secure the continued existence of export crops.

The issue of how emancipated slaves were to become stimulated by *self-interest* was closely related to consideration of the *status* that they should be given. There were two questions: was it possible within the plantation system to secure highly productive work from free wage laborers without the level of this pay undermining the profitability of colonial cultivation; and was it preferable, in seeking to develop their eagerness to work, to allow the new workers to acquire the status of more or less autonomous agents?

NOTES

1. Pierre-Paul Le Mercier de La Rivière, *L'ordre naturel et essentiel des sociétés politiques* (1767), Fayard, Paris 2001, p. 365.
2. Adam Smith, *Wealth of Nations*, vol. 1, Liberty Classics, Indianapolis 1981, pp. 340–341.
3. Émilien Petit, *Traité du gouvernement des esclaves*, Knapen, Paris 1777, chap. 3.
4. David Duval de Sanadon, *Discours surs l'esclavage des Nègres, par un colon de Saint-Domingue*, Amsterdam 1786, pp. 41–43.

5. The example held in the National Archives carries an attribution to M. Tournu-Montagné (Archives nationales, Paris, AD VII 21 B), undated. It is included in a series of pieces published during the first years of the Revolution.
6. Ibid.
7. Colonists of the eighteenth century and also of the nineteenth often made use of climatic arguments, whether explicitly or implicitly. Among those who openly cite Montesquieu are two pamphlets: *Considérations politiques sur les esclaves des colonies de l'Amérique, et sur leurs gens de couleur libres*, 1791, pp. 56; and *Le vrai patriote à MM. les patriotes des Antilles françaises*, De l'imprimerie de la colonie, Pointe-à-Pitre 1792; Le Pelletier Du Clary, *Du travail libre et du travail forcé aux colonies françaises*, impr. d'Ad. Bondeau, Paris 1841, pp. 79; Carteau, *Soirées bermudiennes* (two quotes from *L'Esprit des lois* are placed in the epigraph for the book, and there are many others in the body of the text).
8. Montesquieu, *L'Esprit des lois* [1748], in *Œuvres completes*, t. II, Gallimard, Paris 1951, book XIV, chap. 2.
9. M. de Saint-Cyran, *Réfutation du projet des Amis des noirs, sur la suppression de la traite des nègres et sur l'abolition de l'esclavage dans les colonies*, Devaux 1790, p. 21.
10. Louis-Elie Moreau de Saint-Méry, *Considérations présentées aux vrais amis du repos et du bonheur de la France à l'occasion des nouveaux mouvements de quelques soi-disant amis des noirs*, Imprimerie nationale, Paris 1791, p. 56.
11. Jean Barré de Saint-Venant, *Des colonies modernes sous la zone torride et particulièrement celle de Saint-Domingue*, Brochot, Paris 1802, pp. 46–50.
12. François-Richard de Tussac, *Cri des colons contre un ouvrage de M. l'évêque et sénateur Grégoire, ayant pour titre "De la littérature des nègres,"* Paris 1810, pp. 221–226.
13. André-C. de Lacharrière, delegate of Guadeloupe, *Observations sur les Antilles françaises*, Impr. de Auguste Auffray, Paris 1831, pp. 56–58.
14. J.-B. Le Pelletier Duclary, President of the Colonial Council of Martinique, *Rapport fait au nom de la commission chargée de répondre à celui de M. de Tocqueville, relative aux esclaves des colonies*, Impr. de Thounens, 1841, pp. 50–52.
15. Alphonse Maynard, *La Martinique en 1842, intérêts coloniaux, souvenirs de voyage par M. le comte de la Cornillère* (pseudonyme), Gide libraire-éditeur, Paris 1843, pp. 220–221.
16. S.-J. Ducœurjoly, *Manuel des habitants de Saint-Domingue*, t. 1, Lenoir, Paris 1802, Introduction, p. cxxxv.
17. It was elaborated particularly in responses made by parish heads to a survey conducted in 1836 by the Guadaloupe administration seeking to establish the situation of new freedmen who had been emancipated since 1832 (ANOM Généralités Box 160, file 1320). See also the text by abbé J. Hardy, *Liberté et travail ou moyens d'abolir l'esclavage sans abolir le travail*, Dentu, Gaume, Debécourt, Adrien Leclère, Paris 1838, pp. 122–124, as well as that by the President of the Martinique Colonial Council Le Pelletier Duclary, *Du travail libre et du travail forcé*, op. cit., p. 58.
18. Article 19 of the law of April 24, 1833, empowered colonial councils to nominate, during their first session, seven delegates from the colonies (two for Martinique, Guadeloupe, and Bourbon, one for Guyana) and to set their remuneration. Their term of office was equal to that of the colonial council that had appointed them. Every French man aged 30 and above enjoying civil and political rights could make a choice. These delegates met in Paris and were required to give the government of the king information relating to the general interest of the colonies and then monitor the effect of its deliberations and the statement of the colonial councils.

19. Saint-Cyran, *Réfutation du projet des Amis des noirs*, p. 24.
20. Anon., *Un mot sur les Noirs et leurs amis*, undated memorandum, p. 11.
21. Guadeloupe Colonial Council, *Rapport de la commission constituée de MM. de Bovis, Reiset, Rochoux, à la fin de Juillet 1843, sur le rapport de la commission instituée par le ministre sur les questions relatives à l'esclavage* (Commission de Broglie), ANOM, Généralités 171.
22. As we have already seen, the hypothetical budget for the free slave was established by Cochut in 1845 using these three headings.
23. Fernand Braudel, *Civilization matérielle, économie et capitalisme* XVe-XVIIIe *siècle*, vol. 1, Armand Colin, Paris 1979, *Les structures du quotidien*, p. 12.
24. Ibid., t. II, *Les lieux de l'échange*, p. 7.
25. Charles Dupin, *Mémoire sur la situation sociale et politique des colonies françaises, en 1844, et sur le système que le gouvernement doit adopter à leur égard*, Firmin Didot Frères, Paris 1844, p. xix.
26. Montesquieu, *L'Esprit des lois*, book XV, chap. 8.
27. Pierre Poivre, *Voyage d'un philosophe ou observations sur les mœurs & les arts des peuples d'Asie, d'Afrique et de l'Amérique*, Yverdon 1768, p. 94.
28. Cited in abbé Guillaume-Thomas Raynal, *Histoire philosophique et politique des établissemens et du commerce dans les deux Indes*, t. 6, J.-L. Pellet, Geneva 1781, pp. 180–181.
29. Condorcet and Clavière, among others, clearly distanced themselves from this climatic theory.
30. Charles Comte, *Traité de législation ou exposition des lois générales suivant lesquelles les peuples prospèrent, dépérissent ou restent stationnaires*, vol. IV, A. Sautelet et Cie, Paris 1827, p. 468.
31. Ibid., p. 412.
32. Sismondi, "De la condition dans laquelle il faut placer les nègres en les affranchissant," *Revue mensuelle d'économie politique*, December 1833, pp. 415–416.
33. Victor Schœlcher, *Abolition de l'esclavage*, Pagnerre, Paris 1840, p. 151.
34. Victor Schœlcher, *Des colonies françaises, abolition immédiate de l'esclavage* [1842], Editions du CTHS, Paris 1998, p. 283.
35. Ibid., p. 287.
36. Agénor de Gasparin, *Esclavage et traite*, Joubert, Paris 1838, p. 43.
37. See chap. 5, pp. 126–128.
38. Abbé Sébastien-André Sibire, *L'Aristocratie négrière, ou Réflexions philosophiques et historiques sur l'esclavage et l'affranchissement des Noir*, Lesclapart et Desray, Paris 1789, p. 108.
39. J.-B. Rouvellat de Cussac, *Situation des esclaves dans les colonies françaises*, Pagnerre, Paris 1845, p. 234.
40. Benjamin-Sigismond Frossard, *La cause des esclaves nègres et des habitans de la Guinée, portée au tribunal de la justice, de la religion, de la politique ou Histoire de la traite et de l'esclavage des nègres, preuves de leur illégitimité, moyens de les abolir sans nuire ni aux colonies, ni aux colons*, Lyon 1789, p. 270.
41. Comte, *Traité de législation*, pp. 467–468.
42. *Commission instituée, par décision royale du 24 mai 1840, . . . Rapport fait au ministre secrétaire d'Etat de la marine et des colonies*, Imprimerie royale, Paris 1841, pp. 230–231.
43. Jean-Baptiste Say, *Traité d'économie politique ou simple exposition de la manière dont se forment, se distribuent et se consomment les richesses*, Déterville, Paris 1803, p. 216.

44. Schwartz, *Réflexions sur l'esclavage des Nègres*, Société typographique, Neuchatel, pp. 21, 23.
45. Antoine-Jean-Thomas Bonnemain, *Régéneration des colonies ou moyens de restituer graduellement aux hommes leur état politique et d'assurer la prospérité des Nations; et Moyens pour rétablir promptement l'ordre dans les colonies françaises*, impr. du Cercle Social, Paris 1792, pp. 52–53.
46. Comte, *Traité de législation*, vol. 4, p. 442.
47. Jean Charles Léonard Sismondi, *Études sur l'économie politique*, 1837–1838, t. I, Slatkine, Geneva 1980, p. 290.
48. Tocqueville, article published in *Le Siècle*, November 8, 1843, in *Ecrits et discours politiques, Œuvres complètes d'Alexis de Tocqueville*, Gallimard, Paris 1962, p. 95. Other writers developed the same approach to the British islands: see André Cochut, "La société coloniale—Abolition de l'esclavage," *Revue des deux mondes*, t. III (1843), p. 178f., and Hyppolite Carnot, *De l'esclavage colonial*, Au bureau de la revue indépendante, Paris 1845, p. 39.
49. Plans for slave emancipation generally treated free labor as a factor in the "moralisation" of black workers—see Caroline Oudin-Bastide, *Travail, capitalisme et société esclavigiste*, La Découverte, Paris 2005, pp. 317–336.
50. Gasparin, *Escalvage et traite*, pp. 146–147.
51. Ibid., pp. 187–188.
52. *Pétition à MM. Les membres de la Chambre des députés. Abolition de l'esclavage, division des terres, indemnité; par un propriétaire d'esclaves*, Hachette, Paris 1836, pp. 12–13.
53. Appendix to "Commission chargée d'examiner la proposition de M. de Tracy relative à l'abolition de l'esclavage," Hearing of July 10, 1839, pp. 81–86.
54. Schœlcher, *Des colonies françaises*, p. 284.
55. Schœlcher, *Des colonies étrangères et Haïti*, t. II, p. 265.
56. Abbé Henri Grégoire, *De la littérature des nègres, ou Recherches sur leurs facultés intellectuelles, leurs qualités morales et leur littérature*, Maradan, Paris 1808, p. 59.
57. Jean-Baptiste Say, *Traité d'économie politique, Œuvres complètes de J.-B. Say*, Economica, Paris 2006, p. 918.
58. Ibid.
59. Ibid., pp. 917–918.
60. Schwartz, *Réflexions sur l'esclavage des Nègres*, pp. 63–72.
61. In a much less elaborate proposal than that of Condorcet, Viefville des Essars argued that it was wrong to think that Europeans were unfitted for cultivation in the colonies; if the black slave, born under the scorching sun, was stronger, then acclimatized whites would be capable of doing most of the work done by black slaves. All that would be needed would be to change the hours of work and, above all, to destroy the detestable prejudice that agricultural labor was too degrading for a European living in the islands to undertake. What would happen to the mass of emancipated slaves, lacking any property? "They will live from their labour and their services, as do our unskilled workers, day workers and servants. Need and necessity will compel them to do so. But it is not a question of suddenly giving them their freedom: this should be done in stages, paying due attention to the type of each slave, whether in giving him land to cultivate or to clear, or otherwise." (*Discours et projet de loi pour l'affranchissement des nègres ou l'adoucissement de leur régime et réponse aux objections des colons*, Imprimerie nationale, Paris 1790, p. 11). He suggested that uncultivated land should be distributed as small plots to emancipated slaves who, with a small

investment, could make the best of it and would not be slow in repaying the government and becoming wealthy.

62. The abbé Grégoire named him in the dedication of his book *De la littérature des nègres*, op. cit., and Comte in his *Traité de législation* very often cites him.
63. Charles-César Robin, *Voyages dans l'intérieur de la Louisiane, de la Floride occidentale et dans les isles de la Martinique et de Saint-Domingue pendant les années 1802, 1803, 1804, 1805 et 1806*, t. 3, Buisson, Paris 1807, pp. 227–228.
64. Comte, *Traité de législation*, pp. 497–498.
65. Ibid., p. 498—our emphasis.
66. Pierre-Armand Dufau, *De l'abolition graduelle de l'esclavage*, Bureau central de la *Revue Encyclopédique*, Paris 1830, pp. 117–118.
67. The idea that blacks would acquire the majority of land was not absent in the eighteenth century. Viefville des Essars thought that within a century the greater part of colonial property would be in the hands of "that class of men accustomed to work a great deal and spend little." He assumed that a revolution would lead all the colonies into independence, a process that would be favorable for the metropoles who would no longer have to bear the immense administrative costs created by their old colonies, conducting trade with them to the great satisfaction of their mutual needs. *Discours et projet de loi pour l'affranchissement des nègres*, pp. 17–18.
68. Gasparin, *Esclavage et traite*, chap. V.
69. Schœlcher, *De l'esclavage des Noirs*, pp. 85–94.
70. Ibid., p. 85.
71. Schœlcher, *Des colonies françaises*, note 1, pp. lxxvi–lxxviii.
72. Ibid., p. xlvii.
73. Ibid., pp. lxxiii–lxxiv.
74. Anne Girollet, *Victor Schœlcher, abolitionniste et républicain*, Karthala, Paris 2000, p. 285.
75. For details of this project, see Oudin-Bastide, *Travail, capitalisme et société esclavagiste*, p. 327.
76. Slaves worked for their masters at least nine hours per day, not including the time spent working on their own accounts; it is hard to imagine, therefore, how their working time might be doubled.
77. Alexandre Moreau de Jonnès, *Recherches statistiques sur l'esclavage colonial*, Imprimerie de Bourgogne et Martinet, Paris 1842, pp. 238, 241, 243–244.
78. On January 13, 1842, a commission was established by ministerial decree to study the project for the colonization of Guyana harbored for some time by Lechevalier, who had managed to win the support of some colonists. Lechevalier's book that we cite here was published with several other pieces, among them extracts from the hearings of the commission.
79. Jules Lechevalier, *Note sur la fondation d'une nouvelle colonies dans la Guyane française ou premier aperçu d'un nouveau mode de population et de culture pour l'exploitation des régions tropicales, suivi de plusieurs pièces et documents*, Firmin Didot frères, Paris 1844, p. 21.
80. Ibid, appended text: "Explications à la commission de colonisation de la Guyane française, extrait de procès-verbal de la séance du 4 mars 1842," p. 105.
81. Ibid., p. 108.
82. Ibid., pp. 21–24.
83. Duval de Sanadon, *Discours sur l'esclavage des Nègres*, p. 27–36.
84. Anon., *De la nécessité d'adopter l'esclavage en France*, Baillio, Paris 1797, p. 13.

85. Malouet, *Mémoire sur l'esclavage des nègres*, pp. 92–94.
86. Oudin-Bastide, *Travail, capitalisme et société esclavagiste*, pp. 92–94.
87. Albert Hirschman, *The Passions and the Interests*, Princeton University Press, Princeton, NJ 1977.
88. Gasparin, *Esclavage et traite*, p. 188. Rémusat, in his report on the work of the commission examining Passy's proposal on the circumstances of slaves in the French colonies (1838), de Broglie in the report of the commission established by royal decree on May 26, 1840, to investigate the relationship between slavery and the political constitution of the colonies (1843), and Schœlcher in his book of 1842 all recommended the creation of savings funds to hold the sums of money set aside by workers before or after abolition.

CHAPTER 8
Status and Interest

How might a stable and hard-working labor force be secured for colonial plantations? This was the question to which abolitionists had to find an answer. The majority of calculations made by those advocating slave emancipation presumed that the process of emancipation itself, by replacing coercion with self-interest as the incentive to labor, would greatly improve labor productivity. Discussion over the options available for the cultivation of colonial land was accordingly underwritten by ideas about the most suitable ways in which liberated slaves might be allowed to enjoy the fruits of this transformation, while at the same time securing to the plantations a supply of labor and avoiding the collapse of export-oriented agricultural production. Since colonists insisted that slavery ensured both the welfare and the labor of black slaves, those opposed to slavery endeavored to develop a legal and economic framework that would demonstrate how the logic of self-interest would in practice work to the advantage of both proprietors and workers.

Whether a free colonial labor force was black or white, Du Pont had argued that it would be composed of day laborers. There was, however, no evidence to support this claim. Opinions were divided on the future *status* of the free laborer in the colonies. Some thought that it would be necessary to restrict, at least temporarily, the full property of the freed slave in his/her person so that it would be possible to compel former slaves to sell their labor power on the market as day laborers. Others thought there to be no need to reduce the freed slaves to the condition of proletarians without house or home if they were attached to the estate and enjoyed a share in the benefits of collective labor through participating in work, impelled by their own self-interest. The pursuit of personal gain on the part of former slaves would lead them to work hard for the planter in order to become affluent. Yet others envisaged a more expansive role for self-interest: they linked the desire for personal gain to the interest that the cultivator took in his or her land, in the attachment to a piece of land and the care and effort that resulted from this. This therefore envisioned a possible future in which emancipated slaves would acquire full property in cultivable land or, alternatively and more likely, one where they were transformed into tenant farmers or sharecroppers.

SLAVERY AS THE BEST OF ALL CONDITIONS FOR BLACK PEOPLE

Colonists ceaselessly insisted that slavery was the sole way in which colonial agricultural production oriented to exports could be sustained, for the most part citing climatic and racist factors such as the appalling level of mortality of whites in the tropics or the inherent indolence of the blacks. Moreover, the conditions in which slaves found themselves were said to be superior to those enjoyed by very many European workers—this following a line of argument originally developed by Petit, Malouet, and Duval de Sanadon.

In 1790 Dubuc de Marentille compared slaves successively to European peasants suffering woes both physical and spiritual; to soldiers who, subordinated to the hardest work and discipline, most often ended up living as beggars in some remote part of the world; and to sailors who, having faced the dangers of the sea and the maladies of their occupation, eked out their final days in neglect. This author would have us believe that the condition of slaves was infinitely happier than any of these three types, citing as evidence that the blacks considered themselves superior to sailors or soldiers whom they refused to treat as white.[1]

In the same year Saint-Cyran published an idyllic portrait of slavery:

> It has already been demonstrated on many occasions that the condition of slaves in our colonies is generally less hard than that of day-laborers in France; that above all they possess, beyond the latter, the advantage of being cared for in infirmity and old-age, that in such circumstances food for their wives and children will be assured; and that, besides their hours of work, they enjoy perfect liberty.[2]

He added that they also enjoyed the possession of huts and gardens, and owned chickens, pigs, and other goods; that many had never had even the slightest punishment inflicted upon them; that they came together to dance at least twice a week; those who were industrious could be welldressed, and share sumptuous meals together; their weddings and funeral processions being especially opulent. Most of them would be very surprised to learn what Parisian philosophers said about their condition. As for colonists, they maintained that the situation of black slaves was better than that of the free laborers that some wished to force upon them. Emancipation would not therefore bring about any transformation through self-interest.

Arguments of this kind persisted until slavery was ended. The most elaborated version was definitely that of Adolphe Granier de Cassagnac, a major colonists' spokeperson, published in 1840 in his *Lettres à M. de Lamartine*. For him, slavery should be celebrated for the way in which no one was allowed to die of hunger; it was the negation of the beggary to which free labor reduced the worker. Slavery might even be more moral, having a more effective civilizing influence than liberty, associated as it was with the great moral and economic evils—the dissolution of custom, and poverty:

> [The regime of liberty and isolation] has produced in the working classes who live from day wages a burden, a disorder, a spirit of dissipation that saps and degrades them. Already, in the great centres of population these classes, descended from the emancipation of slaves and serfs during the Middle Ages, are no longer able to produce sufficient to cover their outgoings; and independently of public charity which has been regularly provided by hospitals ever since Christianity extended enfranchisement, it has been necessary every winter, and even with the least public commotion reacting upon industry, to increase the giving of alms for the support of this exhausting, barren and impracticable regime of freedom without organisation, that is to say, a regime of isolation.[3]

In France, said Granier de Cassagnac, where landlords represent twelve-fifteenths of the active population, the proletarians were terrible: "[T]hey are drops of water, but drops of water vaporised by the sun of incendiary theories, bursting the social machine [of the country]."[4] How would things stand in the colonies where there would be one landlord for every two hundred day laborers? European workers without savings were not able to resist the regime in which they lived. They were only able to avoid dying of hunger while working on dreadful tasks that the blacks did not want to do. He proposed the establishment of "life tenancies" that would give slaves the legal enjoyment of the civil rights that they did de facto already enjoy (marriage, recognition of transactions made by mutual agreement), coupled with the granting of an indemnity to masters who would no longer have the right to sell slaves. Hence the sole difference between blacks and European tenants would be that the former always worked for the same employer, while the latter hired out his labor to many; this being a difference of advantage to blacks because an enduring tenancy created a connection between master and worker and allowed arrangements to be made for retirement, protecting older workers from the fate of a pauper's death in a hospital.[5]

Slavery was therefore represented by colonists as one form of an "immemorial contract made by the rich with the poor,"[6] a "lifetime engagement,"[7] an "association" within which a man worked his entire life for one master who undertook to support him from cradle to grave,[8] a "service contract"[9] by virtue of which, in return for a number of hours' work five days a week, the slave was fed, clothed, and cared for both in ill health and during an unproductive old age. This relationship did not assume the legal form of a contract—equality of parties, freedom to enter into the contract or not—but it had advantages for the slaves since it provided them with something that the day worker or free peasant did not have: security for the worker's family members without a need to assume responsibility for them. Granier de Cassagnac never ceased repeating that slavery was a system of *solidarity*, whereas free labor engendered *isolation*.

Following this logic to its conclusion, colonists would have had to advocate the reintroduction of slavery in Europe. For the most part they did not seek to go this far. Malouet noted that very many of Europe's poor would gladly become slaves voluntarily, but it was not appropriate for all landowners to engage in such contracts between the members of a free and proud nation, an arrangement that would in any case quickly lead to the enslavement of all. The approach could not be applied to a free people; every pauper had to retain the prospect, however remote, of becoming a proprietor; and this prospect, available to all, was a consolation to the poor that no one had the right to deny.[10] This was a line of argument that undermined Malouet's defense of slavery: if the subordination of slaves were similar to that of day laborers in France, why deny to the first a "consolation" allowed to the second?

Granier de Cassagnac did, on the other hand, push the argument to its limit:

> It will be no more than half a century before France, wearying of providing alms to debauched and idle proletarians, will *compel* these people to work, taking control of their incomes in the same way the army does with its soldiers.[11]

This is a curious statement from a man who, four years earlier, had written that, unlike slaves, "civilised men" were patient, industrious, and imbued with a sense of order.[12]

Those opposed to slavery refused to go along with these ideas of slave "welfare," but their concern for economic efficiency and social peace led them to develop ideas that would enable emancipated slaves to remain on their plantations, while protecting them from the lack of security and poverty from which European popular classes suffered.

HOW MIGHT A FREE LABOR FORCE BE PERSUADED THAT THE PLANTATION SYSTEM BE MAINTAINED?

The plantation system was based on large properties upon which slaves worked in teams which in the French colonies were called *ateliers* or *bandes*. Many abolitionists thought that this form of landed property and exploitation had to be retained, being the only system capable of working on a large scale, at least for the main export crops.

During the early years of the French Revolution the idea of "participatory labor" or "associated labor" emerged in response to a dual objective: to guarantee the stability and high level of labor productivity on plantations, each being necessary to meet the interests of emancipated slaves and plantation owners.

In 1789 Daniel Lescallier, an administrator in Guyana, put forward a series of proposals that would lead to the emancipation of slaves: abolition of the slave trade; emancipation of domestic slaves together with those in village and town who were not vital to cultivation; freeing of mulattos; the creation of humane and uniform estate administration; and in particular, *the allocation to slaves of 10 percent of what they produced*. He wrote that

> It is more than probable that this apparent sacrifice on the part of proprietors of part of their income will be returned to them at the same rate, since the self-interest of the blacks will prompt them to work with greater will, [t]aking a lively interest in the progress of plantations, the exploitation of food crops, preventing theft, the loss of time, and the many abuses that the hard regime of slavery multiplies.[13]

This percentage could be progressively increased to *one third of the net revenue* so as to improve the comfort and ease of producers and stimulate their productivity. The export trade would increase in the same proportion thanks to the increased consumption of blacks who would appreciate their advantages and love their masters. A new colonial code providing for the equal rights of proprietors and their "vassals" could be introduced after a dozen years; it could be designed in such as way as to convince colonists that what was being proposed to them was neither impossible nor harmful to their interests.

First of all, a system of "glebe servitude" would initially substitute for slavery. Families that had sufficient savings, and which had therefore demonstrated themselves capable of good conduct in a condition of liberty, could buy themselves out, through either a one-time payment or an annual fee. A definite increase in population would permit them to leave the estates and settle on land granted to them by proprietors or the government where they could raise cattle and livestock, grow food, cotton, indigo, tobacco, or even, when there were sufficient numbers of emancipated slaves, establish new sugar plantations together. Lescallier's project did not aim at the parcelization of large plantations; instead, freed slaves were to be encouraged to assume the status of small peasant proprietors, or to found co-operatives to exploit previously uncultivated land. It is not entirely clear how this writer thought that a free labor force might be retained on plantations through this virtuous circle, since all "vassals" would in principle be induced to purchase their freedom.

A system of participation linked to extremely coercive measures intended to attach workers to the land was introduced by decree in some colonies during the first period of abolition. For instance, the provisions imposed in 1793 by the French colonial commissioner Léger-Félicité Sonthonax for northern Saint Domingo specified that, after deduction of taxes, one-third of the revenue would go to proprietors, one-third for various costs including those for management and hospitalization, and the remainder to workers attached to estates that also had a garden. In 1799 Edme Étienne Borne Desfourneaux the new governor of Guadeloupe was met with complaints from newly liberated slaves who supported themselves solely from the concession of a garden and a free Saturday, as they had when they were slaves; Desfourneaux responded by decreeing that cultivators would receive, in addition to their garden, *one quarter of net profits*.[14]

Colonists therefore set about demonstrating how inefficient the participatory labor system was. In 1802 Barré de Saint-Venant railed against "this new way that has misled one and all, this quarter of all produce upon which one so confidently counts, and by means of which it is hoped to induce negroes to work."[15] Reasoning on the basis of data from 1788, a year of great prosperity when Saint Domingo produced nearly 30 million *livres* and had almost 340,000 slaves, he calculated that the sum flowing to each worker would be 88 *livres* per annum, or rather less than 4 *sous* 10 *deniers* per day, a sum that was too small to overcome the indolence of black slaves. Even distributing the entire product to workers—each receiving 19 *sous* 4 *deniers*—would be without effect, given the behavior of older freed slaves who were rarely prepared to work for a daily wage of 40 *sous*, the only thing that would make them work being extreme need. He came to the same conclusion as the other colonial calculators: colonial resources were insufficient to allow a transition to free labor.

The idea that black workers could be motivated by paying them out of the product of the estates did, however, remain a recurring element in nineteenth-century abolitionist discourse. In 1814 the idea was promoted by Colonel Malenfant, a colonist, as one of the measures by which the old colony of Saint Domingo could be linked to France: by giving *one quarter of the income* from estates to free workers in their *ateliers* planters could get active agricultural laborers working and even punish the lazy whose lack of enthusiasm would reduce their share from any distribution.[16] We can find the same idea from the pen of Dufau in 1830; sketching a plan for the abolition of slavery, he proposed that each slave attaining adulthood be attached for ten years as a free laborer in the service of his master, so long as he had no valid reason for refusal, in which case he would, however, be engaged on the same terms by another planter. The wage received by the emancipated slaves for their work on the estates would, following the Haitian rural code, amount to one quarter of the estate's product distributed proportionately among the workers according to their status and the degree of utility of the work that they performed. There would, however, be the addition of a personal tax, to be fixed according to local conditions.[17]

Schœlcher's 1842 plan for abolition assigned a major role to the system of association, presenting as a whole the legislative project developed by Judge Boyer, amending it in some respects. Where estates had more than twenty active workers these could, if they and the proprietor so wished, become associates of the latter. Half of the gross income from work on the estate would flow to the proprietor who would have to build accommodation and make major repairs, *and half would be allocated to labor*. A fifth of this second portion would be used by the planter to pay managers (if any were employed), while the surplus would be divided between the workers (who retained their enjoyment of a piece of land) in proportion to days worked. The sums of money needed to replace agricultural equipment and draft animals would be top-sliced from the total revenue. Schœlcher commented that this system of shared working

> . . . merited serious attention since the negro is infinitely more attached to work whose product can be attributed directly to him than to any other. This is the system that the republic has established in place of slavery. In this way the laborer is attached to the soil. There is hardly any further need to supervise

> the workers, they supervise themselves, each of them is interested and no one succumbs to idleness.[18]

He did, though, emphasize the limits of this proposal: there was a risk that masters would refuse to associate themselves with blacks, and there was the fear on the part of workers that they would be duped in the process of dividing up the income, coupled with their inability in their present condition to bear any losses.

In 1845 Lechevalier published *Réorganisation des colonies à esclaves* (*Reorganization of Colonies with Slaves*), apparently having abandoned his earlier project for European immigration. He now proposed a "French procedure" for the emancipation of black slaves, with the first experiment to be conducted in Guyana. Before joining this new regime planters would become shareholders in a "Company" for which the state would guarantee a minimum return of 4 percent on capital employed over a period of forty-seven years. The former slaves would be concentrated in "municipalities" subject to civil and political legislation, and in "industrial corporations" subject to the general administration of the Company. Each new freed slave would receive a grant of 150 francs (70 francs for initial subsistence, 40 francs for equipment, and 40 francs to open a savings account). Work would be organized by task or piece, and paid in two parts: one fixed, and the other variable based on 25 percent of the Company profits set aside for this purpose. Newly freed slaves would be permitted to acquire land, but in plots of limited scale; here they would be permitted to grow only export crops, the Company monopolizing the production of foodstuffs.

Cochut vigorously applauded this proposal, since it secured the necessities of life to emancipated slaves while luring them on with the prospect of a significant share in profits, "entangling them once more in the ties of personal interest."[19]

By contrast, Schœlcher was outraged by the idea, denouncing it as "a false emancipation of slaves,"[20] an "odious juggling":[21]

> Here the blacks are enchained by a new forty-seven year lease. . . . They will receive a wage, they will have a 25% share in the net profits. That is all very good; but by allowing that the profits will not be mopped up by functionaries, by the payment due to those first employed, like Messieurs Lechevalier, Saint-Quantin and Sauvage,[22] ultimately by the wages of jailer and overseer, what will they do with it? At best they will be able to improve their material well-being a little. And that is all. They will remain no less men of the glebe, serfs, slaves, without any means of ever gaining, either for themselves or their children, true independence, of becoming proprietors for example. How, whatever their talent and

> economy may be, can they escape membership of a caste of labourers? On the one hand, the manual work to which they are statutorily condemned separates them from any intellectual labour; on the other, the Company, which has at its disposal the entire country, will never make the error of selling one inch of land to a black. Its own interest will prevent it from so doing: the company well knows that this would forever empty its *ateliers* of the black labour on which they depended. The Company is very clear that the worker will not be able to quit the status of helot and become a proprietor, since it has in advance fixed the price of land that it is prepared to sell at a minimum of 2,800 francs.[23]

While a very great many colonists safeguarded their privileges right up to the end of the slavery system, considering as a duty not to abandon a single part of it, some of them, like Adolphe de Saint-Quantin and Henri Sauvage, were conscious that emancipation was inevitable and showed an active interest for the participatory system. In an "Appeal to French Colonists" published in the *Démocratie pacifique* of May 1847, Louis de Lucy, a member of a noted Martinique creole family, called for thought to be given to the way in which estate work might be maintained. He was certain that the proletarian system could not work in the colonies, for it would immediately shatter the ingrained habits and practices of a black population that had to be regarded as childlike, its intelligence at the point of formation. He therefore proposed a connection of capital and labor during a period of transition to emancipation:

> We have to make the black understand that it is in his interest not only to increase the annual product of our estates through his own efforts, but also, and above all, keep a constant check on the work done by each of his brothers. Association creates solidarity among the workers.[24]

In an "Address to the King" dated July 10, 1847, the Guadeloupe Colonial Council offered to accompany France on the journey to emancipation, stating that they had already appointed a commission whose task was to prepare a plan for reorganizing labor on the foundation of "the principle of association, a principle whose application was perhaps impossible in Europe but which could be realised in those countries where groups of family and society could already be found."[25] The project drafted by this commission provided for the establishment of a register held in the town hall of every commune which would record all individuals involved in agricultural or industrial work, day laborers of either sex being required to wear on their clothing a leather tag carrying their registration number, the initials of their occupation, and the name of their commune. In 1849

Schœlcher commented ironically that this amounted to the glebe plus a tag worn round the neck, just like the collars of dogs on which was written the name of the person to whom the dog belonged.[26]

These participatory and associationist proposals for the colonies claimed to provide a complete social and economic resolution for all the problems arising from emancipation. The division of the product would secure the continued existence of the plantation but also the alliance of capital and labor, creating a relationship of mutual confidence between proprietor and workers. Such proposals involved a dual perspective: first, they are *pragmatic*, addressing the concerns of those familiar with colonial problems (like Lescallier and Malenfant),[27] but also issues raised by some French colonial administrators during the first period of abolition (Sonthonax on Saint Domingo, Desfourneaux on Guadeloupe) regarding the way in which the destruction of export production, even the loss of the colonies, might be avoided. Those colonists who did accept the associationist principle during the final years of slavery—the success of which they supposed to consist in the attachment of newly emancipated slaves to the glebe—signed up to what was thought a realistic perspective. Second, during the final days of slavery this *pragmatic perspective* collided with *theoretical approaches* regarding the relation of capital and labor. The idea of association played a key role in the thinking of reformers like Charles Fourier[28] and Louis Blanc.[29] We can also note that this idea can be found in the works of liberal economists who were concerned about the social effects of the industrial system. Michel Chevalier, a former Saint-Simonian who had become a liberal economist, suggested in his lectures at the Collège de France that capital and labor should join in association together with the aim of preventing the emergence of "an industrial feudalism in which the laboring masses, treated like mutineers, will be once again condemned to servitude."[30] The liberal periodical *Journal des économistes* began publication in 1842 with an editorial by Louis Reybaud, an economists who treated the idea of association as the most important question to be studied in the search for solutions to industrial problems:

> Will this principle be one day as fecund, as infallible as is believed, will a satisfying formulation ever be found? These questions remain enigmas. Science might seek to understand them, providing solutions if it finds them, dissipating illusions if it finds none.[31]

While we would not go so far as to claim that Schœlcher and Lechevalier thought of experimenting with Fourier's *phalanstère* in France's American colonies,[32] it is true that these authors and others like them were very much marked by the ideas of their time. Lechevalier became interested in Fourierism, having been a Saint-Simonian. Schœlcher, who accused Lechevalier of betraying his (Saint-Simonian) masters,[33] developed his own ideas in a number of publications, writing many pieces for *La Réforme*, founded by the republican radical Alexandre Ledru-Rollin, while not hesitating from occasional collaboration with *L'Atelier*, a Christian-social publication, and with *Siècle*, representing constitutional monarchists, as well as organs of the liberal press such as *Le Courrier français* or the *Journal des économistes*. He regarded the proposal for participatory labor (borrowed from Boyer) as continuous with the policy that the Republic had pursued in its colonies during the period of the first abolition.[34] His approach to working in association differed from the majority of other writers in its emphasis on *consent*, amending Boyer's text in this respect. He was disgusted by the absence of this essential condition from Lechevalier's projects, or from the writings of some colonists who wished to attach the newly liberated slave to the glebe. This was an attitude that corresponded exactly to the liberal position. During 1848 Horace Say published in the *Journal des économistes* an analysis of the report of the commission that had been established to prepare the legislation for abolition, citing at length the passage in the report relating to the freedom to work; these lines, he wrote, reflected the "generous ideas that one is used to finding in the writings of Victor Schœlcher." H. Say was very much in agreement with this refusal to countenance any compulsion for labor, although he did regret that the commission had not taken a position on the need to renounce a superannuated colonial system which was one of the greatest obstacles to French maritime commerce.[35] For Schœlcher, freedom of labor was also the condition for upward social mobility; if the worker were attached to the glebe, blacks would not be able to "rise." While he did not defend economic egalitarianism, Schœlcher did support republican principles of civil and political liberty and equality whose existence at least gave everyone the hope of moving up the social scale.

During the final days of slavery the British experience of emancipation led abolitionists to consider in greater detail the way in which the supply of labor could be secured for plantations. They were concerned that emancipated slaves might disperse themselves to the many uncultivated parts of the colonies, and that the resulting shortage of labor might prompt an excessive rise in labor costs that could well choke off the competitiveness of colonial products on the world market. Consequently, the question of the appropriation of land became central to debate.

In 1838 Gasparin maintained that only Antigua possessed the full range of conditions favorable to the survival of the export trade in agricultural goods: general emancipation of slaves, the moral and religious education of former slaves and their families by the Moravian Brethren,[36] and the appropriation of all land. In his view this last condition was *essential*. When there was not an inch of land without an owner there was nowhere for emancipated slaves to go where they might grow their own food, so making the dispersion of the labor force impossible:

> Forced labour necessarily survived slavery, the newly-freed slaves remaining tied to their former masters who could ransom them at will, and who set their wage rate at such a level that, in order to live, they had to work just as many hours as they had when they were slaves.[37]

In this respect the Antiguan experience was exemplary. Planters had fixed wages at a rate that allowed workers to pay for their food by working for a little more than four days of the week; for their part workers, who also enjoyed access to a hut, a garden and free medical care would therefore tend to restrict their work to this. The majority of workers were, however, led to work more hours on the plantations by the threat of a reduction in their pay; a threat, Gasparin noted, that had to be made quickly in order to "provide a constraint through need that could no longer be inflicted with the whip."[38] In Antigua, or also in Barbados where whites also owned all the land, blacks would be condemned to a lifetime as proletarians and workers. This was a state of affairs that Gasparin seems to have thought regrettable, but necessary.

Tocqueville took the same position in 1839. He considered that the lack of inclination on the part of free blacks to continue working in the same way for planters was prompted in part by the hatred and mistrust that took root during their period of apprenticeship, something that made it very difficult to determine a fair wage rate; but above all by the fact that blacks had in fact become small proprietors, retaining the right to allotment and garden that had been their right under slavery. The lesson that he drew from this was a simple one:

> If it is thought that, to preserve the cultivation of colonial foodstuffs and the permanent settlement of the white race in the Antilles, the negro must lease his services on a permanent basis to large landed proprietors; then it is also necessary to deny to the negro a domain in which he could live at ease and work only for himself.[39]

The Broglie Commission was clearly aware of this problem. It contrasted the case of Antigua, which it approached in the same way as Gasparin,[40] to other British colonies, especially Trinidad. Here emancipated slaves had used the small amounts that they had been able to save during their period of apprenticeship to buy uncultivated land very cheaply from the government or from indebted colonists. On this land they were able to grow food and other products for local consumption, making enough through abundant harvests for themselves and their families to be able to live in some comfort. As the rapporteur for the Commission wrote:

> This tendency for newly-emancipated slaves to rise from the status of day labourers to proprietors, instead of emerging spontaneously, instead of developing according to the natural laws of the human heart, has been fostered by the imprudence of their former masters, managed and supported by the intervention of missionaries, and sanctioned by the approval of the authorities.[41]

To moderate this problem the project for emancipation endorsed by the majority of the Commission involved three measures designed to attach a low-cost labor force to plantations:

1. The former slave would be obliged to reside in the colony in which he had been freed for five consecutive years from the date of emancipation;
2. the former slave had to enter into a contract for at least one year with one or several employers for the same period of time;
3. maximum and minimum wage rates would be fixed annually by decree of the governor and his privy council.[42]

In 1843 Tocqueville argued that, rather than introduce these exceptional measures, it would be "more simple, tidy and perhaps more effective" to require the government to commit itself to apply the laws against vagrancy in all their rigor; while at the same time forbidding for a fixed number of years emancipated slaves from buying or occupying land. "By preventing negroes from possessing land for the time being, what does one achieve? They are placed artificially in the same position as the worker in Europe naturally finds himself."[43] He added that this would certainly not be tyrannical, and that the person on whom this path out of servitude was imposed did not seem to have any grounds for complaint.

Cochut noted with some acuity how sugar production had diminished in the British colonies because very many emancipated slaves, no doubt those of greatest intelligence, had been able to acquire uncultivated land at a very low price and speculate on their own account in the sale of foodstuffs: "*The mass of labour has not been reduced, but displaced*, and wages have risen to a ruinous level in the islands where the desertion of former workers has not been immediately dealt with."[44] He considered that Lechevalier's project for the colonization of Guyana was the best way to resolve the problem. Combined with the fixing of wages by the government, the granting to the Company of control of cultivation and a monopoly on the sale of foodstuffs was the foundation of the system: "[T]here is no other way of preventing blacks from seeking in their gardens an independence that will lead, in the majority of cases, back into savagery."[45] While this was considered an economic necessity, the production of export crops here becomes presented as the condition for newly freed slaves to gain access to civilization. Cochut added that preventing former slaves from growing their own food was frowned upon by some abolitionists who imagined that this was a proposition entertained by "a company of ruthless stockjobbers driven by a desire to starve workers and reconstruct an industrial slavery more perfidious than legal slavery":

> What they fear for their dear protegés will come about much earlier in the British colonies, exposed as they are to all the hazards of free commerce. The excessive increase of the wages and the fortunes of some negroes in countries where there has been a shortage of hands have been but accidental phenomena. In the islands where there is no shortage of labour, in Antigua, Dominica, Nevis, and Montserrat, from the very first the daily wage of the labourer was 60 cents. Let the demon of competition be permitted to do its work, and a way will be found to increase the supply of hands, and in turn dictate the price of wages.[46]

During the final days of slavery, therefore, the strategy of prohibiting former slaves from acquiring land served two distinct, but closely connected, goals. Exclusion from the possession of this essential means of production was clearly intended by the leading abolitionists as an approach capable of securing to landed proprietors the amount of cheap labor they needed in order to *maintain the production of export crops*. Lacking access to land and so unable to acquire independent means of providing their own foodstuffs, blacks would be forced into the labor market where they would discover the benefits of working for gain and so be able to satisfy their growing needs in this way. They would, ultimately, become enmeshed in the *logic of self-interest*.

Nonetheless, the decrees of April 27, 1848, relating to the abolition of slavery did not involve any such restraint on the rights of new citizens to acquire property in land and to cultivate foodstuffs. The "Decree Suppressing Vagrancy and Pauperism and Anticipating the Creation of Disciplinary Workhouses in the Colonies" did, however, exert pressure on emancipated slaves to continue working on plantations. Besides suppressing vagrancy by assigning to *workhouses* established by public authorities for three or six months vagrants who were defined as those without occupation, or beggars (Article 1), this decree confirmed that masters retained full ownership of the huts and gardens that had been assigned to slaves (Article 2), also providing for the expulsion by the police authorities of any individual resident on state land or of a private owner who did not enjoy any right of usufruct, nor was a farmer, tenant, or holder of any other concessionary title (Article 3). All of these measures, which had already been included in Schœlcher's 1842 "Essai de législation propre à faciliter l'émancipation en masse et spontanée" (Essay on the Legislation Favorable to a Spontaneous and Massive Emancipation),[47] were aimed, above all, at preventing former slaves from withdrawing into "material civilization."

PROJECT PLACING THE PLANTATION SYSTEM IN QUESTION

For all of those who favored the various forms of participatory labor, all of which had the advantage of leaving the plantation system unchanged, a *pecuniary interest* was all it took to stimulate productivity. However, several abolitionists question this assumption, arguing instead that an *interest in the land* was a powerful stimulus to labor, involving a love of the land and a resulting care for it. This latter group therefore proposed that cultivators should be able, en masse and within a reasonable amount of time, to acquire property as tenant farmers or as sharecroppers.

Thinking in terms of significant white immigration, Condorcet had suggested the development of smallholdings and tenant farming, harvests being processed in the existing facilities on the plantation, by the indigo plants, or by new public mills established by merchants. He thought that the resulting increase in the gross product of the colonies that would ease the abolition of slavery would be as much the consequence of the exploitation of uncultivated land as of the increase in labor productivity. This fundamental reform of the organization of colonial agricultural production would not at first therefore disrupt the racial hierarchy: the status of owners and farmers would devolve to whites in the same way that slaves would be transformed into day laborers.

Ladebat did not propose encouraging European agricultural workers to move to the colonies; it was the former slaves who should be provided with an attachment to this land. Having become free men, slaves would form a new class of "glebe serfs": "This progression is quite natural. When slaves had not been emancipated by victory, or when they remained shackled to the yoke of the conqueror, they were 'glebe serfs' before being freed; such were the slaves among the Germans, according to Tacitus."[48] Ladebat went on to suggest that entry to this "glebe serf" category would be dependent on the payment of a sum that the slave would acquire by working for six or seven years without payment. Black workers would then have the right, once they had gained this status, of receiving a wage fixed by statute. Every man who gained this first stage of liberty would be able to secure the same status for his wife by paying a sum that was reduced by the number of children that she had. Only the children born to women who were "glebe serfs" would belong to this class. A "glebe serf" could gain his freedom by purchasing a piece of land if he were able to persuade an owner to sell it to him, by the payment of a fee (which had the effect of transforming him into a tenant farmer), or by payment of a sum sufficiently large for the landowner to continue the work of cultivation by employing someone else. Ladebat concluded that

> This division of the land would quickly increase its product. The products that required processing would be dealt with in the owners' workshops, and subsequently divided up. The direction of these establishments would become more simple and economical; the value of the investment would increase along with liberty.[49]

If Ladebat's proposal seemed similar to that of Lescallier in advocating a stage in which the emancipated slave was attached to the glebe, the outcome he foresaw was different. He was interested in terminating a plantation system that depended upon collective agricultural work, on large workshops, on estates. These estates would instead be broken up and sold in lots to smallholders or, if planters were reluctant to dispose of their land, divided up into farms tenanted by the families of emancipated slaves. In either case, harvests would be processed in the works of the former planters. These new working arrangements would bring about growth in the gross product of the colonies that would benefit the colonists, the emancipated slaves, and also metropolitan France.

Frossard showed himself to be prudent when it came to agricultural reorganization. He argued for the indefinite extension of the garden concession for newly emancipated slaves who had become day laborers—a measure that would allow emancipation to be effected "without fuss, without even being apparent." In addition, he suggested that emancipation would be furthered by the division of large holdings into small farms distributed to the new citizens who merited greatest trust through the payment of a fee that would be accepted by proprietors. He did not think, however, that this arrangement could be extended to the sugar plantations, which required large-scale plant and had significant intermediate running costs. On the other hand, it would be possible to divide up the land used for the production of coffee, cotton, cocoa, achiote, tobacco, and so forth, because these all required less labor for harvesting and less outlay for their cultivation. It would therefore be possible to lease out pieces of land to the most industrious blacks in return for the payment of part of the crop, which was much easier than seeking to be paid in money.[50] These emancipated slaves would have a much higher status than that of day laborers, and would deserve to become farmers and an example to the mass of newly emancipated slaves.

In 1792 Armand Guy Kersaint, a member of the National Convention, invited colonists threatened by general insurrection to think about the only course open to them if they wished to preserve their property and their lives: first, improve the lot of their slaves, then guide them toward a form of liberty resembling that of sharecroppers who would cultivate the lands of the colonists and receive in payment one-half of what they produced.[51]

Setting aside climatic and racial arguments for the sake of debate, some colonists embarked on absurd lines of reasoning, thinking it useful to respond to abolitionist proposals that placed in question the centralization of land and the system of collective labor on the plantations.

In 1788 Malouet argued that the smallholding principle did not apply to the colonies since two hundred arpents of land devoted to sugar production incurred costs and investment—in buildings, animal pasture, and tools—equal to that employed in the cultivation of six hundred—and so subdivision would result in the loss of colonial manufactures. Responding to Condorcet's proposals, which he thought to be no more than vague assertions full of forcible and unfitting comparisons, Malouet conceded that it would have been possible when the colonies were originally founded to have given one settler a simple mill, another a manufactory, and land for cultivation to several others whose produce would be transformed by these establishments.

> But that did not happen. All possible processes and establishments were developed on each of the estates. How can these now be dispersed and sold? Who would want to sell? Who could buy? It defies belief, it is a dangerous irritant to the feelings of honest people to seek to persuade them that the real evils of black slavery could be so easily destroyed.[52]

The following year De Lattre de Montfleury stated that a plantation divided into ten would produce no more than one-third of the previous income; it would therefore not be politic, and was contrary to the interests of colonists and metropolitan France, even more so the division of land if it were decreed by an agrarian law.[53]

For his part, Saint-Cyran tried to prove the stupidity of the abolitionist proposal to break up the estates into smallholdings whose product would be processed in an establishment belonging to a former slaveowner, and also to demonstrate the impossibility of transforming slaves into farmers or sharecroppers working for landed proprietors. The first proposal was void for reasons both economic and social:

> But firstly, how will this transfer of property currently in the hands of one person come about? What proprietor will sell his land to the negro who has nothing, with the certainty of receiving no payment? Who would want to build or maintain an establishment of four hundred thousand *livres* that needs not a press, but a mediocre sugar plant with buildings, tools, oxen, mules, the hire of a large number of workers, hand workers, refiners, and be exposed to the risk that all this expenditure will be useless, if the new owners, or many of them, would prefer to cultivate coffee, indigo, cotton, foodstuffs rather than cane? Would they consult with each other on planting, so that their canes would mature only successively, and at a suitable time so as to provide precisely the quantity needed for processing, and with the uniform continuity that the work of mill and sugar factory absolutely demands? Would they agree among themselves to set land aside for pasture to feed the livestock dependent on the establishment, and about the many operations that can only be directed by one person? Where would they get fertilizer? But we do not have the time to refute such absurdities.[54]

The idea of transforming slaves into farmers or sharecroppers was no more realistic: to continue to be competitive in foreign markets it would be necessary for newly freed farmers or sharecroppers to work just as hard as they had when they were slaves, something that would be impossible to get them to do. And what might they then fear from justice if they failed to fulfill their obligations to the owner, those who lived naked in a reed hut, sleeping on a floormat and using no furniture?

The proposal to subdivide estates into farms, sharecroppers' holdings, or smallholdings was, however, defended by some nineteenth-century abolitionists. The most successful project in this respect was undeniably that of Sismondi, who saw in the colonies after abolition a propitious terrain for experiments in sharecropping. This was an idea that ran through all of his writing, that sharecropping could prevent the emergence of wage-labor, a status that was synonymous with exploitation and was also the source of economic crisis.[55]

In 1833 Sismondi deplored the small amount of attention that metropolitan opinion paid to the issue of slavery, a lack of attention that he attributed to the great calamities that the first attempt at abolition had brought about, the major revolutions that had shaken French society, and the immense distance that separated Europe from those countries in which slavery was practiced. The abolition of slavery in the British Isles had, however, obliged the French to reconsider the question. The process of emancipation had to secure the progress and welfare of those emancipated, while at the same time preserving the fortunes of planters and maintaining civilization in those countries in which great wealth had been created. In this new system prosperity could be based upon either the former culture or a new one; each colony had the right, like any French *département*, to be governed according to its own particular interest. The means employed by Britain in abolishing slavery would not allow these aims to be met: the indemnity of 500 million francs that had been given to colonists was costly, while the system of "apprenticeship" of twelve years imposed on the former slaves was no more than a disguised form of slavery that would only aggravate the situation. Obliged to work, but without a wage of any kind, for three-quarters of a day or a week for their former masters whose interest in them would not even go as far as maintaining them in good health, they would be faced with an exhausting work rhythm that would render them incapable of any activity in the time that they had to themselves. Emancipation having been completed, they would lose their huts and their gardens and would be reduced to the sorry condition of Irish or English wage laborers who, suffering from the surplus of manual labor, "lived from day to day, without hope of any future, and always faced with utter poverty," working on an occasional basis for large farmers who invested capital and managed labor but without becoming directly involved in the work themselves.

To secure the welfare of all and for success in the work carried out "it was necessary that interests would converge on one aim, rather than being set in opposition to each other."[56] The sharecropping system which had in Europe, very fortunately, replaced the ancient slave system seemed to Sismondi the appropriate system to assure colonial prosperity because it mingled the interests of the worker with those of the owner: "For the personal interest of his humble associate will work for him; it will sharpen his intelligence, overcome his idleness, it will achieve what blows never could, what self-interest has done on more than one French province where the peasant is more dense, slower, more obstinate, more alien to any education that is any negro."[57] While the establishment of this form of labor organization was difficult for the British who had abandoned it some four or five centuries previously, it was easy for French colonists to develop it when it only involved a return to the customs of their mother country. It should be encouraged by the payment to the planter of a bonus of 2,000 francs per black of any age and of either sex who had been freed and transformed into sharecropper, a premium that would only be paid after one year when the newly freed slave had given proof of being on the path to prosperity thanks to his industry, sense of economy, and the increased production of the land that had been granted to him. Seduced by the hope of selling their slaves to the public authorities at a price higher than that of the market, the masters would want to see the experiment succeed, encouraging them to select the most robust, active, and intelligent blacks as sharecroppers. The price of redeemed slaves would be reduced during subsequent years for two reasons. First, where the new system had been introduced, those plantation workers who were not selected at the time the plantation had been established would be worth less than those retained by the master to secure the viability of the plantation. Second, those settlers who had not taken the risk of overcoming the difficulties inherent to this new system would not deserve the substantial payment of 2,000 francs. In order to protect freed slaves from any abuse it should be decreed that the cultivation be conducted for half shares, publishing and sanctioning the conditions of the farm lease as was established custom in the most prosperous provinces of France. Sismondi concluded:

> May France raise in the West Indies an industrious, although black, class of peasants, fond of the soil that it cultivates, showing affection for the master with whom it shares its products, serene about its fate, assured of its future, raising its children with confidence and with certain knowledge of the fate and the position destined for them, so that the new generation always remains in proportion to the old! May these beautiful climes that have known such suffering and so many crimes after experiencing those of slavery, never know those of competition, where many struggle to gain sufficient work and very little bread, as do today the inhabitants of cottages in Kent and in Ireland, in the midst of opulence and in the name of liberty.[58]

Four years later Sismondi repeated the same proposal in his *Études d'économie politique* (*Studies in Political Economy*), without, however, mentioning the incentive payment of 2,000 francs. Nonetheless, this condition was original and significant given the way in which it provided an incentive for the introduction of sharecropping, distinct therefore from payment in compensation for expropriation that was advocated by most abolitionists. He dwelt at length on the reasons for thinking the sharecropping contract to be more suited to the slave colonies than tenant farming. This system seemed to him perfectly in keeping with the nature of colonial cultivation (perennials and shrubs). The sharecropper would, in association with his master, devote to each plant care proportionate to the yield that he expects, while the farmer would be obliged to use day laborers who, by their negligence, would quickly bring about the ruin of the plantation. He also thought that the freed slave would be unable to bear the risks faced by a farmer; the latter required a level of vigilance and activity too great for a man recently released from slavery. Linked to a proprietor, the sharecropper benefits from his knowledge and experience. Finally, Sismondi emphasized the fact that the distribution of capital in the colonies left the black with no alternative than that of being a sharecropper; he came out of slavery "absolutely naked," and the newly freed slave would not have the necessary initial capital to be a farmer. By becoming a sharecropper he remained under the control of a proprietor who would advance to him the means of production necessary for the exploitation of the land conceded to him.[59]

Unlike England, which had transformed slaves into proletarians, France had to elevate the black to the status of the French peasant. The division of the plantation into as many shareholdings as it contained families would lead to an increase in productivity—each cultivator finding in himself "his own spur to activity"; the half of the harvest that would be returned to him would secure to him means for his subsistence more abundant than those he had had while a slave. It was, however, probable that sugar and coffee would become, through this form of activity, less exclusive crops: the new peasants would think a little more about their own needs and those of the population of the colony, and a little less about the needs of European consumers. However, the decline of the export trade, even the cessation of the production of colonial commodities, would not be detrimental to the prosperity of the colony; the sharecropping system would enable the settlers to escape from their debt, to enjoy their incomes, and to sell their land easily. The system would ensure the comfort of the farmers, demographic growth in proportion to the lands remaining to be cleared, as well as an increase in consumption.

Baron de Cools, a delegate from Martinique, responded in 1834 to the project developed by Sismondi. Having applauded his very accurate criticism of the British Emancipation Bill in respect of property rights, and supporting Sismondi's concern to preserve colonial cultivation, he addressed himself to opening Sismondi's eyes to the "illusions that animate his generous soul." His argument was organized in four points.

He dwelled initially on the way that the climate shaped the paucity of the black's needs, noting that "because [British] partisans of emancipation have not dared to rely upon the stimulation to work *through pure need*, they decided to impose an initial period of apprenticeship before complete liberation, a period during which colonists had an obligation to subsidise in part the subsistence of those of their manual workers who were not able to support themselves by using the free time that the law had given them." [60]

He then attacked the hypothesis upon which Sismondi's system was based: the possibility of exploiting the land, as in Tuscany, by the families of sharecroppers. This was inappropriate in that the family, necessary for the future of any social organization, did not exist among slaves. The black slave seemed, either for lack of moral progress or by inner repugnance, to fear the responsibilities that domestic affection imposed. Time and moral education would be needed to create the family as an institution in the colonies before it could be used as a building block for other projects.

Experience, which Cools thought Sismondi could not ignore, had in any case preceded argument. This theory had first been tested in Guadeloupe and Guyana during the first abolition of slavery, as in Saint Domingo and Trinidad. Cools here amalgamated, in good or bad faith, participatory work (which does not divide up the land and keeps work in *ateliers*) and the sharecropping system which presupposed a division of the estate into smallholdings each run by a family of an emancipated slave.[61] The problem, he added, was evident: blacks never worked except under the threat of government bayonets; many left the estates, preferring marauding to regular work. Reduced to poverty, after the initial abolition of slavery they returned to the plantations without regret, happy to find peace and care of all kinds that they had long enjoyed, in health and in sickness, before the abolition of slavery![62]

Cools did, however, admit that Sismondi's proposed 2,000-franc bonus could encourage settlers to adopt his system. But, he asked, "If at the end of the trial year the work of the freed slave did not fulfil the hopes and enlightened directions of his former master, by what right could M. de Sismondi claim that the owner must remain stripped of his property without receiving any compensation?"[63] In anticipation of this probable failure it would be necessary to provide for an indemnity which, according to the proportion voted by the English Parliament, would raise 200 million francs for the 280,000 slaves owned by the French planters, and not 140 million as Sismondi assumed.

Cools concluded by arguing that it would be necessary to give up all attempts to resolve social difficulties by a priori arguments and "let time tell." Only a gradual abolition—decided case by case by the planters—could allow the admission of a black into society on the condition that he demonstrated productive industry and presented, through the constitution of family and property, the moral and political guarantees necessary for the formation of any prosperous and sustainable society.[64]

The experience of the abolition of slavery in British colonies did not add anything to French debate on the status of emancipated slaves. Apprenticeship as envisaged in the Act for the Abolition of Slavery was clearly aimed at the transformation of the slave into a free wage laborer, the status of farmer, sharecropper, or smallholder not even being raised. Although he was clearly interested in the issue, Macaulay did not bring to the attention of his French readers any example based on the British experience of abolition. In Ch. V of his *Faits et renseignements prouvant les avantages du travail libre sur le travail forcé* (*Facts and information demonstrating the advantages of free labor over constrained labor*) (1835) he simply reproduced extracts from the two articles published in 1833 and 1834 in the *Revue mensuelle d'économie politique* (*Monthly Review of Political Economy*) where Sismondi had defended his proposals about sharecropping.

In the early 1840s the acquisition of property by former slaves in some British colonies was thought to represent a hindrance to colonial cultivation, not a means of maintaining it. According to the committee of the House of Commons appointed to inquire into the State of the West India Colonies (1842), the fall in production "arises partly from the high wages which the insufficiency of the supply of labor, and their competition with each other, naturally compel the planters to pay; but is principally to be attributed to easy terms upon which the use of land has been obtainable by the Negroes." "The Cheapness of land," it was added, "has thus been the main cause of the difficulties which have been experienced."[65] During the hearings many British planters expressed the same view. In a memorandum on the condition of Jamaica addressed to the Ministry of the Navy and of the Colonies in January 1842 the French writer Layrle was quite frankly pessimistic: "In Jamaica there is a great deal of land; a few gourdes is enough to become a proprietor; and all these smallholders are so many hands lost to large-scale cultivation. The ease with which the black can cut himself off, reducing the labor available for the estates, will be the ruin of the colony; but this is an evil that it is impossible to cure.[66]

However, during the same period there was some development in the discussion about the status of freed slaves in the British colonies. In January 1842 Henry James Ross, the owner of a coffee plantation on Grenada, published a pamphlet entitled *Thoughts on the Objectionable System of Labour for Wages in the West India Colonies; and on the necessity of substituting a System of Tenancy and Allotment of the Staple Cultivation.* Following Sismondi, he recommended the introduction of sharecropping to the British colonies. In his evidence to Parliament he stated that he had adopted the system in 1840 with the aim of preventing workers deserting the plantation. Ross claimed that former slaves had received this innovation favorably, being able to organize their working time to suit themselves and because of their interest in the result of the labor—payment being made to each in cash at a rate of one-third or one-quarter of the total. The system had been adopted by other sugar producers.[67] A note sent by Sir Charles Metcalfe, Governor of Jamaica, to Lord Stanley, Minister for the Colonies, included a recommendation that sharecropping be introduced to Jamaica, citing the example of sharecropping in the French *département* of the Gironde, and the system established under the Haiti Rural Code. Metcalfe declared himself attracted to the idea, suggesting that, since Jamaica had never tried this particular system, it might be of interest to planters lacking the means to make the considerable advance payments in cash that wage labor required.[68] In spite of the encouragement of Lord Stanley, who thought that workers had to have a commitment to the product of plantations, planters in the larger colonies were ultimately reluctant to establish a sharecropping system, which was adopted only in the sugar plantations on the smaller British islands (Nevis, St. Lucia, and Tobago in particular).

There were, however, positive echoes from Sismondi's project. Besides glebe servitude and sharecropping as systems of emancipation in which the state had no right to intervene in private transactions,[69] the Broglie Commission defended the idea that the establishment of sharecropping could, if established by mutual agreement, be of benefit to everyone. Without leaving the plantation, blacks would obtain an almost independent position, the difference between the status of sharecropper and that of the owner being amply compensated by the advantage of keeping their savings, and being freed of the need to clear uncultivated land and raise their own capital. Nothing would prevent them from owning a field not far away which they could work during their free time. The landlords would be relieved of the difficulty that could arise from variations in wages and the need to put by a cash reserve to ensure the daily or weekly payment of labor. All they would need to do was to ensure that at harvest time they had enough cash to pay their sharecroppers, sums that could be advanced to them against a particular yield. The cares of agriculture work and its supervision would no longer take up the greater part of their time. Finally, metropolitan France, supposing that it had any interest in the extension of colonial cultivation, would see it increase, "the blacks working, apparently, infinitely more and infinitely better for themselves than they work [in slavery] for their masters."[70]

The terrible earthquake that destroyed the city of Pointe-à-Pitre and a large number of sugar manufactories on Guadeloupe led Schœlcher to develop his ideas about the possible forms of labor organization after abolition. In an article published in April 1843 in the *Journal des économistes*, he noted that this catastrophe offered an opportunity to reorganize sugar production on the island, based on the separation of manufacturing activity and cane cultivation.[71] Manufacturing activity would be centralized, while cane cultivation would be conducted on a small scale by former slaves working on plots formed from the breaking up of large estates. Not unaware of the dangers of an indefinite division of property, he wrote that he would adopt this solution "as the only way forward that could replace the dreadful present colonial regime," adding that the day would come when social science would further increase profits through the association of the manufacturer, the small and the large owner, the craftsman, and the laborer.[72] Refusing the forced association advocated by some colonists, the report of the Commission established to prepare legislation for the eventual abolition of slavery in 1848 did not ultimately envisage the fragmentation of property, but presupposed the creation of several different forms of organization that would profit both the former black slave and also the entire society: work by task or by day, free association or partible colonization, this last mode of tenure finding among former slaves "a favour which makes all hope for the future."[73]

Unlike proposals for participatory or associationist working, those involving the development of smallholdings (linked with the separation of sugar-making and cane cultivation), of tenant farming or of sharecropping involving estates or uncultivated land, deal with the problem of abolition through both social and economic measures. They were underpinned by the question of the relationship between labor and capital that had since the Restoration played an increasing role in French political debate. While working in association—as proposed for the colonies—did not call into question the strict separation between capital and labor whose interests it claimed to reconcile, these options did on the contrary presume *some greater degree of access to means of production* (land and the goods needed to develop it), linked to greater levels of worker autonomy. In any case, this greater autonomy permitted the worker to escape the subjection associated with the wage system.[74] Sismondi's exposition of why he considers sharecropping more suited to the situation of the former slaves than arming is particularly enlightening in this respect. The farmer leases land from the owner against the payment of a cash rent and cultivates it with his own capital, his labor and that of day laborers whom he hires as he needs. His independence derives from his contribution of fixed and circulating capital and not from the ownership of land, which does however remain a desirable objective. While the sharecropper does not own any capital, his status confers on him "*all enjoyment, all security of property*, although only half of the yield belongs to him."[75] While the laborer is subordinated to his employer, the sharecropper is *associated* with the owner: "Both want to benefit equally from the knowledge, experience and ability of each other."[76] The black sharecropper will gradually gain autonomy: if his deference toward a planter accustomed to command will at first be complete, the experience that he gradually acquires will lead the owner to loosen the bridle.

* * *

Anti-slavery discourse on the status acquired by newly freed slaves sought to solve two problems: to prevent the former slave fleeing to uncultivated land that they could appropriate in order to produce food; and to avoid the creation of a proletariat without hearth and home that would become dangerous because of their unjustified poverty. Understanding the advantages of what we now call economies of scale—repeatedly cited by colonists to highlight the devastating impact of any breaking-up of large plantations—abolitionists advanced their own proposals for the continuation of large-scale cultivation.

The diversity of these proposals shows the difficulty that their authors had identifying a way out of slavery.

Some looked to history for ways of organizing the transition from slave to free labor. According to Ladebat, glebe servitude corresponded to the *course taken by nature*. For Sismondi the establishment of sharecropping in Western Europe showed that it was possible to terminate slavery "without disturbance, without violence, without rebellion, even when the emancipation came suddenly," while the maintenance of the working population of Eastern Europe in an intermediate condition of serfdom advanced "neither the wealth of the landowners, nor the happiness of the laborers, nor the civilization of the country."[77] Tocqueville for his part envisaged a temporary ban on access to property in land as a means of artificially placing the former slave in the same position as that which European workers naturally found themselves. Commenting on this proposal, Aimé Césaire exclaimed: "Cynicism and intelligence. Exact understanding of the genesis of capitalism and wage labor. One word too much: *naturally*. The historian Tocqueville pretends to ignore the success of violence and atrocities in fifteenth-century Europe, to tear away from their rural roots vast masses of people so that they might be thrown into the labor market, rootless, defenceless, vendible proletarians."[78] He undoubtedly based this statement on his reading of *Capital*, where Marx described the process by which, from the later fifteenth century to the eighteenth, English peasants were expelled from the lands they cultivated as proprietors or farmers and deprived of communal property that they possessed with the same feudal title as their masters, becoming proletarians without hearth or home. Marx wrote in 1867 that in the ordinary course of things the laborer was abandoned to "the natural laws of society, to a "dependence upon capitalism engendered, guaranteed and perpetuated by the very mechanism of production. It is different during the historical genesis of capitalist production."[79] Like Ladebat, but unlike Sismondi, Tocqueville used references to history to *naturalise* the path of transition between servitude and free labor that he advocated.

The debate on the status to which freed slaves should be admitted must be placed in context: that of the *indignity* of wage labor. Robert Castel has outlined how, at the end of the Ancien Régime, the structure of wage labor "reflected extremely diverse situations that can almost exclusively be characterised as social activities that have been imposed by need and conditioned by relations of dependency."[80] In the first part of the nineteenth century "the proletarian condition represented a situation of quasi-exclusion from the social body. The proletariat is an essential link in the nascent process of industrialisation, devoted to working to reproduce itself, 'encamped in society without being part of it.' "[81] The condition of the day laborer and of the manual worker is characterised by poverty, insecurity, dependence, characters that make his condition one of *indignity*. This is how Saint-Simonian thinkers thought of the question when they argued that slavery would be succeeded within the framework of the exploitation of man by man by the wage relationship.[82] Commenting a little later on an America on the verge of Civil War, Pierre-Joseph Proudhon thought that "slavery and the proletariat [were] incompatible with republican mores," and called for the abolition of both of them.[83]

This indignity of wage labor allowed colonists to assimilate it to slavery, and even to assert that the second offered the individual a better life than the first. If we were to believe them, the slave was provided for by the benevolent tutelage of the master, enjoying total security and the satisfaction of his few needs. The abolitionists obviously rejected this assimilation using various arguments: the slave has no chance of escaping the dominance of his master, unlike the laborer; the slave's "happiness" can at best only be comparable to that of the beast of burden that his owner keeps. However, incorporating the idea of the indignity of wage labor, emancipation projects usually claimed that the former slave would enjoy better conditions than that of the day laborer. Sismondi's proposal is exemplary in this respect: critical of European wage labor, he aimed not only to give former slaves a degree of ease and comfort, but also to provide them with a stable situation and relative autonomy from their former owner.

The status of a sharecropper would, in a way, reconcile the advantages of working for oneself with those of working for others. Schœlcher was the herald of free labor whatever the conditions: he wrote in 1842 that "Between the slave and the proletarian there is the difference between a tool and a worker. If the worker is unhappy that is a reason to improve his lot, but not a reason to forego passing from the condition of a human tool to that of a worker."[84] His equivocation as to the status to be granted to former slaves—participatory work in 1842, smallholdings (associated with the establishment of central factories) in 1843, acceptance of the idea of partial colonization in 1848—does, however, reflect his distrust of wage labor. Beyond the desire to maintain and even increase export crops, the ambition to offer free settlement workers a more dignified status than that of laborers was a characteristic of abolitionist discourse.

NOTES

1. Dubuc de Marentille, *De l'esclavage des nègres dans les colonies d'Amérique*, Pointe-à-Pitre Guadeloupe 1790, pp. 6–7.
2. M. de Saint-Cyran, *Réfutation du projet des Amis des noirs sur la suppression de la traite des nègres et sur l'abolition de l'esclavage dans les colonies*, Devaux 1790, pp. 4–5.
3. Adolphe Granier de Cassagnac, *De l'émancipation des esclaves, Lettres à M. de Lamartine*, Delloye, Paris 1840, pp. 16–17.
4. Ibid., p. 48.
5. Ibid., pp. 67–68.
6. Pierre-Victor Malouet, *Mémoire sur l'esclavage des nègres dans lequel on discute des motifs proposés pour leur affranchissement, ceux qui s'y opposent, et les moyens praticables pour améliorer leur sort*, Neuchatel 1788, p. 26.
7. Dubuc de Marentille, *De l'esclavage des nègres dans les colonies d'Amérique*, p. 6.
8. Adolphe Granier de Cassagnac, *De l'émancipation des esclaves, Lettres à M. de Lamartine*, Delloye, Paris 1840, p. 5.
9. Alphonse Maynard, *La Martinique en 1842, intérêts coloniaux, souvenirs de voyage par M. le comte de la Cornillère* (pseudonyme), Gide libraire-éditeur, Paris 1843, p. 215.
10. Malouet, *Mémoire sur l'esclavage des nègres*, pp. 36–37.
11. Granier de Cassagnac, *De l'émancipation des esclaves*, p. 87.
12. Granier de Cassagnac, "Colonies françaises, de l'esclavage et de l'émancipation," *Revue de Paris* (1836), p. 258.
13. Daniel Lescallier, *Réflexions sur le sort des noirs dans les colonies*, n.p. 1789, pp. 52–53.
14. Léo Elisabeth, "Rémunération du travail libre et question agraire à la Martinique et dans les colonies françaises d'Amérique de 1842 à 1851," in Marcel Dorigny (ed.) *Esclavage, résistances et abolitions*, éditions du CTHS, Paris 1999, pp. 310–311; and Frédéric Régent, *Esclavage, métissage, liberté*, Grasset, Paris 2004, pp. 342–344.

15. Jean Barré Saint-Venant, *Des colonies modernes sous la zone torride et particulièrement celle de Saint-Domingue*, Brochot, Paris 1802, p. 53.
16. Colonel Malenfant, *Des colonies et particulièrement de celles de St-Domingue, Mémoire historique et politique*, Audibert, Paris 1814, pp. 130–131.
17. Pierre-Armand Dufau, *De l'abolition graduelle de l'esclavage dans les colonies européennes et notamment dans les colonies françaises, considérée à la fois dans l'intérêt des esclaves, des maîtres, des colonies et de la métropole*, Bureau central de la Revue Encyclopédique, Paris 1830, pp. 111–112.
18. Victor Schœlcher, *Des colonies françaises, abolition immédiate de l'esclavage* [1842], Editions du CTHS, Paris 1998, pp. 400–404.
19. Cochut, "De la colonisation de la Guyane française," *Revue des deux mondes*, t. 11 (1845), p. 522.
20. Victor Schœlcher, *Histoire de l'esclavage pendant les deux dernières années* [1847], t. 2, Emile Désormeaux, Pointe-à-Pitre 1973, p. 424.
21. Ibid., p. 426.
22. Saint-Quantin and Sauvage were two Guyanan colonists who supported Lechevalier's project.
23. Schœlcher, *Histoire de l'esclavage*, pp. 428–429.
24. Nelly Schmidt, *Abolitionnistes de l'esclavage et réformateurs des colonies, 1820–1851*, Karthala, Paris 2000, Document 73, p. 631.
25. Ibid., Document 196, p. 954.
26. Schœlcher, *La vérité aux ouvriers et cultivateurs de la Martinique*, Pagnerre, Paris 1849, pp. 195–196.
27. Lescallier claimed to have extensive experience in the colonies of several European nations. Colonel Malenfant was on friendly terms with many large-scale planters in Saint Domingo, and considered that calm persuasion was the best means of returning the mulattos and blacks of this independent island to French rule.
28. In his *Traité de l'association domestique-agricole* (Paris 1822), Fourier envisaged the division of product in the phalange as follows: 5/12 to labour, 4/12 to capital, and 3/12 to talent.
29. Louis Blanc, *Organisation du travail*, Bureau de la société de l'industrie fraternelle, Paris 1839; 5th edition 1848.
30. Michel Chevalier, *Cours d'économie politique fait au Collège de France*, Capelle, Paris 1855, pp. 23–24.
31. Louis Reybaud, "Introduction," *Journal des économistes*, t.1, vol. 1, January 1842, p. 8.
32. According to Schmidt, Schœlcher's proposals involved a "colonial Fourierism," envisaging the transformation of colonial exploitation into *phalanstères* based upon the association of agricultural workers (*Victor Schœlcher*, Fayard, Paris 1994, p. 55). Léo Elisabeth argues that in promoting the Boyer plan, Schœlcher did, like Lechevalier and his disciples, envisage the transformation of French American colonies into a kind of *phalanstère* ("Rémunération du travail libre et question agraire à la Martinique et dans les colonies françaises d'Amérique," in *Esclavage, résistances et abolitions*, p. 309). The *phalanstère* project, or at least Fourier's idea of the phalange, was based on association not only in work, but also in the daily life of families both rich and poor. The aim was the creation of true community. There is no sense of this in the proposals made by Lechevalier and Schœlcher.
33. Schœlcher, *Des colonies françaises*, p. 402.
34. Ibid.

35. Horace Say, "De quelques mesures récentes touchant les finances," *Journal des économistes*, April-July 1848, p. 212.
36. The Moravian Brethren were Protestants from Moravia, today in the eastern part of the Czech Republic.
37. Agénor de Gasparin, *Esclavage et traite*, Joubert, Paris 1838, pp. 143–144.
38. Ibid., p. 144.
39. Alexis de Tocqueville, *Rapport fait au nom de la commission chargée d'examiner la proposition de M. de Tracy, relative aux colonies*, 1839, *Œuvres complètes d'Alexis de Tocqueville*, t. III, vol. 1, Gallimard, Paris 1962, p. 46.
40. [Commission de Broglie], *Rapport fait au ministre secrétaire d'Etat de la marine et des colonies*, Imprimerie royale, Paris 1843, p. 157.
41. Ibid., p. 305.
42. Ibid., p. 364.
43. Tocqueville, article published in *Le Siècle,* December 6, 1843, in *Ecrits et discours politiques, Œuvres complètes d'Alexis de Tocqueville*, p. 105.
44. Cochut, "De la colonisation de la Guyane française," p. 538—our emphasis.
45. Ibid., pp. 538–539.
46. Ibid., p. 539.
47. Schœlcher, *Des colonies françaises*, pp. 397–398.
48. André Daniel Laffon de Ladebat, *Discours sur la nécessité et les moyens de détruire l'esclavage dans les colonies*, Bordeaux 1788, p. 24.
49. Ibid., pp. 27–28.
50. Benjamin-Sigismond Frossard, *La cause des esclaves nègres et des habitans de la Guinée, portée au tribunal de la justice, de la religion, de la politique ou Histoire de la traite et de l'esclavage des nègres, preuves de leur illégitimité, moyens de les abolir sans nuire ni aux colonies, ni aux colons*, Lyon 1789, p. 280.
51. A.-G. Kersaint, *Moyens proposés à l'Assemblée Nationale, pour rétablir la paix et l'ordre dans les Colonies*, impr. du Cercle social, Paris 1792, pt. 2, p. 25. Less radical, Bonnemain during the same year proposed that when slaves were emancipated measures should be taken "that the interest of colonist and former slave would require": that emancipated slaves should continue to enjoy the use of a hut, their tools, and a small plot of land; land would be ceded to them on payment of a fee, or they would work for a daily wage (Antoine-Jean-Thomas Bonnemain, *Régénération des colonies ou moyens de restituer graduellement aux hommes leur état politique et d'assurer la prospérité des Nations; et Moyens pour rétablir promptement l'ordre dans les colonies françaises*, impr. du Cercle Social, Paris 1792, p. 80).
52. Malouet, *Mémoire sur l'esclavage des nègres*, p. 114.
53. MDLDMFY, *Mémoire sur l'esclavage des nègres contenant réponse à divers écrits qui ont été publiés en leur faveur*, 1790, pp. 49–50, note G.
54. Saint-Cyran, *Réfutation du projet des Amis des noirs*, pp. 24–25.
55. Richard Arena, "Sismondi et la transition de l'esclavage au métayage," *Economies et sociétés*, série *Œconomia*, 2009.
56. Sismondi, "De la condition dans laquelle il faut placer les nègres en les affranchissant," *Revue mensuelle d'économie politique*, December 1833, p. 415.
57. Ibid., p. 421.
58. Ibid., p. 427.
59. Jean Charles Léonard Sismondi, *Études d'économie politique*, 1837–1838, t. I, Slatkine, Geneva 1980, pp. 297–301.

60. Baron de Cools, *De l'agriculture coloniale en réponse à M. de Sismondi, lettre adressée à M. le rédacteur en chef de la Revue mensuelle d'économie politique*, Imprimerie de Moquet et Cie, January 1834, p. 4.
61. Ibid., p. 23.
62. This description is made even more tendentious by the fact that in Guadeloupe slavery had been very bloodily restored.
63. de Cools, *De l'agriculture coloniale*, p. 29.
64. Ibid., p. 32.
65. This report is reproduced in the *Report of the Acting Committee to the Standing Committee of West India Planters and Merchants*, Maurice & Co., London, December 1843, p. 67. The French translation is in *Précis de l'abolition de l'esclavage dans les colonies anglaises*, vol. 5, p. 157.
66. *Précis de l'abolition de l'esclavage dans les colonies anglaises*, vol. 5, p. 99.
67. Ibid., pp. 297–302.
68. Ibid., pp. 303–307.
69. *Commission instituée, par décision royale du 24 mai 1840,. . . Rapport fait au ministre secrétaire d'Etat de la marine et des colonies*, pp. 146–147.
70. Ibid., pp. 352–353.
71. He based his proposal on the works of Paul Daubrée, *La question coloniale sous le rapport industriel*, Malteste, Paris 1841.
72. Schœlcher, *Histoire de l'esclavage*, tome 2, p. 380. Gustave Du Puynode made a very similar proposal in 1847. He also added that, especially in British Guyana, blacks had bought up very large estates to cultivate in common. He considered that these associations combined the advantages of large-scale cultivation and that of smallholding—Gustave Du Puynode, *De l'esclavage et des colonies*, Joubert, Paris 1847, pp. 76–77.
73. Cited by Horace Say, "De quelques mesures récentes touchant les finances," *Journal des économistes*, April-July 1848, p. 211.
74. Wage labor is thus a relation of hire, which is itself a commercial relationship like any other, but with a negative connotation since it implies a form of subordination similar to that of master and servant. Article 1779 of the 1804 Civil Code states that "There are two main kinds of hire of work and industry: 1. hire of working people who engage with someone to provide services; 2. carriers by land or by water who conduct the carriage of persons or goods." In his study of the interconnection of economic and legal doctrine Jean-Michel Poughon makes the following comment on this: "Although the legal definition seems to give precedence to the wills of the parties involved, economists tend to include the object of this contract itself, labour, so that analysis would as a consequence include the hiring of services in the domain of exchange." *Histoire doctrinale de l'échange*, Libraire Générale de Droit et de Jurisprudence, Paris 1987, p. 131. It was not until the end of the nineteenth century that this aspect of economic subordination was recognized as part of the labor contract. See Vatin and Steiner, "Après l'abolition de l'esclavage: mise au travail, contrainte et salariat," *Economies et sociétés*, série *Œconomia*, 2009.
75. Sismondi, "De la condition dans laquelle il faut placer les nègres en les affranchissant," p. 418. Our emphasis.
76. Sismondi, *Etudes sur l'économie politique*, tome 1, pp. 300–301.
77. Sismondi, "De la condition dans laquelle il faut placer les nègres en les affranchissant," p. 413.

78. Aimé Césaire, Introduction to *Esclavage et colonisation par Victor Schœlcher*, Presses Universitaires de France, Paris 1948, p. 9.
79. Marx, *Le capital, critique de l'économie politique*, French translation, vol. 1, Gallimard, Paris 1968, p. 1196.
80. Robert Castel, *Les métamorphoses de la question sociale. Une chronique du salariat*, Fayard, Paris 1995, p. 155.
81. Ibid., p. 323. The exact passage runs as follows: "The proletariat is encamped in the midst of Occidental society without being housed in it" (Auguste Comte, *Système de politique positive, ou Traité de sociologie instituant la religion de l'Humanité*, vol. 2, Larousse, Paris 1851–1853, p. 411).
82. "Ultimately, the exploitation of man by man that we have shown existing in the past in the form of slavery, its most direct, most uncouth form, continues at a much higher level in the relationship of proprietors to workers, or masters and wage workers. . . . The relationship of master to wage worker is the final transformation of slavery. If the exploitation of man by man is no longer as brutal as it was in Antiquity; if it appears to us today to have moderated, it is no less real." Saint-Amand Bazard and Prosper Enfantin, *Doctrine de Saint-Simon. Exposition. Première année*, 2nd edition, Au Bureau de l'Organisateur, Paris 1830, pp. 174–175. The same argument is taken up by Proudhon in his sixth study—Work—of his major text *De la justice dans la Révolution et dans l'Eglise. Nouveaux principes de philosophie pratique*, vol. 2, Garnier Frères, Paris 1858, pp. 147–148.
83. "In a federal republic the proletariat and slavery appear to be equally inadmissible: there must be a tendency to their abolition." Pierre-Joseph Proudhon, *Du principe fédératif* [1863], in *Œuvres complètes de P.-J. Proudhon*, Librairie Marcel Rivière, Paris 1959, p. 538. To effect this, he proposed "to attack the white proletariat at its source, taking control of wage labourers and by organising, besides political guarantees, a system of economic guarantees." It should be noted that at this time slavers in the Southern states denounced the situation of workers in the North as "wage slavery"—Eric Foner, *Free Soil, Free Labour, Free Men. The Ideology of the Republican Party before the Civil War*, Oxford University Press, New York 1970.
84. Schœlcher, *Des colonies françaises*, 1998, p. 61.

CHAPTER 9
Justice and Utility

While economists, abolitionists, and colonists questioned the relationship between justice and utility, they obviously did not all understand this relationship in the same way.

Following Du Pont, a great number of economists and anti-slavers proclaimed the harmony of utility and justice for all parties: the interests of plantation owners, slaves, the nation—indeed, all mankind—could join together and move forward; all would benefit, both morally and economically, from the abolition of slavery. Some did think that interests diverged, at least in the short term. They sought therefore to determine a hierarchy between the various agents to determine a *general interest* which could counter some particular interests. This was an exercise that was all the more delicate since political economy after Adam Smith maintained that it was by allowing the free play of private interests that one most effectively realized the collective interest. The coincidence of justice with utility was ultimately recognized more by those who, like Du Pont, based their arguments on a deontological conception of justice than by authors such as Say and Comte who, adopting the utilitarian philosophy of Jeremy Bentham, rejected the idea of natural rights.

Colonists were most definitely part of this debate. They too mobilized a hierarchy between the various agencies set in play by the relationship of justice and utility, a hierarchy that differed from those of economists and abolitionists with regard to the role and extent of involvement of the nation.[1]

THE STRENGTH OF MORALITY AND ECONOMIC SELF-INTEREST

Having proclaimed the primacy of morality over economic self-interest, Du Pont asserted that "Injustice is a bad housewife; she buys everything too dearly. Justice does not pay nothing, but (as the word suggests) pays a just price. It is benevolence that gets everything cheap."[2] For Du Pont, political economy contributed greatly to the triumph of justice by highlighting the common interests of slaves, masters, colonies, and nation. Calculation reinforced morality by showing that, properly understood, self-interest indicated no more than what has to be done.

Nineteenth-century abolitionists saw in the coincidence of justice and utility the means to support one line of argument with another. When in 1814 Sismondi published his pamphlet *De l'intérêt de la France à l'égard de la traite des nègres* (*France's Interest related to the Slave Trade*), he was praised in the French press for treating the slavery question solely from the standpoint of economic interest, disregarding all moral conditions. Sismondi responded to this praise as follows:

> I spoke the language that I thought most appropriate to be heard. If violent passions had not been excited, if the obstinacy of the party spirit did not stifle the lights of reason and those of the gospel, I would have spoken to the French in a language worthy of them and which I believe they are still prepared to hear; I would have repeated to them the motto of their former knights: *Do what you must, come what may.*[3]

The argument from utility was presumed to be the most effective line for public debate, the one most adapted to the way that European society thought, and where the language of interest was accepted in step with the development of trade and industry. It was of value only to the extent that it could eventually assist in the triumph of the moral principle.

Breaking with the predominant deontological morality of abolitionist thinkers, Say followed Bentham in rejecting the theory of natural law. According to him, a moral decision followed from a well-made calculation, a calculation in which all the relevant circumstances of the problem were taken into account and, above all, in which all the consequences of the proposed solution were contained. If there was a marked difference between deontological and utilitarian conceptions at the level of principles, this did not apply to the conclusions that Say derived from these principles. For him, a moral principle, properly applied, dictated the solution to the political problems of his time in the same way as had happened in ancient Greece. In his *Essai sur le principe de l'utilité* (*Essay on the Principle of Utility*), developed from his teaching at the Athénée Royal in the early days of the Restoration and later published after his death, he linked political and moral sciences closely together. Having presented Bentham's modern utilitarianism, he based his argument on the nature of interests:

> When virtue prescribes the sacrifice of a *lesser* interest to a *major* interest; of a *passing* interest to a *durable* interest; of a *precarious* and doubtful interest to an *assured* and untroubled interest, this is only another way of expressing our *well understood interest*.

Public morality, therefore, does not differ from private morality:

> It is agreed that those who manage the interests of nations sacrifice what is honest to what is useful; and let us say quite frankly that this morality, far too usual and commonly pursued, is detestable; this is what has brought down the greatest evil upon nations. No, even in the relations between peoples, there is no difference between the useful and the honest. What is honest is, moreover, what is most useful.[4]

Moreover, Say never tried to use the utilitarian calculus in the way Bentham had prescribed, for any such calculation was technically impossible.[5]

Comte also took an unusual position in analyzing the slave system from a utilitarian point of view. Before going on to denounce those who, following Smith, believed that to judge the impact of slavery on wealth it was sufficient to compare the cost to the contractor of work performed by a slave with that done by a free man, he stated that any assessment by an economist must be based on the interest of humanity, and not on that of particular groups:

> We, who do not know what the legitimate price is for the ability to do violence to men, to children or to women . . . ; we, in whose eyes slaves are men just as much as their masters, and who must calculate the cost of a product not to this or that individual, but to the entire human race; we, who cannot discount the violence and miseries to which people are subjected for the pleasure of a small number of individuals—we must reason in a different way to the way in which the owners of men do.[6]

If the economist has to explain the effects of slavery on the increase or decrease of wealth he must not forget that wealth is only a *means* that must be evaluated in terms of the qualitative effects that it has on nations.[7] Comte therefore slid from a *calculation* of the wealth produced in the slave regions to a *judgment* of the influence of slavery on production in such regions. He abandoned the quantitative approach so that he might take into account the way in which wealth was distributed among the various classes of the population; the consequences of these various modes of distribution on consumption; and finally, the total cost of the time and the trouble taken in acquiring such wealth.[8] This judgment led to a *total evaluation of the economic phenomenon* viewed from the perspective of its moral condition of existence, that which makes it a *legitimate economic act*.

Whether this coincidence of morality and political economy was gained as a result of a utilitarian calculation or was based upon natural law, this coincidence was a principle to which economists were especially attached. Joseph Droz placed political economy immediately after morality in the hierarchy of sciences;[9] Cochut wrote the entry "Morality: concordance with political economy" in the *Dictionnaire de l'économie politique* showing that the framework of analysis and the solutions offered by the two sciences were similar.[10] In his book *Le juste et l'utile ou rapports de l'économie politique avec la morale* (*Justice and Utility, on the relation between Political Economy and Morals*), Henri Dameth reviewed the contribution of political economy to the slavery question ten years after it had been abolished. He argued that political economy had shown that the work of the slave was more costly and less productive than free labor, that the land cultivated by slaves produced less than those cultivated by free labor, that slavery presents an almost insuperable obstacle to the improvement of agriculture and industry, to the growth and diffusion of wealth, and lastly, that it is the multiplication of capital and the employment of machinery that furnish the means of emancipation. He concluded by asking:

> If political economy has demonstrated all this, has it not done more for abolition than all moralists taken together, ancient and modern? Why did Plato and Aristotle conclude that slavery was an eternal institution, while at the same time identifying justice and utility, if not because they were unaware of what political economy found?[11]

To put it in the words of Henri Baudrillart: "The correspondence of justice and utility is the polar star of political economy; one must always be guided by its light."[12] Economists and militant abolitionists were, for the most part, guided by this star.

However, in this entanglement of morality and economic calculation, morality had the dominant role. If the cost of free labor proved to be higher than that of slave labor, Du Pont was clear that it would be necessary to pay more for sugar, or even to do without it, "rather than violate so cruelly the rights of humanity."[13]

THE NATION AND THE HIERARCHY OF INTERESTS

The primacy of justice over utility was a major element in debate over the relation of nation and colonies. The phrase "Rather the colonies perish than principles!" was the most extreme expression of this primacy. The idea was expressed in a short article written by Louis de Jaucourt for the *Encyclopédie*: "Traite des Nègres. Commerce d'Afrique,"[14] and it resurfaced in a striking fashion during a debate in the Constituent Assembly on the question of citizenship for persons of color that took place between May 11 and 15, 1791. Confronted with a threat of secession on the part of colonists, Du Pont took his argument of twenty years previous to its logical conclusion:

> If [the secession of the colonies] has to happen, if you find yourselves with a pressing need to sacrifice either justice or humanity, I say to you that your unique power is that of equity: that if you abandon this foundation, then you risk the safety of all the illustrious works that you have done for humanity; and so your interest, that of Europe, that of the world demands that you do not hesitate at all to sacrifice a colony rather than a principle.[15]

Responding to Moreau de Saint-Méry, who had proposed an amendment limiting the legislative powers of the National Assembly with respect to the status of slaves "to a formal and spontaneous demand to colonial assemblies," Maximilien de Robespierre defended the idea that any such amendment would dishonor the Assembly:

> There is great interest in the preservation of our colonies; but this interest is not without a relationship to our constitution; and the supreme interest of the nation and of the colonies themselves is that you preserve your liberty, and that you do not by your own hands undermine the foundations of this liberty. Rather that these colonies perish if you preserve them at such a price. Yes, if it is necessary to lose either our colonies, or our well-being, our glory, our liberty, I will repeat: let our colonies perish.[16]

In his commentary on this public debate published in his periodical *Les Révolutions en France*, Camille Desmoulins drew attention to the similarities in the positions adopted by two men whose politics were otherwise quite at variance. He thought the formulation to be sufficiently striking to repeat it in his conclusion: "In any case, we must always return, as does Du Pont, to the system of Robespierre and Pétion: let the colonies perish, rather than the principles!"[17] Freedom, natural right, prevails over usefulness; *moral and political interest*, the supreme interest, thus outweighs the *economic interest*.

Although the repeated opposition of settlers to this famous formula can be read as proof of their criminal blindness, many nineteenth-century abolitionists did not hesitate to adopt it during the final days of slavery to make clear that they would not want to retain colonies at the cost of maintaining slavery. Gasparin wrote to this effect in 1838,[18] as did Schœlcher and Puynode in 1842 and 1847.[19]

Besides the declamations made in the National Constituent Assembly, this famous phrase highlights the central role played by the *nation* in the debate on slavery, especially when interests diverge.

Three significant voices—those of Turgot, Condorcet, and finally Say—were raised in protest against the idea, developed by Du Pont and subsequently adopted by most of the abolitionists, that there was a coincidence of interest between slave-owners and the nation.

Turgot expressed himself briefly and privately. He sought to curb the computational impulses of his friend Du Pont, assuring him that injustice could be useful and could even happen without incurring the remorse of those who benefited from it, insofar as they did not mean to act unfairly and that they were not condemned by public opinion. Who benefited from crime in the case of modern slavery? Masters and merchants, for one, who could quickly make their fortune thanks to slave labor. They did harm to the colony since the interests of planters and trade were satisfied at the expense of the interests of the population at large (both in terms of its growth and its well-being, we can assume). In seeking to support his argument with empirical evidence of the very high wages enjoyed by free skilled workers in the West Indies, Turgot ultimately presented a tragic conception of the ever-possible dissociation of justice and utility.

In both editions of his book, Condorcet decoupled the planter interest (related to the amount of the net product) and that of trade and the nation (which depended on the growth of the gross product):

> The destruction of slavery would ruin neither colonies nor commerce; it would render the colonies more flourishing, it would increase commerce. It would do no more harm than prevent some barbarous men from fattening themselves with the sweat and blood of their brethren; in a word, the whole mass of men

would gain, while a few individuals would lose only the advantage of being able to commit with impunity a crime useful to their interests.[20]

Unlike Turgot, Condorcet did not dissociate utility from justice; he established, like Say and Comte would do later, a hierarchy of interests based on the principle that the economic interest of humanity—in this case that of the colonies and the nation—takes precedence over that of individuals. Justice and utility then march in step to the extent that calculation is only legitimate if it is applied to all men and women.

While Condorcet presumed that the productivity of the free worker would be greater than that of the slave, while also maintaining that the use of the latter was more profitable for the master, Say developed a more radical argument. A convinced abolitionist, he maintained that the master could, by violence, triumph over the idleness natural to every human being, while the self-interest of the free worker was too weak a spring to raise the productivity of the free laborer to the level of the slave. Although he forced the slave to work by using a whip, the planter was a good judge of his own interest, knowing how to preserve his human flock by tempering the severity of the abuse that he inflicted upon it. Matching the violence he inflicted on the slave against the gain he wanted to obtain, the master showed himself capable of *optimizing* (a term that Say obviously does not use) the product of the plantation. In so doing he adopted a behavior similar to that of the employer seeking to determine the optimal level of monetary incentive for work. Say was also saddened to come to conclusions that supported the arguments made by settlers. His chapter on "The profits [the gain] made from the slave" ends with this harrowing sentence: "For how long should books of political economy contain chapters like this one?"[21] He seems here to be closer to the tragic vision developed by Turgot than to the optimism of the utilitarian philosophy that he professes elsewhere. His refusal to align the interests of slaves, masters, and the nation was, as we have seen previously, very badly accepted by the abolitionists. The basis of his opposition to slavery and colonialism was the higher interests of the nation. The nation at issue here in political economy was formed of consumers seeking to obtain the goods they consumed at the best price in a free trade context, and therefore regardless of their place of origin. This is how the greatest utility can be obtained. The protectionist and fiscal system established to support production and trade with the West Indies enriched traders and settlers to the detriment of consumers who paid more for sugar than it would cost if bought from foreign producers. The elimination of taxes on imported sugar (at a rate of 50 percent of their value) would, according to Say, provide annual savings of 25 million francs that the French could devote to other purchases without reducing trading profits and the receipts of the exchequer: he added that "It is even probable that trade and the Treasury would receive more; for a fall of one quarter in the price of this commodity would considerably increase consumption.[22] The changing economic climate and the associated decline in the profitability of estates during the 1820s helped Say out of the dilemma in which his defense of the productivity of slave labor had placed him.[23] The enrichment of settlers was not a sign of a higher level of utility achieved by French society; it was no more than the counterpart of what was levied on French sugar consumers. Say is here in line with Smithian political economy, which continued to denounce the harmful consequences of mercantilist politics for international trade and the absurdity of colonial rule: "The enslavement of our colonies, far from providing us with new outlets for our products, serves only to limit them."[24] To those who objected that this policy protected the interests of Caribbean producers, Say responded by calculating the profit and loss for the nation arising from the maintenance of colonial rule. The gain made by the nation was equal to that made by traders and settlers, to which must also be added taxes collected in the colonies, subtracting the costs of administration and defense. According to the figures at his disposal, the West Indies did not cover the costs that they engendered. The harmonization of justice and utility (this being understood as the realization of the general interest) required the establishment of a system of exchange freed from state intervention and the private exploitation to which it can give rise. Pellegrino Rossi, successor to Say in the chair of political economy of the Collège de France, also established a hierarchy of interests, a particular interest—in this case that of those who owned slaves—being revealed as often contrary to the general interest, which was the increase of national wealth, the sole concern of public economy.[25]

This denunciation of the very principle of a colonial economy remained a minority view in French abolitionist discourse. It had, however, already been argued vigorously by the Comte de Mirabeau and Étienne Clavière during the Revolutionary period.[26] Gasparin would repeat it again in 1838.[27] Like Say, these authors sought to show that colonies cost the nation more than they brought in; like him, they advocated free trade, and the end of exclusive colonial trade.

For Turgot, Condorcet, and Say, the planters derived from their slave labor a higher profit than they would have obtained if they had employed free laborers. However, justice and utility usually coincided, at least for the latter two writers, since abolition, failing to satisfy the interest of the planters, permitted the realization of the general interest. Everybody would benefit. A desire that justice and utility triumph on a global level was not peculiar to these authors. Many abolitionists linked the emancipation of colonial slaves with the reform of the international division of labor. The "African project"[28] testifies to this.

THE NATION AND THE AFRICAN PROJECT

The beneficial effects of the abolition of slavery could be extended beyond the French nation. According to Du Pont, it could establish a new division of labor on a global scale, based on the transfer of European knowledge and capital to Africa where sugar refineries could be established, while the colonies, their lands exhausted by the cultivation of cane, could undergo an agricultural reconversion.[29] Du Pont called upon citizens to take up this idea, which would ensure the eternal glory of the first sovereign to put it into practice.

The idea was not entirely new. In 1763 Nicolas Baudeau, a fervent physiocrat, had advocated free trade in France's commerce with Africa and East Asia.[30] He set his project within the framework of the French colonial empire: the idea was to make the islands of France, Réunion, and Madagascar the center of cultivation and manufacturing for Africa and Eastern Asia. The territory of these colonies being immense, it was necessary to introduce a great number of Africans and Asians who, bought anywhere that they were available for sale, would not be transformed into slaves but into free workers, into citizens of the colonies, civilized and disciplined. Free persons, including the French who wanted to settle in these colonies, would find there all possible safety and comfort. The mission of the East India Company would be reduced to two objects: on one hand the establishment of a maritime communications service between the metropolis and the colonies, but also between these and the various "posts" in Africa and East Asia; and on the other hand, the increase of the population of the three islands together with the development of suitable crops and manufactures. The French "posts" located in the various regions would be a "refuge" for French merchants who would find there suitable and safe houses protected militarily from occasional outbreaks of disorder. They could never take over the territory or claim exclusive trading rights to the detriment of France or other European nations.

In volume XII of his *Histoire générale de l'Asie, de l'Afrique et de l'Amérique* (*General History of Asia, Africa and America*), published the same year as the two texts by Du Pont on slavery, Pierre-Joseph-André Roubaud, member of the physiocratic school, also advocated the establishment of a new international division of labor. His argument followed two axes. First, he invoked the political and moral principles developed by Physiocracy, foremost among which was personal freedom, the inalienable right of every human being. Secondly, he applied the logic of interest to European trade and not, as did Du Pont, to the slave owner. This perspective perhaps explains Turgot's praise for his text, even though he deplored Du Pont's computational approach. The abandonment of a slave trade that was depopulating Africa and creating wars would be of benefit to Europe, and it would enable the creation of new trade with a continent capable of supplying sugar, coffee, indigo, cotton, syrups, woods, and the skins that the American colonies produced: "It would obviously be to the interest of Western Europe to introduce into this land the cultures and arts and the knowledge that it lacks; and the ruinous establishments it maintains, sword in hand, in the two Indies."[31] The meeting with Africa had to be effected under the seal of the friendship, as an alliance; it was necessary to trade with the Africans, to bring them enlightenment, to teach them how to make use of their soil and their products, all of which were, after all, recommendations similar to those formulated by Du Pont. Like Du Pont, in his peroration Roubaud urged Europeans to understand where their true advantage lay:

> If the self-interest of others [that of Africans] does not move them, will they resist the evidence of their own self-interest, because instead of heroically unjust designs, plans will be put to them whose success requires only patience, equity, which are natural virtues. I do not want to believe it; I will speak as if they are understanding me.[32]

The idea took off. It can be found in the abbé Raynal's *l'Histoire philosophique des deux Indes* (*Philosophical History of the two Indies*), in the abolitionist writings of the abbé Sibire, of Frossard, of Lescallier, of Lanthenas, of Bonnemain, of Clavière, of Mirabeau, in Condorcet's *Esquisse d'un tableau historique des progrès de l'esprit humain* (which extended the project to Asia, following the example of Baudeau), in the writings of the abbé Grégoire and, much later, in those of Hippolyte Carnot, a French stateman, and of Schœlcher.[33] On November 28, 1792, the National Convention, sensitive to anti-slavery arguments, had also referred to its committees for Commerce and for Colonies Kersaint's proposal to examine the condition of the agricultural establishment founded by the English Society of Friends of the Blacks in Sierra Leone, and to provide it with means for developing the production of colonial commodities in Africa. Later Carnot and Schœlcher added the example of Liberia to that of Sierra Leone, praised by the abbé Grégoire. A modern historian observed that

> One can just as well . . . discover [in this project] the premises of the future colonial empire of the nineteenth century—when the most brutal conquest purified itself through the pretext of exporting human rights—that it was the beginning of a policy of cooperation between peoples based on the development of trade.[34]

The abolitionists adopted, no doubt sincerely, the second approach. Based on the free labor and the consent of peoples, the African project once again shows the convergence of justice (which a civilized Europe has to propagate) and utility: "We do not halt," exclaimed the abbé Sibire, on the coasts of Guinea;

> let us penetrate the interior of this land. Let us look not for men, but things. Leave in peace the hands that cultivate it, and not force them into the eternal rest which we prescribe for them, in bloody abductions that we gladly carry out, devouring ourselves. . . . The need for trade will bring industry, and human victims will no longer be currency or commodity. Yes, let us cease being ferocious, we'll be all the richer for it.[35]

A USELESS REFORM

Colonists sought to justify the continuation of slavery by questioning the notion of utility used by those whom they contemptuously called "philosophers" and "philanthropists." The aim of their own calculations was to demonstrate that it would be impossible to maintain the plantation system if slaves were replaced with free labor, so ruining the colonial economy and hence weakening the power and wealth of the nation.

They argued that the question of justice could not be answered without taking account of a racial hierarchy, the existence of which was said to be demonstrated by the behavior of blacks. Their indolence and lack of interest in what the future might bring were presented as symptoms of a native inferiority.

Félix Patron, a colonist, stated in 1831 that the "negro" was "*in his very essence* idle and ferocious," that European "philanthropists" who demanded the abolition of slavery did not know what blacks were like, and so were as a consequence unable to judge what might be of advantage to them, or what might harm them. Liberty, as the example of Saint Domingo showed, necessarily led them to commit the most horrible crimes and plunged them into poverty.[36]

In 1843 Bovis, the rapporteur for the commission set up by the Guadeloupe Colonial Council to advise on the Broglie report, maintained that

> we intend neither to blame nor degrade the slave. We put him in his proper place: for us slavery becomes a social function, a social function most fitted to the aptitude of the negro, because for them there is no aptitude for intelligence equal to ours.[37]

He went on to add, while making little effort to conceal his incredulity:

> We must believe, we must at least hope that through increasing contact with our own intelligence this indolent and limited intelligence will grow and develop. Well! Let the bridle loose; if and when the negro performs well, we will not be obliged to make him do so; it will be of advantage to all and society will gain by it; since physical forces remain the same, new intellectual faculties would come to our assistance.

According to Bovis, slavery is the most suitable condition for the black while awaiting this hypothetical evolution. In perfect harmony with his nature, this cannot be unjust.

Malouet put forward a much more subtle justification for the continuation of slavery. In 1788 he argued that "it is no doubt awful to calculate the price of men in this way, men who have become commodities, and to find oneself drawn by the imperious law of necessity to such tragic results."[38] Persuaded that the institution would one day perish, he went against the opinion of the larger planters of Saint Domingo in favoring state intervention to moderate slavery, an easing of conditions that would preserve the interest of the masters while gradually improving the status of slaves. Jacquemard's *Réflexions* expressed a similar sentiment: "Nobody will deny that slavery is an evil. It is to be hoped that this can be completely remedied by the complete liberation of the Negroes."[39] He stated that this is the position of the colonists: "If one simply asks: is slavery an evil? Is it not fair to prevent the Negroes from being deprived of their liberty? There is not a single American planter for whom the evidence of his own senses would not force him to confirm this."[40] Presenting himself as an Anglo-American planter, he asserted that several planters living in London, "as commendable by their humanity as they are distinguished by their fortune," were ready to cooperate "zealously in the modification of slavery, giving the signs that only they can supply."[41]

The unjust nature of slavery was often recognized by colonists so that they might better explain the relative nature of this injustice. Comparison of the living conditions of slaves with those of day laborers in Europe—slaves, they argued, being happier because their existence was less precarious than that of day laborers—only went to show that the logic of domination prevailed in all societies, whatever the system of work adopted. Colonists thereby used the rhetorical strategy that Hirschman called the thesis of "inanity": it is of no use to proceed with reforms that a law more powerful than human decision—in this case, domination of the poor by the rich—renders ineffective.[42]

"The best is the enemy of the good." This phrase formed the epigraph for an anonymous pamphlet that in 1791 claimed to represent the perspective of all French colonists in the Americas, and which summarized a second form of argument for slavery. The point was simple: the abolition of slavery would lead to a situation worse than that which already existed—according to Hirschman, another typical line of reactionary argument.[43] This assertion also implied the existence of a calculation in the sense of both categorization and quantification: one has to make sure of the reality of the evil that one proposes to fight, measuring the gains and the negative effects, to make sure that by striving for the best one does not end up with the worst.

Petit had already proposed the general principle:

> We can only praise those who seek to reduce the miseries of humanity; but we must ascertain the reality and the greatness of the evil so that we can put ourselves in a position to deal with it; then propose practical means to stop the evil; propose them in good time; balance advantages and disadvantages; and if the principle of evil has no remedy, if the sum of good outweighs the sum of evil; limit the effort to diminishing the sum of evil.[44]

Brushing aside the idea that the colonies exist only for the enrichment of the colonists and the pleasure of consumers eager for sugar, he maintained that one had to look elsewhere for the prime purpose of the colonies and of the slave trade:

> The maintenance and the increase of a navy, the sale of commodities and of goods from the metropolis, the balance of trade between nations, the useful employments that result from this commerce for many men of all kinds; the sustenance for so many families against whom fortune turns its face in Europe; all of these have in France led to an imperious law directing that every possible means be pursued so that the exclusive possession of these commodities be not left to rival nations, or enemies of her power.[45]

Malouet analyzed the hypothesis of the abolition of the slave trade from a similar point of view:

> If we renounce the slave trade, they [all the other people of Europe] will not give it up. They would replace, by increased cultivation, the withering of ours;

so there would be on the globe the same sum of slaves; humanity would gain nothing from it.

Ruined by this unilateral gesture, France would lose outlets for its agriculture and its manufactures, plus its economic, military, and political power. His conclusion is unforgiving:

> It is with regret that I thus rebel against the spirit of beneficence, which disseminates and accredits the opinions I have here opposed. There is a kind of shame or courage in presenting the need to maintain the established order for the cultivation of the colonies, the usefulness of which is undoubtedly balanced by vicious results; but which cannot be abandoned without the result of greater evils.[46]

Jacquemard protested: "Enthusiasts will cry out in vain: perish all arrangements incompatible with morality and justice! The statesman cannot do the same; he is not always allowed to shape his conduct according to the exact theory of moral rectitude."[47] Duval de Sanadon, who did not shrink from printing in his book of 1786 an epigraph taken from the Roman poet Terence—*Homo sum: humani nihil a me alienum puto*[48]—denounced the "fiery declaimers," the "rigorous moralists," the "speculative philosophers" who proposed their unworkable systems with an insulting smile: "It is indeed easier to imagine a beautiful ideal, and to modify it at will, than to present palpable truths, and to render the good possible."[49] Three years later he set out his view in this regard, concluding that it was ultimately a question of "verifying the good that was presented as the real, and of realizing the best thought to be possible."[50]

In 1802 C. Belu, a colonist, bluntly stated that the interest of France had to take precedence over that of slaves:

> In truth, if you follow them at work, the severity that one is forced to apply, you will see in the background that humanity turns its eyes away; but notes that she looks upon France with a sense of consolation. Indeed, she finds there many workshops in which industry and existence are closely related to the condition of the Negroes.

And he goes on to cite the French philosopher Claude-Adrien Helvetius, who maintained that humanity is at times pitiless toward individuals, and that the question of public safety renders everything legitimate, and even virtuous[51]; which would be an incautious quotation when one knows that Helvetius, in the name of humanity and having made a basic utilitarian calculation, advocated the renunciation of the consumption of sugar, a "pleasure bought by the tears and the death of so many unfortunate people."[52]

Until the end of slavery the colonists relied on the primacy of national interest to explain the need to preserve the system.

The most successful presentation of the effects of abolition on the greater collective good can be found in Dupin's writings, whose evaluation of the productive forces of France and England[53] makes him one of the greatest calculators during the first half of the nineteenth century. His calculations were aimed at demonstrating that the reactionary thesis formulated as "the best is the enemy of good" had solid foundations.

Dupin was a major asset for colonists in their controversy with abolitionists, since he never missed an opportunity to argue in favor of cane sugar production using the slave system. While he made extensive use of his talent for calculation, he never sought to answer the arguments of his adversaries regarding the relative costs of free and slave labor. The three memoranda he published in 1844 and 1845 exemplify the way in which he defended colonial interests.[54]

The first opens with a denunciation of the position adopted by "narrow-minded and mistaken theoreticians" since the Restoration who saw only a loss of colonial production and who "invited us to allow other countries to produce on their own land the colonial commodities that are indispensable to us; and to receive from their hands what we ourselves could produce through our activity, our constancy and our industry on a soil that has become French."[55] The wisdom of government having protected France from this "anti-national error," the colonies enjoyed the great prosperity that had fostered the development of the merchant navy, which was in turn indispensable for the development of the navy and national greatness. Dupin argued in terms of the national interest when he maintained that the colonies must enjoy the same protection as did the metropole: a perspective opposed both to protectionists—who, in the debate on the sugar question, argued that protection of the metropolitan sugar beet industry was a priority as a source of employment for nationals—and to the views of liberals who advocated free trade. Having made the colonial question one of national defense, Dupin then calculated the losses suffered by England following the emancipation of 1833. He added together the additional costs in the production of sugar, rum, and coffee; the amount of compensation; the capital cost of the apprenticeship period; and the losses incurred by British trade, arriving at a total of 2.5 billion francs, a sum shared equally between the colonies and the metropolis. Modest in his triumph, he concluded that he would "not add one word to these calculations;

it is up to the government in its wisdom to weigh such considerable losses in regard to a goal attained with so many imperfections."[56]

The following memorandum continued the argument by establishing the connection between the national perspective as he understood it and the conservative position adopted by the colonists: in seeking the best, abolitionists would bring about a situation worse than that of the present, also for slaves who were already freed. Once again basing his argument upon the experience of British colonies after emancipation, he too deplored the rash and sudden increase of wages and the reduction in the quantity of work that followed, "this excessive level of payment only ensuring that the number of blacks quickly diminished."[57] Abolition had led to the ruin of colonists and, as a result, also of the blacks. The progressive reduction in the export from Britain to its colonies of fabric and leather during 1839–1841—spending on clothing being "one of the most reliable indicators of a population's well-being or poor situation"—demonstrated how serious the situation had become. Blacks had ceased working after emancipation, the population of the British colonies had been led to reduce its expenditure on clothing, Dupin pointed to the 47 percent fall in the importation of fabric.

Applying the same criteria to living conditions in the French colonies, and using data from the first four years of the decades 1820s, 1830s, and 1840s, he calculated that there had been an increase in the volume of exported fabric and leather from France to its territories during the previous twenty years. He emphasized that the volume of luxury fabrics (silk and wool, extra-fine linen, and cotton) had fallen, while that of ordinary cotton, linen, and hemp had risen. The cause was clear:

> Placing these two facts together demonstrates that it is generally the lower orders of society, in a word workers and blacks, who prompt an increase in ordinary fabrics. To convince oneself of this important fact one need only ask after the situation of impartial and skilled observers: but it is more satisfying to see, as we will demonstrate, that the most authentic official documents lend this fact the significance of a truth shown most rigorously.[58]

To complete his argument Dupin demonstrated the improvement to slave nutrition in the French colonies using data on the growth in the import of cod between 1830 and 1841. He arrived at a rate of increase of 15 percent: "And so by way of a remarkable reconciliation negro slaves receive a quantity of animal food that is rather superior to that of our urban populations, and three times as great as that of our rural populations."[59]

Not only had emancipation in British colonies ruined the planters and checked the prosperity of the metropole, but it also had impoverished blacks, placing them in a situation that was deplorable by comparison with that of slaves in the French colonies. Proof of this was supplied through the calculation that a search for a better future had led to a worse present. All that Dupin had to do in his third memorandum was to praise the quality of French colonists in the army, navy, the sciences, letters and arts, and in the service of the monarchy. He finished by vilifying those modern economists who employed a British instrument—political economy—to attack the development of the navy and the colonies on which Britain had, however, founded its omnipotence; while Britain sought to overcome its miscalculations and persuade other nations to emancipate their slaves so that they might suffer the same losses, the same disasters that Britain had.[60]

During the final decade of slavery the idea that the slave was more fortunate than the laborer or the poor European peasant and had an interest in preserving his position recurred in colonial discourse. Proposing to grant civil rights to blacks while keeping them on the plantations through compulsory labor, Granier de Cassagnac claimed to be working in their favor:

> It is therefore in the interest of the slaves that I speak; it must be so, since philanthropists speak only for the sake of their vainglorious little sect and their doctrine of demolition. They claim that they wish to sacrifice the colonies to a principle; they are in error, and they lead those who listen to them into the same error. I too say, let the colonies perish, let the world perish, rather than a principle; because a principle is truth, and truth is God; but their system of emancipation is a folly and not a principle, for it is not true that slaves, even if they are hard-working and organised in families, are in a condition to resist the difficulties of a free and isolated life.[61]

By becoming a proletarian, the slave would suffer a degradation of his material and moral situation. According to Granier de Cassagnac, his proposed "emancipation" would prevent the ruin of the colonies without compromising the principles of morality and human dignity: "I do not know," he concludes, "if it is philanthropic; but I know it is right."[62]

Two years later Alphonse Maynard, a publicist, stated that emancipation was both "unjust and impolitic."[63] It was impolitic because it ruined cultivation, and it involved a serious assault on the maritime connections that should be the preserve of France, and on the prosperity of French ports and manufactures. It was unjust because it deprived the planter of the labor he needed, despoiling him under a vain pretext and without sufficient compensation for property acquired under the guarantee of law, but also because it "removed the black from a paternal regime only to subordinate him to an inflexible law, tearing him from "a contract . . . infinitely more gentle than this presumed liberty enjoyed by the French proletarian."[64] The colonists finally managed to align all interests but reached a conclusion diametrically opposed to that of Du Pont!

* * *

If all the actors in this debate agreed on the need to make justice and utility coincide, they differed on how to bring about this convergence, and how the philosophy of calculation might be applied. Two elements emerge from an examination of the ways in which justice and utility might be reconciled.

The significant difference between Kant's deontological morality and Bentham's utilitarianism played no significant role, since authors with an allegiance to the latter approach would not risk embarking on a calculation whose result would define what was just. Taking refuge in the idea that the right of the individual to self-determination is a *useful* right that is violated by slavery, they ultimately ended up in a position that was little different from that of the proponents of deontological morality.

The position of Du Pont and those who followed him among the abolitionists was based on the strong assumption of a perfect alignment of interests that only ignorance or lack of insight could mask. This position very much simplified the calculation, but some abolitionists went further and sought to establish a hierarchy between groups, and to explain that all might benefit from an undermining of the colonists' interests. The role of the nation and its extent is then of great importance, because for the largest group the interest of the nation outweighs that of the settlers and slaves with which everything had begun. In the peaceable and free-market vision of the world that was then dominant among economists, the colonies were a cost borne by consumers and French citizens, a cost that should be reduced or simply eliminated for the more daring of those who envisaged the emancipation of the colonies and the termination of colonial projects. The nation, made up of consumers, gained by buying at the best price, whatever the nationality of the producers might be. The interest of the colonists, who were neither economically efficient nor morally defensible, could not counter this line of argument. For the colonists the nation includes both colonies and metropole, together being part of a global power game in which maritime trade and the navy played a crucial role. Tropical exports were a decisive national asset in the struggle between France and the British Empire, respect for the interests of planters guaranteeing the interests of the various classes of the metropolitan population, and even those of . . . the slaves!

The border between these different conceptions of the nation would prove fragile. Faced with the Algerian question, the anticolonialism of

Say faltered: calling on the Enlightenment in his final writings, he left the door to European expansion open: to Asia through the British East India Company, as in Algeria.[65] Half a century later, liberal economists would be in favor of colonial expansion in the name of the logic of power which European nations had adopted. This would be an oxymoron for which the discourse of Paul Leroy-Beaulieu provides the most complete example.[66]

NOTES

1. The idea was suggested by Pétré-Grenouilleau, but he has not investigated this dimension for the period considered here—Pétré-Grenouilleau "Abolitionnisme et idée nationale: divorce et compromis, France, 1789–1831," in Pétré-Grenouilleau (ed.) *Abolir l'esclavage, Un réformisme à l'épreuve (France, Portugal, Suisse, XVIIIe-XIXe siècles)*, Presses Universitaires de Rennes, Rennes 2008.
2. Pierre Samuel Du Pont, "Observations importantes sur l'esclavage des nègres," *Les Éphémérides du citoyen*, vol. VI (1771), p. 218.
3. Sismondi, "Nouvelles réflexions sur la traite des nègres," [1814] in Sismondi, *Écrits d'économie politique, 1799–1815, Œuvres économiques complètes*, vol. 3, p. 407.
4. Say, *Leçons d'économie politique, Œuvres complètes de Jean-Baptiste Say*, vol. 4, Économica, Paris 2006, p. 140.
5. Jeremy Bentham, *An Introduction to the Principles of Morals and Legislation* [1789], Hafner Press, New York 1948, pp. 29–31. According to Bentham, the measurement of pleasure and pain could be effected in four dimensions: intensity, duration, certainty, and proximity. If one wanted to apply this to *action that produced* pleasure and pain there would be seven dimensions that Bentham would require to be taken into account, adding fecundity, purity, and extension to the original four. The plurality of dimensions of utility conceived in this way makes it very hard to identify a single metric allowing this list of dimensions to be transformed into a synthetic numerical indicator.
6. Charles Comte, *Traité de législation ou exposition des lois générales suivant lesquelles les peuples prospèrent, dépérissent ou restent stationnaires*, A. Sautelet et Cie, Paris 1827, p. 242.
7. Ibid.
8. Ibid., p. 244.
9. Joseph Droz, *Economie politique ou principes de la science des richesses*, 2nd edition, Renouard, Paris 1846, p. 2.
10. Cochut, "Morale," *Dictionnaire d'économie politique*, vol. 2, Guillaumin, Paris 1853.
11. Henri Dameth, *Le juste et l'utile*, Guillaumin, Paris 1859, p. 105.
12. Henri Baudrillart, *Manuel d'économie politique*, Guillaumin, Paris 1857, p. 33.
13. Pierre Samuel Du Pont, "Observations importantes sur l'esclavage des Nègres," *Les Éphémérides du citoyen*, vol. VI (1771), pp. 217–218.
14. "Perhaps it will be said that the colonies will quickly be ruined if negro slavery is abolished. But if that is so, is it necessary to conclude that this kind of human being must be so horribly mistreated so that we might become rich, or to provide us with our luxuries? It is true that the purses of highway robbers would be empty if theft were completely abolished; but do men have the right to make themselves

rich by cruel and criminal methods? By what right does a brigand steal from passers by? To whom is it allowed that they should become wealthy by harming their fellow creatures? Can it be legitimate to strip the human species of its most sacred rights solely for the satisfaction of his own avarice, his vanity, or his personal passions? No . . . rather let European colonies be destroyed than to render so many unfortunate!"

15. Speech by Du Pont to the Assemblée Nationale, May 13, 1791, *Archives parlementaires de 1787 à 1860, Première série (1787 à 1799)*, Société d'imprimerie et librairie administratives et des chemins de fer, Paris 1887, tome 25, p. 50, col. 1.
16. Speech of Robespierre to the Assemblée Nationale, May 13, 1791, *Archives parlementaires de 1787 à 1860, Première série (1787 à 1799)*, Société d'imprimerie et librairie administratives et des chemins de fer, Paris 1887, p. 60, col. 2.
17. Cited by Florence Gauthier, *Périssent les colonies plutôt qu'un principe. Contribution à l'histoire de l'abolition de l'esclavage 1789–1804*, Société des études robespierristes, Paris 2002, p. 101.
18. Gasparin, *Esclavage et traite*, pp. 51–52. Gasparin also stated that renunciation of the principle was not purely a problem of morality, but that it could ultimately harm the material interests of the nation.
19. Victor Schœlcher, *Des colonies françaises, Abolition immédiate de l'esclavage* [1842], Editions du CTHS, Paris 1998, 1842, p. 385.
20. Schwartz [Condorcet], *Réflexions sur l'esclavage des nègres*, Neuchatel 1781, p. 26.
21. Jean-Baptiste Say, *Traité d'économie politique ou simple exposition de la manière dont se forment, se distribuent et se consomment les richesses*, vol. 2, Déterville, Paris 1803, p. 249.
22. Say, *Cours complet d'économie politique pratique. Ouvrage destiné à mettre sous les yeux des hommes d'État, des propriétaires fonciers et des capitalistes, des savans, des agriculteurs, des manufacturiers, des négocians, et en général de tous les citoyens, l'économie des sociétés*, 1828–1830, in *Œuvres complètes de Jean-Baptiste Say*, vol. 1, Économica, Paris 2010, p. 253.
23. Say, *Traité d'économie politique*, vol. 2, p. 409.
24. Say, *Cours complet d'économie politique pratique*, vol. 1, p. 649.
25. Pellegrino Rossi, *Cours d'économie politique*, t. 2, Guillaumin, Paris 1865, p. 373.
26. Benot, *La Révolution française et la fin des colonies*, La Découverte, Paris 1987, pp. 111–114.
27. Gasparin, *Esclavage et traite*, pp. 53–76.
28. This position was more difficult for abolitionists to maintain in the eighteenth century, when planters demanded freedom of trade, than in the nineteenth when they invoked the colonial pact in order to secure protectionist measures with regard to foreign cane sugar and sugar beet producers. Clavière denounced the colonists' duplicity in claiming that colonial trade was indispensable for French producers, while demanding that their exclusive relationship be ended. See Étienne Clavière, *Adresse de la Société des amis des noirs à l'Assemblée nationale*, Imprimerie du Patriote François, Paris 1791, p. 61.
29. Du Pont, "Observations importantes sur l'esclavage des nègres," *Ephémérides du citoyen*, t. VI, (1771), p. 244.
30. Abbé Baudeau, *Idées d'un citoyen sur la puissance du roi et le commerce de la nation dans l'Orient*, Amsterdam, 1763.
31. Abbé Roubaud, *Histoire générale de l'Asie, de l'Afrique et de l'Amérique, contenant des discours sur l'histoire ancienne des peuples de ces contrées, leur histoire moderne et la description des lieux, avec des remarques sur leur histoire naturelle, et des observations*

sur les religions, les gouvernements, les sciences, les arts, le commerce, les mœurs, les caractères, etc., des nations, vol. 12, Des Ventes de la Doué, Paris 1770–1775, p. 205.

32. Ibid., p. 210.
33. Benot, *La Révolution française et la fin des colonies*, pp. 194–196; Dorigny, "Intégration républicaine des colonies et projets de colonisation de l'Afrique: civiliser pour émanciper?," in Bénot and Dorigny (eds.) *Grégoire et la cause des Noirs (1789–1831), combats et projets*, Société française d'histoire d'outre-mer, Association pour l'Etude de la Colonisation Européenne, 2000, pp. 89–104; Caroline Oudin-Bastide, "L'Afrique dans le discours abolitionniste de Victor Schœlcher," *Afrique & histoire*, 2005.
34. Bernard Gainot, "La Société des amis des noirs et des colonies, 1796–1799," in Dorigny and Gainot (eds.) *La société des amis des noirs*, pp. 312–313.
35. Abbé Sibire, *L'Aristocratie négrière, ou Réflexions philosophiques et historiques sur l'esclavage et l'affranchissement des Noirs. . .* , Lesclapart et Desray, Paris 1789, pp. 116–117.
36. F*.P. (Félix Patron according to Barbier), *Des noirs, de leur situation dans les colonies françaises, L'esclavage n'est-il pas un bienfait pour eux et un fardeau pour leurs maîtres?* Charles Mary, Paris 1831, pp. 23–24.
37. Conseil colonial de la Guadeloupe, "Rapport de la commission constituée de MM. de Bovis, Reiset, Rochoux, à la fin de Juillet 1843, sur le rapport de la commission instituée par le ministre sur les questions relatives à l'esclavage (Commission de Broglie)," ANOM, Généralités 171.
38. Pierre-Victor Malouet, *Mémoire sur l'esclavage des nègres dans lequel on discute des motifs proposés pour leur affranchissement, ceux qui s'y opposent, et les moyens praticables pour améliorer leur sort*, Neuchatel 1788, p. 13.
39. Nicolas-François Jacquemard, *Réflexions d'un cultivateur américain sur le projet d'abolir l'esclavage et la traite des nègres*, Londres et Paris 1788, p. 3.
40. Ibid., p. 63.
41. Ibid., p. 87.
42. Albert Hirschman, *The Rhetoric of Reaction. Perversity, Futility, Jeopardy*, Harvard University Press, Cambridge, MA 1991, chap. 3.
43. This is the argument of "perverse effect"—see Hirschman, *Rhetoric of Reaction*, chap. 2. Hirschman notes that this argument is often combined with that of inanity, as here with French colonists.
44. Émilien Petit, *Traité sur le gouvernement des esclaves*, vol. 2, Knapen, Paris 1777, p. 24.
45. Ibid., p. 27.
46. Malouet, *Mémoire sur l'esclavage*, p. 23.
47. Jacquemard, *Réflexions d'un cultivateur américain*, pp. 64–65.
48. "I am human; nothing human is alien to me."
49. David Duval de Sanadon, *Discours sur l'esclavage des Nègres, par un colon de Saint-Domingue*, Amsterdam 1786, p. 7.
50. David Duval de Sanadon, *Réclamations et observations des colons, sur l'idée d'abolition de la traite et de l'affranchissement des nègres*, 2nd edition, 1789, p. 26.
51. C. Belu, *Des colonies et de la traite des Nègres*, Guilleminet, Paris 1800, p. 33.
52. Claude-Adrien Helvétius, *De l'esprit* [1758], Fayard, Paris 1988, p. 37, note e.
53. Charles Dupin, *Des forces productives et commerciales de la France*, Bachelier, Paris 1827. On Dupin's statistical method and his economic approach see Antoine de Falguerolles "Charles Dupin, statisticien" and Steiner "Charles Dupin et

Jean-Baptiste Say: arithmétique politique et économie politique" in Carole Christen and François Vatin (eds.), *Charles Dupin (1784–1873), Ingénieur, savant, économiste, pédagogue et parlementaire du Premier au Second Empire*, Presses universitaires de Rennes, Rennes 2009.

54. Dupin, *Mémoire sur la situation sociale et politique des colonies françaises en 1844 et sur le système que le gouvernement doit adopter à leur égard*, Didot frères, Paris 1844; *Second mémoire—Situation comparée des colonies françaises et des colonies anglaises*, Didot frères, Paris 1844; *Troisième mémoire—Les colonies françaises devant la Chambre des Pairs*, Didot frères, Paris 1845.
55. Dupin, *Mémoire sur la situation sociale et politique des colonies françaises*, p. 2.
56. Ibid., p. 39.
57. Dupin, *Second mémoire*, p. 18.
58. Ibid., p. 29.
59. Ibid., p. 31.
60. Dupin, *Troisième mémoire*, pp. 2–3, 14, 46–47.
61. Adolphe Granier de Cassagnac, *De l'émancipation des esclaves, Lettres à M. de Lamartine*, Delloye, Paris 1840, p. 83.
62. Ibid., p. 90.
63. Alphonse Maynard, *La Martinique en 1842, intérêts coloniaux, souvenirs de voyage par M. le comte de la Cornillère* (pseudonyme), Gide libraire-éditeur, Paris 1843, p. 232.
64. Ibid., pp. 232–233.
65. Philippe Steiner, "Jean-Baptiste Say et les colonies ou comment se débarrasser d'un héritage intempestif," *Cahiers d'économie politique*, vol. 27 (1997), pp. 153–173.
66. Paul Leroy-Beaulieu, *De la colonisation chez les peuples modernes*, Guillaumin et Cie, Paris 1874; "Colonisation au XIXe siècle," in Léon Say, Joseph Chailley (eds.) *Nouveau dictionnaire d'économie politique*, vol. 1, Guillaumin et Cie, Paris 1891.

Conclusion

Freeing the Slaves

While seeking to place a value on the relative costs of free and slave labor, most abolitionist calculators adhered to the primacy of the principle of justice over that of economic interests. They were, however, quickly reassured: the achievement of justice did not impede the realization of utility, but was, on the contrary, its necessary condition. This was not a convenient argument shaped by a struggle against slavery intended to assuage the concerns of colonists, merchants, and government administrators. The coincidence of justice and utility was a universal certainty on which the development of political economy during the eighteenth century had been founded and which can be found, quite intact, in the writings of very many nineteenth-century economists. Moreover, calculation remained very closely linked with the moral opprobrium that, up to 1771, was the basis of anti-slavery discourse, and which would remain one of its essential arguments after that date. It was not at all a matter of covering self-interest with the gloss of justice; the claim of slave emancipation was not a tactical means whose primary aim was to preserve export crops and secure national prosperity nor, as has sometimes been suggested, to defend the interests of indigenous sugar producers. Utility is not the hidden source of anti-slavery discourse; it was, in the understanding of abolitionist calculators, one of the primary supports, along with morality, of the abolitionist cause. This is what lent force to calculation.

The reactionary position of the colonists was, by contrast, based upon a moral pragmatism: justice could not be defined by the application of universal principles; it had to be defined by the impact that "philanthropic dreams" would have if put into practice in a particular time and place. The colonists' calculations were aimed at demonstrating that the emancipation of slaves would ruin both plantations and colonies, have a serious impact on the metropolitan economy, and plunge slaves into poverty. By applying the principle of liberty, in itself unobjectionable, the government would make everyone suffer.

The issue of the cost of labor for the masters was not the only point where the relation of calculation and morality arose in the debate on the abolition of slavery. Calculation as a moral form to which the slave had to conform after emancipation also played an important role here.

Much of the controversy over abolition turned on the capacity of the black to be stimulated by economic self-interest and, if that capacity were admitted, on the means of its employment in a system of free labor. It was a matter of determining whether the *homo servilis* could become a *homo œconomicus*; that is, a man capable of rationally calculating his self-interest with a view to maximizing his economic satisfaction in the market, a form of maximization that depended upon an analysis of the world in which he found himself, and the anticipation of its future.

As far as the colonists were concerned, the answer was a negative one: *homo africanus* was endowed with an indolent nature, had little trouble in feeding himself from a naturally generous environment, and who therefore would not know how to enter into the logic of the calculation of needs. Left to himself, he would live from cultivating a few crops, from hunting and fishing, reverting to the barbarian state of his ancestors. Only the calibrated (so they said) exercise of violence by his master would force him to work. This argument was reinforced by that from the *inanity* of substituting the force of needs for the goad of the whip; by allowing that slaves might be transformed into day laborers one would simply substitute one form of submission for another that was both harder and much more precarious.

From the perspective of the abolitionists, the indolence of slaves had to do not with their nature but with their condition as slaves. Placed in a position where his self-interest was to work as little as possible, the slave had thereby demonstrated his rationality. Liberty would necessarily lead the emancipated slave to try to increase his gains in order to satisfy growing needs. Stimulated by self-interest, the black would deploy his physical and intellectual capacities to support himself and his family, but also to secure a better future for himself and those close to him. In this way he would engage not only with material well-being but also with "arts" and morality—in a word, with civilization. The plans made for the phased abolition in both the eighteenth and the nineteenth century were intended to "prepare" the former slave for this new condition, to transform him almost unconsciously, and so seamlessly, into a *homo œconomicus*.

When they were confronted with the disorganization of work prevailing on some British islands following emancipation, several abolitionists realized that the enactment of this virtuous circle depended on one essential condition: preventing former slaves from acquiring land on which they could grow crops with which they could support themselves. Various solutions were put forward. Some of these solutions drew upon respect for the law of property, limited to withdrawing the concession of a hut and garden from those who refused to remain on the estate working for the planter, and banning the working of uncultivated land belonging either to individuals or to the state. Other solutions were more coercive: Lechevalier advocated a "French procedure" for emancipation that would forbid emancipated slaves from cultivating foodstuffs, granting a monopoly instead to the company charged with cultivating the colony, a measure that Cochut praised as the only one that promised to maintain and develop export crops. For his part Tocqueville did not shrink from suggesting that the government should temporarily debar newly liberated slaves from any access to land. While the slave was forced to work by the threat that at any moment his owner could use violence against him, the newly emancipated slave would be, in Cochut's words, "captive to his self-interest," which he could only satisfy within the framework of the estate.

Within this dynamic approach the European worker represented the future model for the freed slave. Almost all abolitionists maintained that *homo europeanus* had long been a *homo œconomicus*. While they did often denounce the fact that French laborers frequently lived in poverty, marginalized and sometimes idle, it was assumed that if the opportunity presented itself those who were unemployed would immediately become dedicated workers, anxious to increase their income to meet ever-increasing needs. The European immigration projects that some abolitionists developed took this for granted, which comes as a surprise when we think of the trouble nineteenth-century entrepreneurs had in finding workers, especially skilled workers, who were prepared to present themselves on a regular basis—this is something that Say noted. Denis Poulot, a Parisian entrepreneur, wrote how managing workers was not only hard work, it was also very discouraging. In his book *Le sublime*[1] he presents a typology of workers, from which there emerge two main categories: workers and those who are "sublime." It is the number of days worked in a year that provides an almost exact means of distinguishing the two. The assiduousness of the "true worker"—showing up at least three hundred days in the year, plus nights and Sundays if asked—is described as the "mother of all the virtues": sobriety, the inclination to save, love and respect for the family, cleanliness, a republican commitment without blindness to partisanship. The "true sublime," on the other hand, represents all human degradation: working only one hundred and seventy days, he is a drunkard, a show-off, has no thought for the morrow, moody, lies to his employer, and is a bad husband. "The sublime" works only to satisfy his immediate needs and has no care for the future, has no plan; in short, is entirely without morality. The persistence and even the increase during the nineteenth century of the practice of St. Monday supports Poulot's remarks. Throughout Europe workers regularly took Mondays off, sometimes even several days in a row. The days that were not worked were used for entertainment and time with friends and family.

The questions raised by the emancipation of slaves and those raised by the control of the European proletariat are nonetheless somewhat different. The great colonial fear, shared by many abolitionists, that newly freed slaves would leave the plantations to devote themselves to the cultivation of food sufficient for their own subsistence, is not exactly the same as the anxiety of employers about the voluntary unemployment of their workers who cannot be bent to material civilization. There is, however, in both cases a questioning of self-interest as a regulator of economic conduct in the labor market: the European worker does not necessarily think that an improvement in his situation will result from a higher income; once he is satisfied with the needs that matter most to him he takes his leisure and surrenders to enjoyment. He calculates rationally; thinking analogously to *homo oeconomicus*, he reckons up the costs and benefits that working gives him—on the one hand fatigue, dependence, lack of freedom, on the other financial gain, but also the pleasure that can be had from productive engagement. He adopts a calculatory logic without necessarily adhering to the morality that makes the sale of labor on the market a central value.

The fear that emancipated slaves would desert colonial plantations was not an idle one.

After 1848 the cultivation of export crops in the former slave colonies faced a labor shortage. The post-abolition situation in Guadeloupe is exemplary in this respect. Production fell until 1850 and did not return to the level of the year before abolition until 1854. Productivity declined sharply, but rose again in the following years together with production. Faced with the ill will of the newly freed slaves, planters and colonial administrators had solved the problem of the lack of manpower by organizing the mass immigration of workers from Africa, but mostly from India. Although freed slaves formed the majority of cane workers, they were reluctant to settle on the estates; they hired themselves out according to their needs, the type of work offered to them, the amount of the wage, and the time which would be left for them to tend their own crops.[2] As Cochut pointed out and also deplored in his commentary on the post-slavery situation in some British islands, work had above all *shifted*. The dynamic of self-interest did not come about in the way abolitionists had wished. This was because the level of pay usually offered was low, but also because, in spite of the disappearance of the whip, planters kept estate workers in a state of dependence that most former slaves rejected.

How one might create economic behavior that was well adapted to a capitalist economy was an issue that reappeared in the colonies later in the nineteenth and early twentieth centuries. In their analysis of American slave plantations, Fogel and Engerman emphasized that slave labor organized in gangs combined "judiciously" with the stimulants of money and violence was effective.[3] Some years later Fogel suggested that

> the central cultural objective of the masters was the creation of a new kind of worker, well-suited to serve as a cog in the large-scale system of production (the agrobusinesses) that they were building. . . . [I]n this respect masters were similar to the men who developed the factory system; manufacturers also sought to transform the individualistic culture of rural laborers into a new culture of collective discipline.[4]

In his recent global economic history of cotton, Sven Beckert also recognized the importance of forced labor, a central element of what he calls "war capitalism," in the emergence of industrial capitalism.[5] But he modifies its point of application by emphasizing that at the very moment in which the productive potential of labor organization on the plantations of the American Southern states was being developed, early industrial capitalist development relied on the domination of manual labor, a work force of children and young women who were not spared violent treatment. War capitalism, making use of violence in the plantations, was combined with a European industrial capitalism that did not hesitate to employ forced labor and which eventually developed into the formally peaceful organization of labor of today.

This remained an issue after the Second World War. Pierre Bourdieu was a young sociologist working in Algeria when he studied the transition in Kabylie from a traditional economy based upon a logic of honor to a capitalist economy based upon the "spirit of calculation."[6]He maintained that the two types of society involved distinct forms of reasoning that did not valorize the same behaviors. Traditional society mobilized family connections and neighborhood relationships to secure the continued working of agricultural production according to a seasonal rhythm thought to be unchanging in the succession of good and bad harvests—setting resources aside and avoiding monetary expenditure. In the absence of a developed monetary economy it was personal relationships—honor—that allowed someone to gain credit, and not resources that could be exchanged in a market. The mastery of the future through forecasting, calculation using money that enabled varied resources to be valued by the same standard, the relation of saving to investment—all of these were no more part of the economic behavior of the peasants of Kabylie than the reallocation of land that had until then been farmed in common, where "work has no other purpose than to directly satisfy primary needs."[7] According to Bourdieu, the adoption of calculation supposes the possession of stable incomes that are sufficient to supersede any concern for subsistence.

The behavior of nineteenth-century European workers, the freedmen of post-slave colonies, and also the workers of postcolonial Algeria, all of these actors show that initiation into the logic of economic calculation requires that particular social and economic conditions must be realized. If the worker is not placed in circumstances that lead him to adopt the economic calculation and ethic that go hand in hand with this logic (the valorization of work, concern for the future), the worker seeks to retreat into the immutability of material civilization (or traditional society, according to the terminology used by Bourdieu). This ensures the protection of the community or, at least, as with the French proletarian of the nineteenth century, permits an evasion of what capitalist exploitation might otherwise do by limiting personal needs and by cultivating a workers' sociability. In so doing, he does not act irrationally but in accordance with a well-understood self-interest, although different from the the labor ethic set by political economy.

NOTES

1. Denis Poulot, *Le Sublime ou le travailleur comme il est en 1870, et ce qu'il peut être*, Maspéro, Paris 1980.
2. Christian Schnakenbourg, *La transition post-esclavagiste 1848–1883. Histoire de l'industrie sucrière en Guadeloupe aux XIXe et XXe siècle*, Pt. 2, L'Harmattan, Paris 2007, ch. 1. Similar findings for Réunion are in Hai Quang Ho, *Histoire économique de l'île de la Réunion (1849–1881)*, L'Harmattan, Paris 2004.
3. Robert W. Fogel and Stanley L. Engerman, *Time on the Cross. The Economics of American Negro Slavery*, Little, Brown & Co, Boston 1974, pp. 200–205.

4. Robert W. Fogel, *Without Consent or Contract. The Rise and Fall of American Slavery*, W. W. Norton, New York 1989, p. 399.
5. Sven Beckert, *Empire of Cotton. A New History of Global Capitalism*, Allen Lane, London 2014, chs. 5–7.
6. Pierre Bourdieu, "La société traditionnelle. Attitude à l'égard du temps et conduite économique," *Sociologie du travail*, 1963; Bourdieu and Abdelmalek Sayad, *Le déracinement. La crise de l'agriculture traditionnelle en Algérie*, Minuit, Paris 1964; Bourdieu, *Algérie 60. Structures économiques et structures temporelles*, Minuit, Paris 1977.
7. Bourdieu, "La société traditionnelle," p. 40.

REFERENCES

Anderson, James, *Observations on Slavery particularly with a view to its effects on the British colonies in the West Indies*, Manchester, J. Harrop, 1789.

Anonyme, « Lettres d'un voyageur à l'Auteur des *Ephémérides* au sujet des observations sur l'esclavage des nègres insérées dans le sixième tome de l'année 1771 », *Les Ephémérides du citoyen*, 1771, vol. 12, pp. 51–77.

Anonyme, *Liste des ouvrages sur la traite et l'esclavage*, Paris, Imprimerie du Patriote François, 1790.

Anonyme, *Considérations politiques sur les esclaves des colonies françoises de l'Amérique et sur leurs gens de couleur libres*, 1791.

Anonyme, *Le vrai patriote à MM. les patriotes des Antilles françaises*, Pointe-à-Pitre, De l'imprimerie de la colonie, 1792.

Anonyme, *De la nécessité d'adopter l'esclavage en France*, Paris, Baillio, 1797.

Anonyme, *Un mot sur les noirs, à leurs amis*, s.d.

Archives parlementaires de 1787 à 1860, Première série (1787 à 1799), Paris, Société d'imprimerie et librairie administratives et des chemins de fer, 1887.

Arena, Richard, « Sismondi et la transition de l'esclavage au métayage », *Economies et sociétés*, série *Œconomia*, 2009, pp. 1201–1230.

Barré Saint-Venant, Jean, *Des colonies modernes sous la zone torride et particulièrement celle de Saint-Domingue*, Paris, Brochot, 1802.

Baudeau, abbé, *Idées d'un citoyen sur la puissance du roi et le commerce de la nation dans l'Orient*, Amsterdam, 1763.

Baudrillart, Henri, *Manuel d'économie politique*, Paris, Guillaumin et Cie, 1857.

Bazard, Saint-Amand, and Enfantin, Prosper, *Doctrine de Saint-Simon. Exposition. Première année*, 2nd édition, 1830, Paris, Au Bureau de l'Organisateur.

Beckert, Sven, *Empire of Cotton. A New History of Global Capitalism*, London, Allen Lane, 2014.

Belu, C., *Des colonies et de la traite des Nègres*, Paris, impr. de Guilleminet, 1800.

Benot, Yves, *La Révolution française et la fin des colonies*, Paris, La Découverte, 1987.

Benot, Yves, *La démence coloniale sous Napoléon*, Paris, La Découverte, 1992.

Bentham, Jeremy, *An Introduction to the Principles of Morals and Legislation*, 1789, New York, Hafner Press, 1948.

Blanc, Louis, *Organisation du travail*, 1839, Paris, Bureau de la société de l'industrie fraternelle, 5e édition, 1848.

Blanc, Robert, *Un pasteur au temps des Lumières, Benjamin-Sigismond Frossard 1754–1830*, Paris, Honoré Champion, 2000.

Bonnemain, Antoine-Jean-Thomas, *Régénération des colonies ou moyens de restituer graduellement aux hommes leur état politique et d'assurer la prospérité des Nations;*

et Moyens pour rétablir promptement l'ordre dans les colonies françaises, Paris, impr. du Cercle Social, 1792.
Bonnet, Casimir, *Manuel du capitaliste ou comptes faits des intérêts*, Paris, Garnier Frères, s.d. [first edition in 1815].
Bourdieu, Pierre « La société traditionnelle. Attitude à l'égard du temps et conduite économique », *Sociologie du travail*, 1963, pp. 24–44.
Bourdieu, Pierre, *Algérie 60. Structures économiques et structures temporelles*, Paris, 1977, Minuit.
Bourdieu, Pierre, and Sayad, Abdelmalek, *Le déracinement. La crise de l'agriculture traditionnelle en Algérie*, Paris, 1964, Minuit.
Braudel, Fernand, *Civilization matérielle, économie et capitalisme* XVe-XVIIIe *siècle*, vol. 1, *Les structures du quotidien*, Paris, Armand Colin, 1979.
Braudel, Fernand, *Civilization matérielle, économie et capitalisme* XVe-XVIIIe *siècle*, vol. 2, *Les jeux de l'échange*, Paris, Armand Colin, 1979.
Brian, Eric, *La mesure de l'Etat. Administrateurs et géomètres au* XVIIIe *siècle*, Paris, Albin Michel, 1994.
Brougham, Henry, *Inquiry into the Colonial Policy of the European Powers*, Edinburgh, Balfour, Manners & Miller, Archibald Constable, 1803.
Brougham, Henry, *Opinion of Henry Brougham, Esquire, on Negro Slavery*, London, H. J. McClary, 1830.
Cahen, Léon, « La société des amis des noirs et Condorcet », *La révolution française*, n° 50, 1906, pp. 481–511.
Callon, Michel, and Muniesa, Fabian, « Les marchés économiques comme dispositifs collectifs de calcul », *Réseaux*, 2003, pp. 189–233.
Carnot, Hippolyte, *De l'esclavage colonial*, Paris, Au bureau de la revue indépendante, 1845.
Carteau, J.-Félix, *Soirées bermudiennes, ou Entretiens sur les événemens qui ont opéré la ruine de la partie française de l'isle de Saint-Domingue*, Paris, Pellier-Lawalle, 1802.
Castel, Robert, *Les métamorphoses de la question sociale. Une chronique du salariat*, Paris, Fayard, 1995.
Césaire, Aimé, « Introduction » de *Esclavage et colonisation par Victor Schœlcher*, Paris, Presses Universitaires de France, 1948.
Charara, Youmna, *Fictions coloniales du XVIIIe siècle. Zimeo, Lettres africaines, Adonis, ou le bon nègre, anecdote coloniale*, Paris, L'Harmattan, 2005.
Chevalier, Michel, *Cours d'économie politique fait au Collège de France*, Paris, Capelle, 1855.
Clavière, Étienne, *Adresse de la Société des amis des noirs à l'Assemblée Nationale, à toutes les villes de commerce, à toutes les manufactures, aux colonies, à toutes les sociétés des amis de la Constitution. Adresse dans laquelle on approfondit les relations politiques et commerciales entre la métropole et les colonies, etc.*, Paris, Imprimerie du patriote François, 1791.
Cochin, Augustin, *L'abolition de l'esclavage, Ire partie—Résultats de l'abolition de l'esclavage*, Paris, Jacques Lecoffre & Guillaumin et Cie, 1861.
Cochut, André, « La société coloniale—Abolition de l'esclavage », *Revue des deux mondes*, 1843, tome 3, pp. 177–228.
Cochut, André, « De la colonisation de la Guyane française », *Revue des deux mondes*, 1845, tome 11, pp. 519–553.
Cochut, André, « Morale », *Dictionnaire d'économie politique*, Paris, Guillaumin et Cie, 1853, vol. 2, pp. 239–242.
[Commission de Broglie] *Commission instituée, par décision royale du 24 mai 1840, pour l'examen des questions relatives à l'esclavage et à la constitution politique des colonies, Procès-verbaux, Ire partie—du 4 au 18 juin 1840*, Paris, Imprimerie royale, 1840.

[Commission de Broglie] *Commission instituée, par décision royale du 24 mai 1840, pour l'examen des questions relatives à l'esclavage et à la constitution politique des colonies, Procès-verbaux, IIe partie—du 22 décembre 1840 au 12 mai 1841*, Paris, Imprimerie royale, 1841.

[Commission de Broglie] *Rapport fait au ministre secrétaire d'Etat de la marine et des colonies*, Paris, Imprimerie royale, 1843.

[Commission Schoelcher] *Procès-verbaux, rapports et projets de décrets de la commission instituée pour préparer l'acte d'abolition immédiate de l'esclavage*, Paris, Imprimerie nationale, 1848.

Comte, Auguste, *Système de politique positive, ou Traité de sociologie instituant la religion de l'Humanité*, Paris, Larousse, 1851–1853.

Comte, Charles, *Traité de législation ou exposition des lois générales suivant lesquelles les peuples prospèrent, dépérissent ou restent stationnaires*, Paris, A. Sautelet et Cie, 1827.

Conchon, Anne, *La corvée des grands chemins au XVIIIe siècle. Economie d'une institution*, Rennes, Presses universitaires de Rennes, 2016.

Conder, Josiah, *The Wage or the Whip. An Essay on the Comparative Cost and Productiveness of Free and Slave Labour*, London, Hatchard and Son, 1833.

Cools, Baron de, *De l'agriculture coloniale en réponse à M. de Sismondi, lettre adressée à M. le rédacteur en chef de la Revue mensuelle d'économie politique*, Imprimerie de Moquet et Cie, janvier 1834.

Dameth, Henri, *Le juste et l'utile*, Paris, Guillaumin et Cie, 1859.

Desmenier, Jean Nicolas, *Encyclopédie méthodique. Economie politique et diplomatique*, 1784–1788.

Desrosières, Alain, *La politique des grands nombres. Histoire de la raison statistique*, Paris, La Découverte, 1993.

Desrosières, Alain, *Gouverner par les nombres*, Paris, Presses de l'école des Mines, 2008.

Daubrée, Paul, *La question coloniale sous le rapport industriel*, Paris, Malteste, 1841.

Dockès, Pierre, « Condorcet et l'esclavage des nègres ou esquisse d'une économie politique de l'esclavage à la veille de la Révolution française », in Jean-Michel Servet (ed.), *Idées économiques sous la Révolution, 1789–1794*, Lyon, Presses universitaires de Lyon, 1989, pp. 85–124.

Dorigny, Marcel, « Mirabeau et la Société des amis des noirs: quelles voies pour l'abolition de l'esclavage? », in *Les abolitions de l'esclavage: de L. F. Sonthonax à V. Schœlcher, 1793, 1794, 1848*, Paris, Presses universitaires de Vincennes and Éditions de l'UNESCO, 1995, pp. 153–164.

Dorigny, Marcel, « La société des Amis des Noirs: antiesclavagisme et lobby colonial à la fin des Lumières (1788-1792) », in Marcel Dorigny and Bernard Gainot (eds.), *La Société des Amis des Noirs*, Paris, UNESCO/EDICEF, 1998, pp. 13–57.

Dorigny, Marcel, « Intégration républicaine des colonies et projets de colonisation de l'Afrique: civiliser pour émanciper? », in Yves Bénot and Marcel Dorigny (eds.), *Grégoire et la cause des Noirs (1789–1831), combats et projets*, Société française d'histoire d'outre-mer, Association pour l'Etude de la Colonisation Européenne, 2000, pp. 89–105.

Drescher, Seymour, *The Mighty Experiment. Free Labor versus Slavery in British Emancipation*, New York, Oxford University Press, 2002.

Droz, Joseph, *Economie politique ou principes de la science des richesses*, 2nd édition, Paris, Renouard, 1846.

Dubuc de Marentille, *De l'esclavage des Negres dans les Colonies de l'Amérique*, Pointe-à-Pitre Guadeloupe, impr. de la veuve Bénard, 1790.

Duchet, Michèle, *Anthropologie et histoire au siècle des Lumières*, Paris, Albin Michel, 1995.
Ducœurjoly, S.-J., *Manuel des habitants de Saint-Domingue*, Paris, Lenoir, 1802.
Dufau, Pierre-Armand, *De l'abolition graduelle de l'esclavage dans les colonies européennes et notamment dans les colonies françaises, considérée à la fois dans l'intérêt des esclaves, des maîtres, des colonies et de la métropole*, Paris, Bureau central de la Revue Encyclopédique, 1830.
Dupin, Charles, *Des forces productives et commerciales de la France*, Paris, Bachelier, 1827.
Dupin, Charles, *Mémoire sur la situation sociale et politique des colonies françaises en 1844 et sur le système que le gouvernement doit adopter à leur égard*, Paris, 1844, Didot frères.
Dupin, Charles, *Second mémoire—Situation comparée des colonies françaises et des colonies anglaises*, Paris, 1844, Didot frères.
Dupin, Charles, *Troisième mémoire—Les colonies françaises devant la Chambre des Pairs*, Paris, Didot frères, 1845.
Du Pont, Pierre-Samuel, *De l'importation et de l'exportation du blé*, Paris, 1764.
Du Pont, Pierre-Samuel, *De l'administration des chemins*, in *Ephémérides du citoyen*, 1767, vol. 5, pp. 135–187.
Du Pont, Pierre-Samuel, *De l'origine et des progrès d'une science nouvelle*, 1768, Catania, CUECM, 1992.
Du Pont, Pierre-Samuel, « Affranchissement des nègres en Pennsylvanie », *Ephémérides du citoyen*, 1769, vol. 9, pp. 172–175.
Du Pont, Pierre-Samuel, « Observations importantes sur l'esclavage des nègres », *Éphémérides du citoyen*, 1771, vol. 6, pp. 181–246.
Du Pont, Pierre-Samuel, « Lettres africaines », *Ephémérides du citoyen*, 1771, vol. 8, pp. 68–118.
Du Puynode, Gustave, *De l'esclavage et des colonies*, Paris, Joubert, 1847.
Duval de Sanadon, David, *Discours sur l'esclavage des Nègres, par un colon de Saint-Domingue*, Amsterdam et à Paris, Hardouin et Gattey, 1786.
Duval de Sanadon, David, *Réclamations et observations des colons, sur l'idée d'abolition de la traite et de l'affranchissement des nègres*, 2e édition, 1789.
Les Ephémérides du citoyen ou Bibliothèque raisonnée des sciences morales et politiques, Paris, chez Delalain, 1765–1772.
Elisabeth, Léo « Rémunération du travail libre et question agraire à la Martinique et dans les colonies françaises d'Amérique de 1842 à 1851 », in *Esclavage, résistances et abolitions*, Paris, éditions du CTHS, 1999, pp. 305–316.
Espeland, Wendy, and Stevens, Mitchell, « Commensuration as a social process », *Annual Review of Sociology*, 1998, pp. 313–343.
Etner, François, *Histoire du calcul économique en France*, Paris, Economica, 1987.
Faccarello, Gilbert, and Steiner, Philippe, « The Diffusion of the Work of Adam Smith in the French Language: An Outline History », in Keith Tribe (ed.) *A Critical Bibliography of Adam Smith*, London, Pickering and Chatto, 2002, pp. 61–119.
Falguerolles, Antoine de, « Charles Dupin, statisticien », in Carole Christen and François Vatin (eds.) *Charles Dupin (1784–1873). Ingénieur, savant, économiste, pédagogue et parlementaire du Premier au Second Empire*, Rennes, Presses universitaires de Rennes, 2009, pp. 115–127.
Fogel, Robert, W., *Without Consent or Contract. The Rise and Fall of American Slavery*, New York, Norton, 1989.
Fogel, Robert W., and Engerman, Stanley, *Times on the Cross. The Economics of American Negro Slavery*, New York, Norton, 1989.

Foner, Eric, *Free Soil, Free Labor, Free Men. The Ideology of the Republican Party before the Civil War*, New York, Oxford University Press, 1970.
Fourier, Charles, *Traité de l'association domestique-agricole*, Paris, Bossange Père et P. Mongie Ainé, 1822.
F*.P. (Félix Patron d'après Barbier), *Des noirs, de leur situation dans les colonies françaises, L'esclavage n'est-il pas un bienfait pour eux et un fardeau pour leurs maîtres?* Paris, Charles Mary, 1831.
Franklin, Benjamin, *Observations Concerning the Increase of Mankind, Peopling of Countries, &c.*, 1751, in *American Writers Series. Benjamin Franklin. Representative Selection with Introduction, Bibliography, and Notes*, New York, American Book Company, 1936, pp. 216–223.
Frossard, Benjamin-Sigismond, *La cause des esclaves nègres et des habitans de la Guinée, portée au tribunal de la justice, de la religion, de la politique ou Histoire de la traite et de l'esclavage des nègres, preuves de leur illégitimité, moyens de les abolir sans nuire ni aux colonies, ni aux colons*, Lyon, Imprimerie Aimée de la Roche, 1789.
Gainot, Bernard, « La Société des Amis des Noirs et des colonies, 1796–1799 », in Marcel Dorigny and Bernard Gainot (eds), *La société des Amis des Noirs*, Paris, UNESCO/EDICEF, 1998, pp. 301–327.
Ganilh, Charles, *Des systèmes d'économie politique, de leurs inconvénients, de leurs avantages, et de la doctrine la plus favorable aux progrès et à la richesse des nations*, Paris, Xhrouet, Déterville, Lenormand et Petit, 1809.
Ganilh, Charles, *La théorie de l'économie politique, fondée sur les faits résultans des statistiques de la France et de l'Angleterre; sur l'expérience de tous les peuples célèbres par leurs richesses; et sur les lumières de la raison*, Paris, Déterville, 1815.
Gasparin, Agénor de, *Esclavage et traite*, Paris, Joubert, 1838.
Gasparin, Agénor de, *De l'affranchissement des esclaves et de ses rapports avec la politique actuelle*, Paris, Joubert, 1839.
Gauthier, Florence, *Périssent les colonies plutôt qu'un principe. Contribution à l'histoire de l'abolition de l'esclavage 1789–1804*, Paris, Société des études robespierristes, 2002.
Girollet, Anne, *Victor Schœlcher, abolitionniste et républicain*, Paris, Karthala, 2000.
Granier de Cassagnac, Adolphe, « Colonies françaises, de l'esclavage et de l'émancipation », *Revue de Paris*, 1836, pp. 103–130.
Granier de Cassagnac, Adolphe, *De l'émancipation des esclaves, Lettres à M. de Lamartine*, Delloye, Paris, 1840.
Grégoire, abbé Henri, *De la littérature des nègres, ou Recherches sur leurs facultés intellectuelles, leurs qualités morales et leur littérature*, Paris, Maradan, 1808.
Hardy, abbé J. *Liberté et travail ou moyens d'abolir l'esclavage sans abolir le travail*, Paris, Dentu, Gaume, Debécourt, Adrien Leclère, 1838.
Hashimoto, Hitoshi, « Notes inédites de J.-B. Say qui couvrent les marges de la *Richesse des nations* et qui la critiquent », *Kyoto Sangyo University: Economics and Business Review*, 7, pp. 53–81.
Helvétius, Claude-Adrien, *De l'esprit*, 1758, Paris, Fayard, 1988.
Hirschman, Albert, *The Passions and the Interests. Political Arguments for Capitalism before its Triumph*, Princeton, NJ, Princeton University Press, 1977.
Hirschman, Albert, *The Rhetoric of Reaction. Perversity, Futility, Jeopardy*, Cambridge, MA, Belknap Press, 1991.
Ho, Hai Quang, *Histoire économique de l'île de la Réunion (1849–1881)*, Paris, L'Harmattan, 2004.
Hodgson, Adam, *A letter to M. J.-B. Say on the comparative expense of free and slave labour*, London, Hatchard and son, 2nd édition, 1823.

Jacquemard, Nicolas-François, *Réflexions d'un cultivateur américain sur le projet d'abolir l'esclavage et la traite des nègres*, Londres et Paris, Lagrange, 1788.
Jennings, Lawrence, *French Reaction to British Slave Emancipation*, Baton Rouge, Louisiana State University Press, 1988.
Jennings, Lawrence, *La France et l'abolition de l'esclavage, 1802–1848*, 2000, French translation, Paris, éditions André Versaille, 2010.
Jennings, Lawrence, « Abolitionnisme, jeux politique et réforme: France 1814–1848 », in Olivier Pétré-Grenouilleau (ed), *Abolir l'esclavage. Un réformisme à l'épreuve (France, Portugal, Suisse, XVIIIe-XIXe siècle)*, pp. 169–183, Rennes, Presses Universitaires de Rennes, 2008.
Jurt, Joseph, « Condorcet: l'idée de progrès et l'opposition à l'esclavage », in Pierre Crépel and Christian Gilain (eds.), *Condorcet mathématicien, économiste, philosophe, homme politique*, pp. 385–395, Paris, Minerve, 1989.
Kersaint, A.-G., *Moyens proposés à l'Assemblée Nationale, pour rétablir la paix et l'ordre dans les Colonies*, Paris, impr. du Cercle social, 1792.
Lacharrière, André-C. de, *Observations sur les Antilles françaises*, Paris, Impr. de Auguste Auffray, 1831.
Ladebat, André Daniel Laffon de, *Discours sur la nécessité et les moyens de détruire l'esclavage dans les colonies*, Bordeaux, Imprimerie Michel Racle, 1788.
Lapidus, André, « Le profit ou la domination: figure de l'esclave dans l'économie d'Adam Smith », in Fred Célimène and André Legris (eds.) *L'économie de l'esclavage colonial. Enquête et bilan du XVIIe au XIXe siècle*, pp. 47–72, Paris, CNRS éditions, 2002.
Lavollée, Paul, *Notes sur les cultures et la production de la Martinique et de la Guadeloupe*, Paris, Imprimerie royale, 1841.
Lechevalier, Jules, *Note sur la fondation d'une nouvelle colonie dans la Guyane française ou premier aperçu d'un nouveau mode de population et de culture pour l'exploitation des régions tropicales, suivi de plusieurs pièces et documents*, Paris, Firmin Didot frères, 1844.
Le Mercier de la Rivière, Pierre-Paul, *Mémoire sur la Martinique*, 1762, in *Mémoires et textes inédits sur le gouvernement des Antilles*, vol. 2, pp. 104–154, Paris, Éditions du CNRS, 1978.
Le Mercier de la Rivière, Pierre-Paul, *Procès verbal de l'assemblée convoquée en exécution de l'arrêt concernant une imposition de 500 000 livres*, 1763, in *Mémoires et textes inédits sur le gouvernement des Antilles*, vol. 2, pp. 155–168, Paris, Éditions du CNRS, 1978.
Le Mercier de la Rivière, Pierre-Paul, *Observations sur l'imposition ordonnée par le roi*, 1763, in *Mémoires et textes inédits sur le gouvernement des Antilles*, vol. 2, pp. 175–226, Paris, Éditions du CNRS, 1978
Le Mercier de la Rivière, Pierre-Paul, *L'ordre naturel et essentiel des sociétés politiques*, 1767, Paris, Fayard, 2001.
Le Pelletier Duclary, J.-B., *Rapport fait au nom de la commission chargée de répondre à celui de M. de Tocqueville, relative aux esclaves des colonies*, Impr. de Thounens, 1841.
Le Pelletier Duclary, J.-B., *Du travail libre et du travail forcé aux colonies françaises*, Paris, impr. d'Ad. Bondeau, 1841.
Le Play, Frédéric, *Les ouvriers européens. Tome premier: La méthode d'observation*, Tour, Alfred Mame et fils, 2e éd., 1879.
Leroy-Beaulieu, Paul, *De la colonisation chez les peuples modernes*, Paris, Guillaumin et Cie, 1874.
Leroy-Beaulieu, Paul, « Colonisation au XIXe siècle », in Léon Say and Joseph Chailley (eds.) *Nouveau dictionnaire d'économie politique*, vol.1, pp. 448–451, Paris, Guillaumin et Cie, 1891.

Lescallier, Daniel, *Réflexions sur le sort des noirs dans les colonies*, s.n., 1789.
Linguet, Simon-Nicolas, *Théorie des lois civiles, ou principes fondamentaux de la société*, 1767, Paris, Fayard, 1984.
Mably, abbé Gabriel Bonnot de, *Le droit public de l'Europe fondé sur les traités*, in *Collection complète des œuvres de l'abbé de Mably*, imprimerie de Ch. Desbrières, an III, vol. 6.
Macaulay, Zachary, *Détails sur l'émancipation des esclaves pendant les années 1834 et 1835*, Paris, Hachette, 1836.
Macaulay, Zachary, *Suite des détails sur l'émancipation des esclaves pendant les années 1835 et 1836*, Paris, Hachette, 1836.
Macaulay, Zachary, *Faits et renseignements prouvant les avantages du travail libre sur le travail forcé, et indiquent les moyens les plus propres à hâter l'abolition de l'esclavage dans les colonies européennes*, Paris, Hachette, 1835.
Macaulay, Zachary, *Haïti, ou renseignements authentiques sur l'abolition de l'esclavage et de ses résultats, à Saint-Domingue et à Guadeloupe*, Paris, Hachette, 1835.
Macaulay, Zachary, *Tableau de l'esclavage tel qu'il existe dans les colonies françaises*, Paris, Hachette, 1835.
Malenfant, Colonel, *Des colonies et particulièrement de celles de St-Domingue; Mémoire historique et politique*, Paris, Audibert, 1814.
Malouet, Pierre-Victor, *Mémoire sur l'esclavage des nègres dans lequel on discute des motifs proposés pour leur affranchissement, ceux qui s'y opposent, et les moyens praticables pour améliorer leur sort*, Neufchatel, 1788.
Marx, Karl, *Le capital*, 1867, French translation, in *Œuvres, Economie I*, Paris, Gallimard, 1968.
Maynard, Alphonse, *La Martinique en 1842, intérêts coloniaux, souvenirs de voyage par M. le comte de la Cornillère* (pseudonyme), Paris, Gide libraire-éditeur, 1843.
MDLDMFY, *Mémoire sur l'esclavage des nègres contenant réponse à divers écrits qui ont été publiés en leur faveur*, S.l., 1790.
Mirabeau, Marquis de, *L'ami des hommes, ou traité de la population*, 3rd édition, Hambourg, Chrétien Hérold, 1758.
Mirabeau, Marquis de, *Philosophie rurale ou Économie générale et politique de l'agriculture*, Amsterdam, chez les Libraires associés, 1763.
Montesquieu, *De l'Esprit des lois*, 1748, *Œuvres complètes*, vol. 2, Paris, Gallimard, 1951.
Montrol, François Mongin de, *Des colonies anglaises depuis l'émancipation des esclaves et de l'influence de cette émancipation sur les colonies françaises, rapport lu à la Société pour l'Abolition de l'Esclavage*, Paris, Impr. Paul Dupont et Cie, 1835.
Moreau de Jonnès, Alexandre, *Recherches statistiques sur l'esclavage colonial et les moyens de le supprimer*, Paris, Imprimerie de Bourgogne et Martinet, 1842.
Necker, Jacques, *Compte rendu au Roi*, 1785, S.l.
Necker, Jacques, *De l'administration des finances de la France*, 1785, S.l.
Necker, Jacques, *Ouverture des États généraux à Versailles le 5 mai 1789*, Paris, Imprimerie royale, 1789.
Oldroyd, David, Fleischman, Richard, and Tyson, Thomas, « The Culpability of accounting practice in promoting slavery in the British Empire and antebellum United States », *Critical Perspectives on Accounting*, 2008, pp. 764–784.
Oudin-Bastide, Caroline, *Travail, capitalisme et société esclavagiste*, Paris, La Découverte, 2005.
Oudin-Bastide, Caroline, « L'Afrique dans le discours abolitionniste de Victor Schœlcher », *Afrique & histoire*, 2005, pp. 149–173.
Oudin-Bastide, Caroline, « Discours colonial et discours abolitionniste: entre passions et intérêts », in Olivier Pétré-Grenouilleau (ed.) *Abolir l'esclavage, Un réformisme*

à l'épreuve (France, Portugal, Suisse, XVIIIe-XIXe siècles), pp. 247–275, Rennes, Presses Universitaires de Rennes, 2008.

Perrot, Jean-Claude, *L'âge d'or de la statistique régionale française (an IV-1804)*, Paris, Société des études robespierristes, 1977.

Perrot, Jean-Claude, *Une histoire intellectuelle de l'économie politique (XVIIe–XVIIIe siècle)*, Paris, Editions de l'EHESS, 1992.

Petit, Émilien, *Traité sur le gouvernement des esclaves*, Paris, Knapen, 1777.

Pétition à MM. Les membres de la Chambre des députés. Abolition de l'esclavage, division des terres, indemnité; par un propriétaire d'esclaves, Hachette, Paris, 1836.

Pétré-Grenouilleau, Olivier, *Les traites négrières. Essai d'histoire globale*, Paris, Gallimard, 2004.

Pétré-Grenouilleau, Olivier, « Abolitionnisme et idée national: divorce et compromis, France, 1789–1831 », in Olivier Pétré-Grenouilleau (ed.) *Abolir l'esclavage, Un réformisme à l'épreuve (France, Portugal, Suisse, XVIIIe–XIXe siècles)*, pp. 185–206, Rennes, Presses Universitaires de Rennes, 2008.

Petty, William, *Political Arithmetick*, 1690, in *The Economic Writings of Sir William Petty*, New York, A. M. Kelley, 1986.

Piguet, Marie-France, *Classe, histoire du mot et genèse du concept des Physiocrates aux historiens de la Restauration*, Lyon, Presses universitaires de Lyon, 1996.

Poivre, Pierre, *Voyage d'un philosophe ou observations sur les mœurs & les arts des peuples d'Asie, d'Afrique et de l'Amérique*, Yverdon, 1768.

Poovey, Mary, *A History of the Modern Fact. Problems of Knowledge in the Sciences of Wealth and Society*, Chicago, Chicago University Press, 1998.

Poughon, Jean-Michel, *Histoire doctrinale de l'échange*, Paris, Librairie Générale de Droit et de Jurisprudence, 1987.

Poulot, Denis, *Le Sublime ou le travailleur comme il est en 1870, et ce qu'il peut être*, Maspéro, Paris, 1980.

Précis de l'abolition d'esclavage dans les colonies anglaises, Paris, Imprimerie royale, 1840.

Proudhon, Pierre-Joseph, *De la justice dans la Révolution et dans l'Eglise. Nouveaux principes de philosophie pratique*, Paris, Garnier Frères, 1858.

Proudhon, Pierre-Joseph, *Du principe fédératif*, 1863, *Œuvres complètes de P.-J. Proudhon*, Paris, Librairie Marcel Rivière, 1959.

Quesnay, François, « Fermiers. Economie politique », 1756, in *Œuvres économiques complètes*, vol.1, pp. 127–159, Paris, INED, 2005.

Quesnay, François, *Tableau économique*, 3rd version, 1759, in *Œuvres économiques complètes*, vol.1, pp. 412–438, Paris, INED, 2005.

Quesnay, François, *Analyse de la formule arithmétique du Tableau économique*, 1767, in *Œuvres complètes*, vol.1, pp. 527–563. Paris, INED, 2005.

Quesnay, François, *Second problème économique*, 1767, in *Œuvres complètes*, vol.1, pp. 619–635, Paris, INED, 2005.

Ramsay, James, *An Essay on the Treatment and Conversion of African Slaves in the British Sugar Colonies*, London, James Phillips, George Yard, Lombard-Street, 1784.

Ramsay, James, *Objections to the Abolition of the Slave Trade with Answers to which are prefixed Strictures on a late Publication, intitled, «Considerations on the Emancipation of Negroes, and the Abolition of the Slave Trade », by a West India Planter*, London, James Phillips and George Yard, 1788.

Raynal, abbé Guillaume-Thomas, *Histoire philosophique et politique des établissemens et du commerce dans les deux Indes*, Genève, J.-L. Pellet, 1781.

Régent, Frédéric, *Esclavage, métissage, liberté*, Paris, Grasset, 2004.

Rémusat, Charles de, *Rapport fait au nom de la commission chargée de l'examen de la proposition de M. Passy sur le sort des esclaves dans les colonies françaises*, Société française pour l'abolition de l'esclavage, n°9, 1838.

Revue Britannique ou choix d'articles traduits des meilleurs écrits périodiques de la Grande-Bretagne sur la littérature, les beaux arts, les arts industriels, l'agriculture, la géographie, le commerce, l'économie politique, les finances, la législation, etc., etc., Bruxelles, Méline, 1826.

Reybaud, Louis, « Introduction », *Journal des économistes*, t.1, vol.1, janvier 1842, pp. 1–12.

Ricardo, David, *On the Principles of Political Economy and Taxation*, 1817, *The Works and Correspondence of David Ricardo*, Cambridge, Cambridge University Press, 1986, vol. 1.

Robin, Charles-César, *Voyages dans l'intérieur de la Louisiane, de la Floride occidentale et dans les isles de la Martinique et de Saint-Domingue pendant les années 1802, 1803, 1804, 1805 et 1806*, Paris, Buisson, 1807.

Roge, Pernille, « The Question of Slavery in Physiocratic Political Economy », in Manuela Albertone (ed.) *L'economia come linguaggio politica nell'Europa del Settecento*, Milano, Feltrinelli, 2009, pp. 149–169.

Rooke, John, *An Inquiry into the Principles of National Wealth: Illustrated by the Political Economy of the British Empire*, Edinburgh, A Balfour & Co., 1824.

Rossi, Pellegrino, *Cours d'économie politique*, Paris, Guillaumin et Cie, 1865.

Roubaud, abbé, *Histoire générale de l'Asie, de l'Afrique et de l'Amérique, contenant des discours sur l'histoire ancienne des peuples de ces contrées, leur histoire moderne et la description des lieux, avec des remarques sur leur histoire naturelle, et des observations sur les religions, les gouvernements, les sciences, les arts, le commerce, les mœurs, les caractères, etc., des nations*, Paris, Des Ventes de la Doué, 1770–1775.

Rouvellat de Cussac, J.-B., *Situation des esclaves dans les colonies françaises*, Paris, Pagnerre, 1845.

Saint-Cyran, Paul-Edme Crublier de, *Réfutation du projet des Amis des noirs sur la suppression de la traite des nègres et sur l'abolition de l'esclavage dans les colonies*, 1790.

Saint-Méry, Louis-Elie Moreau de, *Considérations présentées aux vrais amis du repos et du bonheur de la France à l'occasion des nouveaux mouvements de quelques soi-disant amis des noirs*, Paris, Imprimerie nationale, 1791.

Say, Horace, « De quelques mesures récentes touchant les finances », *Journal des économistes*, Avril-juillet 1848, pp. 209–217.

Say, Jean-Baptiste, *Traité d'économie politique ou simple exposition de la manière dont se forment, se distribuent et se consomment les richesses*, Paris, Déterville, 1803.

Say, Jean-Baptiste, *Petit volume contenant quelques aperçus des hommes et de la société*, Paris, Déterville, 1817.

Say, Jean-Baptiste, *Cours complet d'économie politique pratique. Ouvrage destiné à mettre sous les yeux des hommes d'État, des propriétaires fonciers et des capitalistes, des savans, des agriculteurs, des manufacturiers, des négocians, et en général de tous les citoyens, l'économie des sociétés*, 1828–1830, *Œuvres complètes de Jean-Baptiste Say*, Paris, Économica, 2010.

Say, Jean-Baptiste, *Leçons d'économie politique*, *Œuvres complètes de Jean-Baptiste Say*, vol. 4, Paris, Economica, 2003.

Say, Jean-Baptiste, *Traité d'économie politique*, *variorum* edition by Claude Mouchot, *Œuvres Complètes de Jean-Baptiste Say*, Paris, Économica, 2006.

Say, Jean-Baptiste, *Manuscrits*, Bibliothèque Nationale, Paris.

Say, Louis, *Etudes sur la richesse des nations et réfutation des principales erreurs en économie politique*, Paris, Renard, 1836.
Schaller, François, *Essai critique sur la notion de productivité*, Genève, Droz, 1966.
Schmidt, Nelly, *Victor Schœlcher*, Paris, Fayard, 1994.
Schmidt, Nelly, *Abolitionnistes de l'esclavage et réformateurs des colonies, 1820–1851*, Paris, Karthala, 2000.
Schnakenbourg, Christian, *La transition post-esclavagiste 1848–1883, Histoire de l'industrie sucrière en Guadeloupe aux XIXe et XXe siècle*, partie 2, L'Harmattan, Paris, 2007.
Schneewind, Jerome, *The Invention of Autonomy. A History of Modern Moral Philosophy*, Cambridge, Cambridge University Press, 1998.
Schœlcher, Victor, *De l'esclavage des noirs et de la législation coloniale*, Paris, Paulin, 1833.
Schœlcher, Victor, *Abolition de l'esclavage*, Paris, Pagnerre, 1840.
Schœlcher, Victor, *Des colonies françaises, Abolition immédiate de l'esclavage*, 1842, Paris, Editions du CTHS, 1998.
Schœlcher, Victor, *Des colonies étrangères et Haïti*, 1843, Fort-de-France, Editions Désormeaux, 1973.
Schœlcher, Victor, *Histoire de l'esclavage pendant les deux dernières années*, 1847, Pointe-à-Pitre, Emile Désormeaux, 1973.
Schœlcher, Victor, *La vérité aux ouvriers et cultivateurs de la Martinique*, Paris, Pagnerre, 1849.
Schwartz [Condorcet], *Réflexions sur l'esclavage des nègres*, Neufchatel, Société Typographique, 1781.
Schwartz [Condorcet], *Réflexions sur l'esclavage des nègres*, 2nd édition, 1788, Paris, L'Harmattan, 2003.
Senior, Nassau William, *Three Lectures on the Rate of Wages, with a Preface on the Causes and Remedies of the Present Disturbances*, London, John Murray, 1831.
Sibire, abbé Sébastien-André, *L'Aristocratie négrière, ou Réflexions philosophiques et historiques sur l'esclavage et l'affranchissement des Noir*, Paris, Lesclapart et Desray, 1789.
Sismondi, Jean Charles Léonard, Simonde de, *De la richesse commerciale* (1803), *Œuvres économiques complètes de Sismondi*, vol. 2, Paris, Economica, 2012.
Sismondi, Jean Charles Léonard, Simonde de, *De l'intérêt de la France à l'égard de la traite des nègres*, 1814, *Écrits d'économie politique, 1799–1815, Œuvres économiques complètes de Sismondi*, vol. 3, Paris, Économica, 2012.
Sismondi, Jean Charles Léonard, Simonde de, « Nouvelles réflexions sur la traite des nègres », 1814, *Écrits d'économie politique, 1799–1815, Œuvres économiques complètes*, vol. 3, Paris, Économica, 2012.
Sismondi, Jean Charles Léonard, Simonde de, « De la condition dans laquelle il faut placer les nègres en les affranchissant », *Revue mensuelle d'économie politique*, décembre 1833, pp. 401–427.
Sismondi, Jean Charles Léonard, Simonde de, *Études sur l'économie politique*, 1837–1838, Genève, Slatkine, 1980.
Skinner, Quentin, *La liberté avant le libéralisme* (1998), French translation, Paris, Le Seuil, 2000.
Smith, Adam, *An Inquiry into the Nature and Cause of the Wealth of Nations*, 1776, Indianapolis, Liberty Classics, 1981.
Société des amis des noirs, *Adresse à l'Assemblée nationale pour l'abolition de la traite des noirs*, Paris, Imprimerie Potier de Lille, 1790.

Steiner, Philippe, « L'esclavage chez les économistes français, 1750–1830 » in *Les abolitions de l'esclavage: de L. F. Sonthonax à V. Schœlcher, 1793, 1794, 1848*, Paris, Presses universitaires de Vincennes et Éditions de l'UNESCO, 1995, pp. 164–175.
Steiner, Philippe, « Jean-Baptiste Say et les colonies ou comment se débarrasser d'un héritage intempestif », *Cahiers d'économie politique*, 1997, pp. 153–173.
Steiner, Philippe, *La « science nouvelle » de l'économie politique*, Paris, Presses universitaires de France, 1998.
Steiner, Philippe, « Les économistes libéraux et l'esclavage (1815–1880): limites et ambiguïtés d'un engagement », in Olivier Pétré-Grenouilleau (ed.) *Abolir l'esclavage, Un réformisme à l'épreuve (France, Portugal, Suisse, XVIIIe-XIXe siècles)*, pp. 225–245, Rennes, Presses Universitaires de Rennes, 2008.
Steiner, Philippe, « Charles Dupin et Jean-Baptiste Say: arithmétique politique et économie politique » in Carole Christen and François Vatin (eds.) *Charles Dupin (1784–1873). Ingénieur, savant, économiste, pédagogue et parlementaire du Premier au Second Empire*, pp. 149–163, Rennes, Presses universitaires de Rennes, 2009.
Steiner, Philippe, and Vatin, François, « Après l'abolition de l'esclavage: mise au travail, contrainte et salariat », *Economies et sociétés*, série *Œconomia*, 2009, pp. 1269–1290.
Steuart, James, *An Inquiry into the Principles of Political Economy: Being an Essay on the Science of Domestic Policy in Free Nations*, 1767, New York, Kelley, 1967.
Sully-Brunet, Jacques, *Considérations sur le système colonial et plan d'abolition de l'esclavage*, Paris, Félix Locquin et Cie, 1840.
Thompson, Ann, « Diderot, Roubaud et l'esclavage », *Recherches sur Diderot et sur l'Encyclopédie*, 2003, pp. 69–93.
Tocqueville, Alexis de, Articles published in *Le Siècle* le 14 décembre 1843, in *Ecrits et discours politiques, Œuvres complètes d'Alexis de Tocqueville*, tome 3, vol. 1, Paris, Gallimard, 1962.
Tocqueville, Alexis de, *Rapport fait au nom de la commission chargée d'examiner la proposition de M. de Tracy, relative aux colonies*, 1839, in *Ecrits et discours politiques, Œuvres complètes d'Alexis de Tocqueville*, tome 3, vol. 1, Paris, Gallimard, 1962.
Tocqueville, Alexis de, *Correspondance anglaise, Œuvres complètes d'Alexis de Tocqueville*, t. 6, vol. 2, Paris, Gallimard, 1991.
Todd, David, *L'identité économique de la France. Libre-échange et protectionnisme 1814–1851*, Paris, Grasset, 2008.
Todd, David, « La liberté, la nation et les colonies dans la pensée de Charles Dupin », in Carole Christen and François Vatin (eds.) *Charles Dupin (1784–1873). Ingénieur, savant, économiste, pédagogue et parlementaire du Premier au Second Empire*, pp. 177–189. Rennes, Presses universitaires de Rennes, 2009.
Tracy, Victor Destutt de, *Développements de la proposition relative au sort des esclaves dans les colonies*, par M. de Tracy, député de l'Orne, Chambre des députés, 2nd session, séance du 12 juin 1839.
Turgot, Anne-Robert-Jacques, *Correspondance avec Du Pont de Nemours, Œuvres de Turgot et documents le concernant*, Paris, Alcan, 1914, 1919, tomes 2 and 3.
Turgot, Anne-Robert-Jacques, *Lettre au Contrôleur Général sur le commerce des grains*, (1770), *Œuvres de Turgot et documents le concernant*, Paris, Alcan, 1919, tome 3.
Tussac, Fr.-Richard de, *Cri des colons contre un ouvrage de M. l'évêque et sénateur Grégoire, ayant pour titre « De la littérature des nègres »*, Paris, Les marchands de nouveautés, 1810.
Vatin, François, *Morale industrielle et calcul économique dans le premier XIXe siècle. L'économie industrielle de Claude-Louis Bergery (1787–1863)*, Paris, L'Harmattan, 2007.

Vatin, François (ed.), *Evaluer et valoriser. Une sociologie économique de la mesure*, Toulouse, Presses de l'Université du Mirail, 2009.

Vatin, François, *L'espérance-monde*, Albin Michel, Paris, 2012.

Vérin, Hélène, *La gloire des ingénieurs. L'intelligence technique du XVIe au XVIIIe siècle*, Paris, Albin Michel, 1993.

Viefville des Essars, *Discours et projet de loi pour l'affranchissement des nègres ou l'adoucissement de leur régime et réponse aux objections des colons*, Paris, Imprimerie nationale, 1790.

Ward, H. G., *Mexico in 1827*, Londres, Henry Colburn, 1828.

Young, Arthur, *Political Arithmetic containing observations on the present state of Great Britain and the principles of her Policy in the encouragement of agriculture*, 1774, New York, Kelley, 1967.

INDEX

Note: The use of "f" after page numbers denotes figures and the use of "n" after page numbers shows a note is there, along with its note number.

www.ingramcontent.com/pod-product-compliance
Ingram Content Group UK Ltd.
Pitfield, Milton Keynes, MK11 3LW, UK
UKHW021134160926
475595UK00020B/54